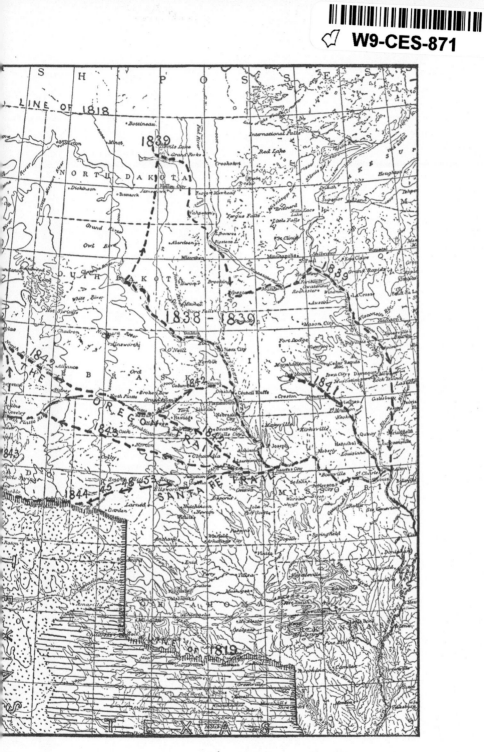

FRÉMONT'S EXPLORATIONS, 1838-1853

FREMONT
Pathmarker of the West

AMERICAN CLASSICS

FREMONT

Pathmarker of the West

By

ALLAN NEVINS

Volume II

FREMONT IN THE CIVIL WAR

FREDERICK UNGAR PUBLISHING CO.
NEW YORK

Copyright 1939, 1955 by
ALLAN NEVINS

Republished 1961 in the
AMERICAN CLASSICS SERIES

Second Printing

PRINTED IN THE UNITED STATES OF AMERICA

Library of Congress Catalog Card Number 61–7088

CONTENTS

Volume I

FREMONT, THE EXPLORER

CONTENTS

Volume II

FREMONT IN THE CIVIL WAR

CONTENTS

APPENDICES

MAPS

ILLUSTRATIONS

Frontispiece: John Charles Frémont, the first United States Senator from California; *Following page 146:* Jessie Benton Frémont; Kit Carson; Thomas H. Benton; Frémont's party attacked by Klamath Indians; San Juan Mountains, 1848; Among the Buffalo; Portsmouth Square, showing Parker House; *Following page 494:* Fillmore

ILLUSTRATIONS

XXII

Starvation and Cannibalism

PASSENGERS on the lake steamboat *Saratoga*, bound from Buffalo westward in the early fall of 1848, saw on its shelter deck an interesting family group: Frémont, in civilian clothes, with close-cropped beard, long mustache, and heavy curling dark hair, slightly grizzled in places; his still girlish wife, carrying a baby in her arms; the little girl of six, Lilly; and a servant. They kept to themselves and invited no approaches. But to one or two fellow travelers who won their confidence they spoke freely. They were on their way to California, with the intention of making it their future home. They frankly admitted that they were poor; they had nothing but Frémont's savings from his small army salary, and they faced the possibility that, if Congress refused to pay the debts he had contracted in his California operations, he would be held responsible for them. However, they hoped quickly to gain a footing in that rich land. Frémont had placed in the hands of Larkin, before leaving to undergo his court-martial, a small sum—$3,000—for the purchase of a ranch; and friends in the East had furnished him credit to send around Cape Horn the agricultural implements and milling machinery he would need there. They had health and courage. It was plain that Frémont was depressed by the verdict of the court-martial, which he regarded as a deep injustice, but Jessie assiduously comforted him. "And it was very pleasant," later wrote a passenger,[1] "to see how he was cheered on and encouraged by the vast prospect of doing good which was opened

[1] Letter of T. C. Rogers, Buffalo *Republic*, reprinted in New York *Tribune*, July 8, 1856.

to them in that new territory. Neither had any other thought or expectation than to obtain an honorable and respected position by their own industry and economy."

They were not going out, however, as mere emigrants. Jessie was accompanying him only as far west as Westport on the Missouri, when she would turn back and take a ship to California by the Panama route. Frémont would meanwhile assume command of a new exploring expedition to cross the Rockies by a southern pass. Nothing shows better the buoyant courage of the man than the fact that, a few months after the court-martial, he had organized his own fourth expedition.

Though it was to prove the least fruitful of all his exploring trips, and though it was destined to end in utter disaster, its objects possessed real merit. Frémont had always wished to cross the continent on a central line intersecting the head of the Rio Grande, and he now intended to do so. But this was not all. Throughout the middle west men were talking of a railroad to the Pacific; some wealthy citizens of St. Louis were interested in making that city the eastern terminus, and Frémont planned to ascertain for them whether a central route was practicable. Since the chief question was whether the snow would be an insuperable obstacle, he had determined to cross the ranges in midwinter. Just how sufficient funds were obtained for the expedition is not clear. Very probably the men planning a Pacific railway subscribed a considerable sum; Senator Benton may have contributed some money; and it seems that several of Frémont's followers, notably Edward M. Kern, recently commander at Sutter's Fort, and his two brothers, furnished their services free. Kern and several of Frémont's other witnesses in Washington had eagerly urged the undertaking, and preparations had been in progress since May.[2]

Thus did Frémont cling to his career as an explorer. The renown he had won in that calling was too great to permit him to give it up. While the court-martial was still fresh in men's minds, he had received from citizens of Charleston a gold-

[2] St. Louis Weekly *Reveillé*, July 3, 1848.

mounted sword and engraved gold scabbard, both of beautiful workmanship, as "a memorial of their high appreciation of the gallantry and science he has displayed in his services in Oregon and California." [3] The bill to pay the various California claims which he had incurred during his military service on the Coast, seven hundred thousand dollars in all, gave a number of Senators, before its final passage, an opportunity to eulogize his work. Benton, of course, was foremost, but Senator Clark of Rhode Island paid him glowing compliments, while John A. Dix of New York declared that he had "exhibited a combination of energy, promptitude, sagacity, and prudence, which indicated the highest capacity for civil and military command," and that his decisive movements had unquestionably "kept California out of the hands of British subjects." [4]

The magazines of the day united in praising him, for nearly all the reviews had by now published appreciative articles upon his explorations. An anonymous writer for the *Southern Literary Messenger* remarked that his reports on the West must always be the basis of scientific information upon the regions he had traversed, "and the name of Frémont is immortalized among the great travelers and explorers, and will doubtless survive as long as those of the Sierra Nevada, or the Sacramento." The *Eclectic Review* gave him many pages. The *Democratic Review* thought that he had been insufficiently rewarded: [5]

The personal merits of Capt. Frémont, in these expeditions, have been great, and evince high talent for command and for enterprise. With an average of 25 men, and no officer to aid him, he has made 10,000 miles of march among tribes of savages, without ever being exposed to surprise or defeat, providing for the subsistence of men and horses, and preserving order, subordination, and cheerful obedience throughout his command. Without the aid of scientific assistants, he has so enriched his report with science as to seem to have been the work of professional savants.... The honorary reward of

[3] Charleston *Mercury*, September 21, 1847; Bigelow, *Frémont*, p. 222.
[4] *Congressional Globe, 30th Cong., 1st Sess.,* Appendix, p. 175*ff.*
[5] *Southern Literary Messenger*, XV, pp. 528, 529; *Democratic Review*, XVII.

brevet captain has been bestowed upon him. Lewis and Clark received something more substantial—double pay, 1,600 acres of land
each, promotion to generals, appointment of government commission
to treat with Indians, and copyright in their Journal. Certainly, as
first explorers, they were entitled to great merit; but they lack the
science which Capt. Frémont carried into his expeditions.

Even abroad he was now well-known; a little later, Baron
von Humboldt, on behalf of the Prussian Government, trans-
mitted to him a gold medal for progress in the sciences, while
the Royal Geographical Society awarded him the Founder's
Medal for distinguished services to geography.[6] It was unfortunate that he did not write a full scientific report of the third
expedition which culminated in the California fighting. Instead,
he contented himself with a careful map of Oregon and California, of which the Senate ordered twenty thousand copies,
and a short *Geographical Memoir* accompanying it. This
Memoir, which was the first publication to give currency to
the phrase "the Golden Gate," might have rivaled the reports
of his earlier expeditions but for the court-martial, and the
inability of Jessie to help him; she served for a time as amanu-
ensis, and then her health broke down. Writing for Frémont
one evening, she suddenly said, "Do not move the lamp, it
makes it too dark," and went into a prolonged fainting fit,
from which she emerged a temporary invalid.[7] Thereafter, Frémont spoke of his task as "the cursed memoir," and dismissed
it as summarily as his conscience would permit him. He offered
to furnish Congress with a much fuller record of his trip, but
although a committee under Senator Breese of Illinois reported
in favor of this, the work was never authorized, and a distinct
gap was thus left in the literature of the West.

Nevertheless, the *Geographical Memoir* was a valuable document, which contained some of the most important of Frémont's
generalizations upon western geography. He divided America
beyond the Great Salt Lake into three regions, the Great Basin,

[6] Bigelow, *Frémont,* 327*ff.*
[7] Jessie Benton Frémont MSS, Bancroft Library.

the Sierras, and the coastal belt; emphasizing the importance of the mountain chain as a divide between the desert on the east, the garden-lands on the west:

> Stretching along the coast, and at the general distance of 150 miles from it, this great mountain wall receives the warm winds, charged with vapor, which sweep across the Pacific ocean, precipitates their accumulated moisture in fertilizing rains and snows on its western flank, and leaves cold and dry winds to pass on to the east. Hence the characteristic differences of the two regions—mildness, fertility, and a superb vegetable kingdom on one side, comparative barrenness and cold on the other.

His description of the partly arid plains of the Great Basin was by far the best yet published. In this he emphasized the importance of the grassy, wooded interior mountains, giving rise to small streams which lost themselves in lakes or the dry plains; and he justly remarked that the region seemed more Asiatic than American, resembling the elevated district between the Caspian Sea and northern Persia. Another illuminating passage was his comparison of the coastal slope of California to Italy; while a very important feature was the emphasis which he laid upon the Humboldt River Valley as a great avenue of communication. As an English scholar has written, the *Memoir* "shows that Frémont was not only a great explorer, but also a geographer with a real understanding of the conception of a region as a natural unit." [8]

Other scientific fruits of the third expedition were of distinct importance. The map which Preuss drew from surveys by Frémont and others was the most accurate yet made of the Far West. More than a thousand botanical specimens had been preserved, and John Torrey's treatise upon them was shortly published by the Smithsonian Institution. [9] Geological specimens had been collected, interesting sketches made of scenery

[8] This *Geographical Memoir upon Upper California* was published as *House Misc. Doc., 30 Cong., 2d Sess.,* No. 5. E. W. Gilbert's comment is in his *Exploration of Western America,* 1800-1850, p. 189.

[9] *Plantæ Frémontianæ, Smithsonian Contributions* (1850).

and animals, and a large number of bird skins prepared with plumage intact. Frémont had been plunged in June, 1848, into a controversy with Captain Wilkes regarding the accuracy of his topographical work and the consequent figures for the California coast line, from which he emerged with enhanced scientific credit. He was regarded as the best American authority upon the great new lands just acquired by the Mexican War and the Oregon Treaty, and his writings were more than ever in demand. When he set out on his fourth expedition, he felt that he was continuing an invaluable national work, and with new discoveries might wipe out old humiliations.

Once more, then, the frontier; once more the free open prairies stretching before the explorer! Years later, in preparing to write the second volume of his *Memoirs,* never published, Frémont jotted down some rough notes upon the adventure which are still kept in his manuscripts:

A winter expedition—about snow obstacles and home for family— preparations at St. Louis—Campbell and Filley—journey up the river—death of the child—Mrs. Frémont at Maj. Cummins—camp on the frontier—Mrs. Frémont's visits to the camp—Scott and the quails.

———

Capt. Cathcart—personnel of the party (33 men)—Godey—the Kerns—King—Brackenridge—Creutzfeldt (when was he with me?) —The two Indian boys Gregorio and Juan—Proue—the three Canadians.

———

Route up the Southern Kansas—the Arkansas bare of timber and exposed to snowstorms—for 400 miles abundant timber, grain, and excellent grass—Valley of the Kansas the best approach to the mountains—the valley soil of superior quality, well timbered, abundant grasses, the route direct—would afford good settlement for 400 miles.

———

The big timber, thirty miles below Bent's Fort—Fitzpatrick and the Indians, six hundred lodges, talks and feasts, Indians report snow deeper than for many years—November 17, mountains show themselves for first time, covered with snow, the country around also—not discouraged.

Thirty-three men, with horses and pack animals, made a large expedition for an almost penniless leader, but numbers were needed, for the Indian tribes before him, the Ute, Apache, Navajo, and others, were hostile or uneasy. The Campbell and Filley here mentioned were Robert Campbell and O. D. Filley, who, with Thornton Grimsley, all three substantial St. Louis business men, furnished financial and other assistance. Campbell had been a traveler, trapper, and pioneer of the Far West; Filley, the manufacturer of a Dutch oven then widely used for baking, gave Frémont a large part of his camp equipment. The expedition included many experienced men. Alexis Godey, Frémont's old friend and companion, was again hunter; E. M. Kern was again artist; Charles Preuss once more went out as topographer. Others who had been with Frémont before were Captain Henry King, Charles Taplin, and three mountain-men, Thomas E. Brackenridge, John Scott, and Thomas S. Martin. Among the new men were three French Canadians well experienced in the West, F. Creutzfeldt, who was employed as botanist, E. M. Kern's two brothers, Richard H. Kern, an artist, and Benjamin J. Kern, a physician, and a roving Englishman, Captain A. Cathcart of the 11th Prince Albert Hussars, who hoped to enjoy some hunting and adventure. Another new recruit was Micajah McGehee, a capable young scion of a distinguished Mississippi family, who kept a diary which in its full manuscript form is an invaluable source of information. Others of the party were L. D. Vincenthaler, who is called by Frémont and others Vincent Haler, Henry Wise, and Raphael Proue. The three California Indians, Manuel, Joaquin, and Gregorio, went along.

At the outset Frémont was saddened by what his notes call the "death of the child"—his before mentioned son, Benton.[10] The little boy had always been delicate and his physicians in

[10] Jessie Benton Frémont MSS, Bancroft Library.

Washington knew that his span of life was likely to be short;
but the young mother (Jessie was still only twenty-four) had
no knowledge of this. The youngster died while the parents
were traveling up the Missouri by steamboat to the starting-
point of the fourth expedition.

The night after Frémont and his party set out from Westport Landing for the west, Jessie and her colored servant slept
at the Indian Agency there. This agency, a queer, irregular
string of log houses, was in the charge of a Major Cummins.
Toward dawn Jessie and her servant were disturbed by the
piteous cries of a mother wolf hunting some cubs which Major
Cummins had just killed, and they had hardly settled to sleep
again when their rest was broken by Frémont himself. In his
usual impetuous way he had ridden ten miles back from camp
to have a final hour with his wife, and Kitty had to get up
and make a pot of tea. "And so," wrote Mrs. Frémont afterward,[11] "with our early tea for a stirrup-cup, 'he gave his bridle
rein a shake,' and we went our ways, one into the midwinter
snows of untracked mountains, the other to the long sea-voyage
through the tropics."

It was October 21, 1848, when Frémont's party set out, and
on November 16th they reached Bent's Fort. Already they had
encountered inclement weather. The Arkansas was full of ice
where they crossed it; they met a blizzard smiting the plains
on the fourth; and at Bent's Fort the snow was a foot deep.
The trappers and Indians at the fort told them that the depth
of the snow, the brilliant aurora borealis, and other signs be-
tokened an early and unusually severe winter. As they went on
the outlook continued gloomy. A short detour took them to the
"Big Timbers" near the fort, where Frémont visited his old
guide Fitzpatrick, now stationed there as Indian agent; perhaps hoping to obtain his services again. According to Frémont's notes, on the seventeenth they sighted the Rockies,
which were heavily mantled in white. Then on November 21st,
they reached Pueblo, a mere hamlet inhabited by a few old

[11] Jessie Benton Frémont, *A Year of American Travel*, p. 20.

mountain-men, some wintering there, some settled for life with their Indian squaws. Once the fur trade had made it the seat of a considerable activity, but now it was in decay.

Here again the old mountaineers warned them against the season; they pointed to the heavy snow all about, declared that the cold in the ranges was unprecedented, and asserted that the high peaks to the west could not be crossed in winter. But Frémont was determined to press on, for a bitter winter season offered just such a test of the practicability of a railroad as he desired. His plan was to march west from the headwaters of the Rio Grande along the line of the thirty-eighth parallel, or near it, for he believed that he would find a good pass over the Sierras between the points marked by Walker Pass and Mono Lake. Certain parts of this region had not then been visited even by trappers, and few men knew that the Cañon of the Colorado cut like a tremendous gash through it. Here, between the upper Rio Grande and harsh western rim of the Utah plateaus, lie some of the worst mountain fastnesses in the United States; formidable even in summer, and to men with the best maps and equipment of the present day. One of the bitterest winters in human memory was descending, and Frémont was heading straight for this forbidding country.

Until he reached Pueblo, Frémont had no guide. Neither Kit Carson nor Fitzpatrick had been available; he had found nobody else. At Pueblo he belatedly engaged the noted trapper and hunter "Old Bill" Williams, a personage rather more typical of the frontiersmen of the time and region than the honest, prudent Carson. Now almost sixty-two, William S. Williams, though spare, lean, and full of endurance, was badly worn by his toils. A tall, stooped man, of hatchet face, nutcracker jaws, small restless eyes, and querulous voice, he was as full of ludicrous eccentricities as any of Cooper's quaint characters, and yet as expert a scout as Leatherstocking himself. Though he had begun life as an itinerant backwoods preacher in Missouri and a missionary to the Osage Indians, his speech was the rough, illiterate lingo of the mountaineer of Southern extraction and Western upbringing; "varmint," "plumb," "nigh onto," "oncet," "haint gotter." His stories had a pic- turesqueness which has been preserved in several verbatim reports. An indefatigable walker, who could cover enormous distances, his gait was a queer, staggering waddle, which car- ried him first to one side and then to another of a straight trail. When he lifted his gun the onlooker had to check a smile at the "double-wabble" with which he brought it into position, but he could hit a coin unerringly at a hundred yards. He rode on his piebald Indian pony with his chest bent over the pom- mel, his stirrups ridiculously short, his trousers hitched up on his bare calves, and his arms flopping up and down over his arched knees. Usually he wore a buckskin hunting shirt, black with dirt and grease, and for headpiece a blanket cap, so roughly tailored that the two corners projected like wolves' ears. In all, he was a remarkable character.

Yet "Old Bill" Williams, despite his age and growing in- firmities, his oddities of speech and bearing, and an erratic quality which kept him from ever gaining the reputation of Carson, Fitzpatrick, or Milton Sublette, seemed an excellent choice for Frémont's purposes. To be sure, he was personally somewhat reckless; he had been in many an Indian fight, and bore the marks of ball and arrow. Earlier in life, after selling a load of furs, he would embark on a wild spree, drinking, gambling, and tossing whole bolts of precious calico to the vociferous squaws in the streets of Taos. He had never been much troubled by scruples in his dealings with other races. He had delighted to lift Indian scalps; at one time, along with other "land-pirates," he had made excursions into California to steal herds of horses from the missions and ranches. But his great merit was that nobody, except perhaps Jim Bridger, knew the Rocky Mountains so well. Twenty-three years earlier he had been the guide of George C. Sibley, who had led the gov- ernment party which in 1825 surveyed a road from the western borders of Missouri to the American boundary in the direction

of Santa Fé. Since then, a man of iron nerve, he had often
gone into the wilderness to live for months alone, trapping,
shooting, and exploring. Like Bridger, Carson, Provôt, and
others, he took an Indian wife (indeed, several squaws followed one another in rapid succession), and ingratiated himself
with various tribes. With the ranges in front of Frémont he
was supposed to be completely familiar. "His knowledge of that
part of the country," declares the scout Antoine Leroux, "was
perfect." McGehee's diary informs us that Williams shared the
misgivings of experienced frontiersmen of the region regarding
a winter passage of the high Rockies; but when Frémont insisted, he concluded to go, believing that the party could fight
its way, though not without great suffering, through the snow-
choked passes.[12]

November 24th found the expedition at a little settlement
called Hardscrabble (Pueblo de San Carlos) at the foot of
the Rockies. Here one of the French Canadians, as McGehee
reports, daunted by the prospect of the deep snow piled on the
peaks, the storms they could see raging there, and the chill
blasts that blew down from the cliffs, abandoned the group,
predicting evil to those who went on. On the twenty-sixth the
party plunged into the mountain defiles, though McGehee
writes that the ranges "presented to view one continued snowstorm." One of the men, George A. Hibbard, looked up at the
icy slopes and storm-wreathed precipices as they slowly picked
their way through the valleys below, and apprehensively remarked: "Friends, I don't want my bones to bleach upon those
mountains." He little dreamed that they would, and that to
some of his comrades death would appear a welcome relief before they were through. Several others, with a premonition of
disaster, climbed to a little eminence that evening to take a
last look at the wintry prairies behind. "The sight was beautiful," wrote McGehee; "the snow-covered plain far beneath us,
stretching eastward as far as the eye could reach, while on the

---

[12] Mr. Stark Young kindly enabled me to obtain the original of McGehee's
diary, a most absorbing document, from his descendants.

opposite side frowned the almost perpendicular wall of high mountains."

Of the character of this "almost perpendicular wall" it is proper to say a word. Pueblo and Hardscrabble lie in south central Colorado, in the valley of the upper Arkansas. To the west looms up that outer escarpment of the Rockies called the Sangre de Cristo or Sierra Blanca Mountains, with an elevation of from seven to fourteen thousand feet. This mountain rampart runs northwestward from upper New Mexico into central Colorado. Beyond it to the west is the valley of the upper Rio Grande, whose headwaters in Colorado form a line which runs sharply northwest, and at times almost west. In crossing the Sangre de Cristo to the Rio Grande, three passes were used by the mountain-men: the most northerly the Williams Pass (now the Music Pass); the central and most direct route from Pueblo the Robidoux Pass; and the southernmost the Sangre de Cristo Pass. All were practicable for a party like Frémont's, but difficult. His intention was to use the central route through the Robidoux Pass, thus passing the outer wall of the Rockies. Having gotten into the Rio Grande Valley, the traveler could push up that river west by north until he found himself confronted by a new wall of mountains, the central chain of the Rockies and true continental divide, called at this point the San Juan Range. It merged toward the north into the Uncompahgre, La Garita, and Sawatch mountains, which successively carried the chain high up into Colorado. From the Rio Grande Valley, the wayfarer had the choice of two routes well known to mountain-men. He could bear northward into the Sawatch Mountains, and cross the continental divide by Cochetopa Pass; or he could bear south into lower Colorado and cross the divide by Cumbres Pass, which is almost on the present-day boundary line between New Mexico and Colorado.[13]

[13] Compare Alpheus H. Favour, *Old Bill Williams: Mountain Man*, pp. 155, 156. The frontispiece shows Old Bill against the background of the Cochetopa Pass.

The first few days of travel beyond Hardscrabble were sufficient to show that the party had embarked upon a grim undertaking. They moved forward on foot, the mules they had
bought in Pueblo carrying one hundred and thirty bushels of
shelled corn. As they pushed into Huerfano Valley, just below
the high Sangre de Cristo peaks, their difficulties grew heavier.
The cold was intense, the ground beneath the fast-deepening
snow was rocky and treacherous, and the storms of sleet were
so terrific that at times it was almost impossible to make the
mules face them. The men suffered from frozen hands, ears,
and toes. Still greater were the sufferings of the animals, which
with no food but dry grain and no water but melted snow,
had to be driven to the last ounce of their strength. One by
one, the mules began to drop down by the trail to die. Every
climb upward made the cold more intense, until the mercury
sank entirely into the bulb of the thermometer and failed to
register the temperature. The men's breath congealed upon
their faces until their beards and eyelashes stood out stiff and
white, and they could hardly speak; the snow clogged the
mules' hooves until it formed balls six inches thick. In this
fashion they managed to cross the Roubidoux Pass, though
a hurricane had completely filled part of their road with a
tangle of fallen timbers—a veritable chevaux de frise, all the
more terrible for being half-concealed by snow. They came
down into the valley; but still, as McGehee writes, their difficulties continued: [14]

We descended into Grand River Valley. The snow lay deep as elsewhere and there was no sign of vegetation. One broad, white, dreary-
looking plain lay before us bounded by white mountains. High, pre-
cipitous, and frozen mountains were behind us, and this broad,
dreary plain lay before us and the Rio Grande, fifty miles ahead of
us. So we entered with the determination of getting through it as
quickly as possible. We traveled late and camped in the middle of
it, without any shelter from the winds, and with no fuel but some
wild sage, a small shrub which grew sparsely around. The cold was

[14] MS Diary.

intense, the thermometer to-night standing at 17 degrees below zero, and it was so cold during the day that Ducatel, a young fellow, came very near freezing to death.

By collecting a quantity of the sage, we made sufficient fires to cook or rather half-cook our supper of deer meat, five of these animals having been killed this evening by two of the men, and bolting down the half-cooked meat, we quickly turned into our blankets, in order to keep somewhat warm and for protection against the driving snow, for since leaving the states we had scarcely ever stretched tents. In the night, as ill-luck would have it, our mules, poor creatures, which stood shivering in the cold with bowed backs and drooping heads, suffering from their exposed situation and half starved, being now reduced to a pint of corn a day, and having no other resources for food, broke loose from their weak fastenings of sage bushes, and started off *en masse* on the back trail in order to obtain the shelter of the mountains we had left the day before or to find some shrubbery they could eat. As soon as it was certain that they were gone, in the middle of the night, we had to rise from our beds, lifting half a foot of snow with our top blankets, and strike out in pursuit of them through the severe cold. We overtook them several miles from camp, and taking them back, made them secure. But we rested little the balance of the night.

The next day we reached the Rio Grande del Norte, which we found frozen over, and camped in the river bottom, which is thickly timbered with cottonwood and willow. We had considerable difficulty in crossing the river, the mules slipping upon the ice and falling or breaking through in places, when we would have to raise them to their feet or draw them over the ice. We found some game, deer and elk, in the river bottom, of which we killed a few. The snow was deeper along here than we had seen it anywhere previously, and our camps, pitched upon it, presented a dreary prospect.

They had reached the Rio Grande at about the site of the present town of Monte Vista, Colorado. It was now December 11th. Before them rose the main chain of the Rockies, the high San Juan Mountains to the west and southwest, the Uncompahgre, La Garita, and Sawatch to the northwest and north. The critical moment for the expedition had arrived—the moment when they must determine by which pass they would scale this mountain wall.

By all accounts, this moment found Frémont and old Bill Williams in fatal disagreement. Although the precise issue between them is not clear, Frémont certainly declared for one route while the scout called for another. According to a story told by T. E. Brackenridge, one of the mountain-men, many years later, and related at second-hand in 1896, Williams wished to go far to the south around the San Juan Mountains, where the continental divide flattens out in northern New Mexico, and then push west on what is now the Colorado-New Mexico boundary. This trail was well known and not difficult; but to have gone so far south would have defeated the whole object of the expedition. The same authority states that Frémont insisted on continuing in a westerly direction along the thirty-eighth parallel, moving up the Rio Grande and past its head. He would thus approach the 9,200-foot pass immediately north of the river-head called the Stony Pass; and if they could get through this, they would prove the thirty-eighth parallel practicable for a railway. It seems probable that Frémont did have this route in mind. But for some reason the party did not really take it; instead, it pushed up the side of La Garita Mountain, whose altitude was 12,000 feet, with some heights beyond even higher. Whose fault was this? On this point the evidence differs, and a clear decision is impossible.[15]

According to Frémont and Alexis Godey, it was Bill Williams who led them astray. He it was who took them toward the impracticable La Garita steep when they should have headed for Cochetopa Pass. They probably did not get as far west as the Gap before he turned them north into the mountains. "The error of our journey," wrote Frémont, "was committed in engaging this man. He proved never to have known, or entirely to have forgotten, the whole region of the country through which we were to pass." Edward M. Kern at the time believed Williams at fault. This is clearly shown by a recently

15 Dellenbaugh, *Frémont and '49*, p. 391*ff.*

discovered letter written February 11, 1849, to Robidoux. In this he states: "We continued a couple of days on the [Rio Grande] del Norte, and then turned up what Williams called your pass on to the Compadne [Uncompahgre?]. In this he was evidently mistaken, for a worse road I never saw." Later, after a quarrel with Frémont, Kern turned about and blamed Frémont. But we also have a full letter written by Alexis Godey in 1856, contradicting Kern's later statement, and upholding Frémont. He wrote: [16]

And now as to the statement made by the Messrs. Kerns, in relation to which you wish my opinion. I will say that every man who was with Col. Frémont on that unfortunate trip to the Carnero Pass [Godey means the Wagon-Wheel] knows it to be untrue. I had the honor of being in command under Col. Frémont on that expedition, and I say now, as I have ever averred, that if there were blame to be attached to any source, on Bill Williams, our guide, and myself should its entire weight rest.

Col. Frémont was, from the time we first came in sight of the Carnero Pass, on the 8th of December, to the 17th, a period of nine days, strongly averse to taking it in our course, preferring to turn off and go through the Cochetopy, a pass some thirty miles to the right; and scarcely a night passed without a consultation took place between the Colonel, myself, Williams, and others; but Williams, who had, as he said, frequently traveled it, evinced so much confidence, and was so strenuous in his efforts to carry his point, that I was completely in his favor, and always told the Colonel that I myself was perfectly willing to trust Williams and follow him; and in this way we traveled on, Frémont unconvinced, yet without any reason to urge, until the 12th instant, when Williams and myself, being ahead, were overtaken by Frémont, who rode up and halted us, and the entire party stopped in the middle of the day. The Colonel then again expressed his fears of trouble ahead, and then it was that Williams told him, that "if he doubted his capacity to carry the party through, say so, and he could get another pilot"; he as-

[16] For this illuminating document see New York *Evening Post*, October 30, 1856. For the very important new letter by Kern, which utterly discredits his later attack on Frémont, see Chapter XXXVII of this book.

serted in the most positive terms that "he knew every inch of the country better than the Colonel knew his own garden." Having every confidence myself in Williams, I advised the Colonel to let him go on, that I was perfectly willing to follow him, and that everything would result favorably.

This was the last consultation on the subject. Frémont acceded to our united arguments, and, the die cast, we pushed on, with what result is well known. For the subsequent misfortunes that befell us, Frémont is not reprehensible. He trusted to his guides, in whose representations he was bound to place confidence, and that they were deceived was no fault of his.

This is strong and circumstantial evidence. Some support for it is furnished by the fact that Bill Williams took special pride in the Wagon-Wheel Pass, which he had discovered, and which many called by his name. In summer it offered a road through the San Juan Mountains to Grand River one day shorter than by the Carnero Pass, and nearly two days shorter than by the Cochetopa. Perhaps Williams did not know that in winter the snows made it quite impassable. He seems to have headed toward it for a time, and then turned blindly up Embargo Creek into the roughest mountain country. On the other hand, several witnesses besides Brackenridge are emphatic that Frémont and not Williams was to blame for going astray. Edward M. Kern's second story, so clearly prejudiced and so flatly at variance with his first, must now be set aside.[17] But Richard Wootton, who was at Taos when the survivors came in and talked to them, declared that if Frémont had taken Williams' advice "he would never have run into the death trap," and that the explorer, having "picked out the route which he wanted to travel over the mountains," stuck to it with blind stubbornness. The same view was expressed by Dr. R. H. Wirz, an army surgeon at Taos at the time. John Scott, a mountain-man with the party, testified that Frémont had insisted on taking the fatal route after Williams proposed the Cochetopa Pass. An even more expert witness, Antoine

[17] Compare Fort Sutter Papers, Huntington Library, MS No. 125.

Leroux, after gathering all the information he could find, wrote
Kern that Williams' knowledge of that part of the country was
excellent, and "the course which was taken by Colonel Frémont was an impracticable one in winter. . . ." [18]

What is certain is that Frémont's party, after pushing up
the Rio Grande cañon for several days, plunged directly into
mountain defiles which offered only a terrible cul de sac. When
they found their way blocked, they turned north into the La
Garita range, forty miles wide, and without any known pass.
Here they soon found themselves in perilous difficulties. The
ascending track lay through deep mountain gorges, amid tower-
ing precipices and crags, and along slopes so steep that again
and again, as they toiled along, a mule would lose its footing
and go rolling to the bottom. They had to cross rough-bottomed
and boggy streams which rushed precipitately down deep ravines, and in which the pack animals would stick tight, sometimes half a dozen in a group. Thereupon Frémont and his men
would turn back, wade in up to their waists in the floating
ice, and shove, haul, and belabor the animals until they scram-
bled, dripping, up the banks. The obstacles multipled as they
went on. Every day the snowdrifts became more appalling in
depth, and the cold more intense. Every night more mules
succumbed and were found stark and stiff at dawn. "It seemed
like fighting fate to attempt to proceed," wrote McGehee, "but
we were bent on our course, and continued to advance."

Once, the men in advance returned with the hopeful news

---

[18] On this vexed question of responsibility, see Favour, *Old Bill Williams*,
Chs. 14, 15, 16; Chauncey Pratt Williams, *Lone Elk, The Life Story of Bill
Williams, Old West Series*, Nos. 6, 7; Dellenbaugh, *op. cit.*; the Fort Sutter
Papers, especially MSS 125-130; Bigelow, *Frémont*, p. 391, which gives
Frémont's letter of December 11, 1849, on the subject. I see no justification
for dogmatic assertions on the immediate responsibility for losing the party
in the San Juan or La Garita Mountains; the evidence is too partial and confused. Brackinridge's testimony was given so long after the event *a priori*
it seems less weighty than Godey's. It must also be remembered that the Kerns
had quarreled with Frémont, and their evidence was surely prejudiced. But
Godey's letter was written in part for campaign purposes. The question admits
of no certain answer. Frémont's larger responsibility for the disaster is of
course beyond doubt.

that there was a clearer prospect ahead and that they thought they saw grass; but when the main party came up, they found that it was only the tops of trees and bushes peering from the all-extending sea of snow. Repeatedly the expedition would break camp in the morning and set off bravely, only to find the tempest of snow too fierce to face. The bitter wind, sweeping across the peaks with incredible velocity, cut like a knife. Sometimes they were mocked at nightfall by a furnace sunset, which seemed to give out cold rather than heat, but for the most part the sky was a leaden pall. On one of the marches into the teeth of a storm, Old Bill Williams was so nearly overcome that he dropped down upon his mule in a drowsy stupor, and was almost senseless when his companions dragged him back to camp.

But it was the tortures which the fierce weather and the rough trail inflicted upon the pack animals which were most heartrending. The corn was now exhausted and the beasts were crazed with hunger. They would roam about ravenously all night, and being too weak to break a new path, would usually wander back along the trail of the previous day, pawing in the snow for vegetation. They began devouring the rawhide lariats with which they were tied; they followed this by eating the blankets which were thrown over them at night, the rigging of the pack-saddles, and finally even one another's manes and tails. They were mere specters of skin and bones; the weaker mules collapsed every fifty yards, and the men, with frozen and lacerated fingers, had to unfasten their packs and lift them up.

Finally they reached the naked, treeless crest of the Great Divide. The cold here was more intense than ever, while the storms on these high rocky ridges were almost incessant. Twice Frémont, with unconquerable resolution, forced his men to attempt a passage. On the first day, they encountered a blizzard or *pouderie*, the dry snow driven so thick by the gale that it was impossible to see more than a few feet in advance, while the roar was deafening and at times it was difficult to catch breath. After a brief fight, the men were forced back into camp.

Dead mules were lying about the fires, and it continued all night to snow steadily. Next day the storm had ceased; they made mauls and, beating a road through the snow, crossed the ridge in defiance of the gale, and pitched camp just below the timber line. "The trail," Frémont wrote, "showed as if a defeated army had passed by; pack-saddles and packs, scattered articles of clothing, and dead mules strewed along." Then the blizzard returned and paralyzed the party. They were now twelve thousand feet above the sea, and in an almost hopeless position. The long rolling ranges and valleys to the westward were buried in snow. It was impossible to go on, and almost equally impossible to turn back. "We were overtaken," Frémont writes, "by sudden and irretrievable ruin."

Under the circumstances, the only hope of escape lay in an immediate retreat. Frémont determined to recross the crest, but very mistakenly decided to try to take the baggage back with him down to the Rio Grande. Along this stream he hoped to find game. On the twenty-second of December they commenced their movement, and being now reduced to man-power, required more than a week to move their camp and equipage over the top of the pass, a distance of two miles, to the head springs of a stream leading to the river. At this altitude the slightest exertion was laborious, and sometimes caused long attacks of nosebleed. The snow was from four to thirty feet in depth; and when they built their camp-fires, cavernous pits were formed, completely hiding the different messes from each other. Deep in these holes the men slept, spreading their blankets upon the snow. In the daytime some of them, half blinded by the pine smoke and the frozen glare, staggered about uncertainly. They had begun to suffer greatly from hunger, and were living in the main upon the carcasses of the frozen mules, which they supplemented by butchering the few feverish animals which remained.

Christmas Day was spent in an atmosphere of deep depression. The men were worn out and utterly discouraged; worse than that, they were grumbling at Frémont for having obstinately thrust them into all this suffering and danger. Three men of the old exploring party, Godey, King, and Taplin, continued loyal and cheerful, but even Kern had become morose and resentful. Reduced to an emergency reserve of macaroni, sugar, and bacon, they did not possess provisions for twenty days. Frémont occupied the early hours of the day in despatching an express party to the nearest settlements to bring relief. Calling for volunteers, and choosing King, Brackenridge, Creutzfeldt, and Bill Williams, he equipped them with rations and instructed them to hurry with all speed to the nearest settlements in New Mexico, and to bring back provisions and mules to an agreed point upon the Rio Grande. Then, after seeing the four men disappear among the snowy pines, he turned back to the circle cowering about his snow-pit camp-fire. He thought of the previous Christmas in Washington, and the merry faces and abundant luxuries of Senator Benton's home. From the Senator's library in the Brant house in St. Louis he had fetched some volumes of Blackstone, to be the foundation for his possible entrance upon the practice of law in California; and, his mind "filled with gloom and anxious thoughts," he now brought these out to read and pass the hours. Then next day the remaining party set about removing the baggage back to the Rio Grande.

Descending along the little stream, over ground so rugged that they averaged scarcely a mile a day, Frémont's men finally reached the Rio Grande again. While they were thus engaged, their last regular provisions had been divided, and they began boiling their rawhide ropes and parfleches to make a gluey soup. The cold seemed to redouble in the final bleak seven miles, and one of the men, Raphael Proue, becoming exhausted, lay down beside the trail and froze to death. The others in transporting the baggage passed and repassed his body, not daring to stop long enough to bury him. At one point Cathcart, McGehee, and two others were imprisoned in a cave for two days by a terrific storm, with no subsistence except some rawhide shoestrings and old wolf-gnawed bones. When at last the expedition made camp on the river, they found as a fresh blow that there was no game, the deer and elk having all been driven off by the deep snow.

Frémont had given the party which he sent under King to seek relief sixteen days as ample time to make the round trip, and for a while simply waited on the Rio Grande. But when the period elapsed, with the ebbing hopes of his men giving way to despair, he grew too uneasy to stay longer. Either King and his men had lost their way, he feared, or had been cut off by hostile Ute or Apache Indians. There was just one course to follow—to set out for relief himself. Taking Preuss, Godey, and two other trusted men, with enough provisions for two or three days, he started down the river. He left orders that the men were to finish bringing all the baggage into camp, and push on with it after him till they were met by the help he would send back. He also made a statement which seems to have increased the mutinous resentment in the breasts of some of his followers: that if they wished to see him they would have to hurry, for he was going on to California.

To tell in detail the horrors which attended the closing days of the ill-fated expedition, now split into three groups, would be unnecessary and repellent. Frémont made rapidly down the ice of the Rio Grande. He hoped to meet the returning party of Bill Williams; or failing that, to reach the Red River settlement one hundred and sixty miles away, and twenty-five miles north of Taos. On the sixth day, led by a friendly Ute whom they met, they discovered a little smoke in a grove of timber near the river bank, and went to investigate it. Here they found the relief party which, twenty-two days earlier, they had sent out from the main camp. Three tottering scarecrows were left, Williams, Brackenridge, and Creutzfeldt, the most miserable objects Frémont had ever seen; and they told him that King had starved to death a few days before. Later on, charges were made that they had partly eaten his body; and Frémont records in his manuscript *Memoirs* a significant remark by Kit Carson that "in starving times no man who knew him ever walked in

front of Bill Williams." [19] Some think this charge of cannibalism dubious, and that if the body had been partly devoured, it was probably by animals or vultures. Placing the three men on some horses which he had obtained from the Utes, Frémont hastened on to the Red River settlement, reaching it on the tenth evening after leaving the main camp. He at once took steps to hurry a relief party under Godey, with pack animals and provisions which he obtained from Rio Hondo and Taos, back to the half-starved men left far up on the Rio Grande.

The word half-starved is a euphemism; for, by Frémont's own statement, the party was left with provisions for only two or three meals, with some five pounds of sugar additional for each man. Its position was desperate, and to stand still was simply to wait for death. Two days after Frémont had left, when they were down to their last crumb, they held a consultation and decided to start down the river at once, hunting as they went along. Each man had a handful of sugar and they divided some bits of candles and rawhide. Trembling from weakness, their feet frozen and bleeding, they marched in gloomy silence. The river was a white streak of snow-blanketed ice; the somber pines on each side were covered with long thick plumes of frost; there was not a sound of life—not the shriek of a jay, not the howl of a wolf. They had not gone far on the first day when the California Indian Manuel, whose feet were turning black, stopped, begged his mates to kill him, and then started back to the camp. A little farther on another man, exhausted and half frozen, threw away his gun and blanket, staggered on a few hundred yards, fell into the snow, and died. That night a third, Carver, raved so violently that his companions became afraid of him, and in the morning, half-crazed, he wandered off into the woods and was never seen again. Thus the survivors went on, the strongest forging ahead, the weakest straggling far behind, while death strode with them. Some of the men were fortunate enough to knock over

[19] Frémont MSS, Bancroft Library. The Red River here mentioned is a small branch of the Rio Grande, and not the well-known river of that name.

two grouse, which they ate even to the entrails, and to find part
of a dead wolf along the river, which they also devoured; some
filled their stomachs with dried buds from the bushes, and
scooped up water bugs where the river ice had melted slightly.
Frémont has feelingly described the fate of several, and the
arrival of relief:

Ferguson and Beadle had remained behind. In the evening, Rohrer
came up and remained with Kern's mess. Mr. Haler learned afterwards from that mess that Rohrer and Andrews wandered off the
next day and died. They say they saw their bodies. In the morning
Haler's party continued on. After a few hours, Hibbard gave out.
They built him a fire, gathered him some wood, and left him without, as Haler says, turning their heads to look at him as they went
off. About two miles further Scott...gave out. They did the same
for him as for Hibbard, and continued on. In the afternoon the
Indian boys went ahead, and before nightfall met Godey with the
relief. Haler heard and knew the guns which he fired for him at
night, and starting early in the morning, soon met him. I hear that
they all cried together like children. Haler turned back with Godey,
and went with him to where they had left Scott. He was still alive,
and was saved. Hibbard was dead—still warm.

When the first far-off halloo told that relief had come, eleven
in all of the thirty-three hardy frontiersmen who had set out
from Pueblo into the mountains had lost their lives, and the
remainder were mere wrecks of humanity.[20] They were so ema-
ciated that they looked like walking skeletons; their hair and
beards were long and tangled; their faces were waxen under
a mask of smoke and grime. Some of them had to be lifted
upon the mules which Godey brought. In this condition they
were all taken down to Taos, and the tragic venture was ended.
While apparently a large part of the blame for the disastrous

[20] Favour in *Old Bill Williams*, p. 168, gives the names: Raphael Proue,
died January 9th; Henry King, January 12th; Henry Wise, January 17th;
Manuel, January 21st or thereabouts; Vincent Sorel. January 22nd; Joseph
Moran, between the 22nd and 28th; E. T. Andrews and Henry Rohrer,
January 22nd; Benjamin Beadle, January 26th; George A. Hibbard and
Carver, January 27th. The remainder arrived in Taos destitute.

failure rests upon Bill Williams, who was unable to impress Frémont with his knowledge of the country, and upon King and Williams jointly for their strange failure later to find the right path down the Rio Grande toward Taos, Frémont himself cannot be acquitted of the principal responsibility. He insisted upon attempting the crossing of the range after he had been warned in the most solemn terms at Bent's Fort and Pueblo that it would be highly dangerous and probably impossible, and after Williams had entered an emphatic protest. It was therefore incumbent upon him, once the passage was under way, to use every precaution to insure the safety of his men. The weight of evidence indicates that instead he clung stubbornly to his plan for moving westward along the upper waters of the Rio Grande and the thirty-eighth parallel after its perils had been forcibly pointed out. But his cardinal error was committed when he turned back deliberately instead of speedily. He should have taken what food and pack animals remained, abandoned the luggage, and made all speed to the nearest settlement, keeping his party a unit. By trying to extricate the baggage, he lost eleven men. A severe critic would say that their lives were upon his head. To be sure, as Godey explained later, he had provisions at the moment for eighteen or twenty days, and felt almost sure that King and Williams would return with help within that time; but he should have taken into consideration the very real risk that they would lose their way or be slain by savages.

Edward Kern later attacked Frémont for not using the frozen mules, after the departure of King on Christmas Day, for food. But Godey is no doubt right in answering that this was impossible, inasmuch as the weather was too severe to permit the men to get the carcasses out of drifts twenty feet deep. As for the failure of King and Williams to keep on the straight path to the settlements, this now seems inexplicable. By Godey's testimony, before they started they and Frémont had fixed and determined every day's journey, and the various camping places, both going and coming; they were experienced,

capable frontiersmen; and Williams supposedly knew the whole region. Yet they did not get fifty miles from their starting place.

It would have been much more in keeping with Frémont's usual gallantry of conduct had he returned up the Rio Grande with the relief party from Taos which, under Godey, did the actual work of rescue. Possibly he was too exhausted; one leg was badly frozen, and reports to the eastern press from a Taos correspondent declared that he was "very severely frosted and scarcely able to get about." Members of his party reported him almost snow-blind. But if he was at all able to travel, he should never have rested while one of his men remained in danger in the wilderness. He took shelter in Kit Carson's hospitable home, where on January 27, 1849, we find him writing Jessie:[21] "This morning a cup of chocolate was brought to me, while yet in bed. To an overworn, overworked, much fatigued, and starving traveller, these little luxuries of the world offer an interest which in your comfortable home it is not possible for you to conceive." He spoke of Kit Carson's care, "constantly occupied and constantly uneasy in endeavoring to make me comfortable." After laying the blame for the debacle upon Williams, he spoke harshly of the want of nerve among many of his party, whose courage in the crisis had "failed fast." Unquestionably, his failure to go back, and the freedom with which he criticized his associates, accentuated the bitterness with which the three Kern brothers and others of his men always spoke of his leadership of the expedition.

Frémont was never a man for useless repining; he wrote Jessie that he had an "almost invincible repugnance" for the task of describing his sufferings, and his whole attention was now centered upon proceeding overland to California. From Major Edward F. Beale, who had been in the California fight-

[21] Bigelow, *Frémont*, pp. 365-376, contains two letters from Frémont to Jessie, one dated January 27th, one February 6, 1849. In the second letter he speaks of "a persistence of misfortune which no precaution has been adequate on my part to avert." It is a pity that he did not detail some of his precautions.

ing, had been Carson's associate in the heroic crawl through the Mexican lines after the battle of San Pasqual, and was now commanding the army forces in northern New Mexico, he received the kindest assistance, including the loan of horses and the sale of provisions from the commissary's department. Almost all his clothing and money had been lost; the saddles, instruments, and baggage had been cached in the mountains. Before leaving Taos, Frémont made an effort to regain this material, but the deep snow prevented the party he sent out from getting through. Other men besides Carson and Beale came to his aid, for Taos was full of old friends—Dick Owens, Lucien Maxwell, and Francis Aubrey among them; and Aubrey lent him a thousand dollars to purchase animals to continue his journey.

Before he left Taos, Frémont told the men of his reunited party that he would be glad to mount and equip all who would accompany him to the Pacific. Most of them, including Godey, volunteered to go. The three Kern brothers, who were impatient to return to the States, Bill Williams, and a few others declined. It may be mentioned that the following spring, Williams and Dr. Kern returned to the scene of the disaster to recover the baggage, Brackenridge's twelve hundred dollars in money, and Edward Kern's collection of specimens in natural history, and that they were attacked and killed, either by Indians or by some treacherous Mexicans who accompanied them. To increase the ill-feeling among those who were left behind, they received the impression that Frémont had made an unfair division of the stores bought from the commissary, though later Godey earnestly denied that this was the fact. It was not until they reached Albuquerque, according to Godey, that Frémont was able to obtain military supplies in any quantity. The new party which the explorer outfitted here and in Santa Fé consisted of twenty-five men and sixty horses, and he planned to use them in going south of the Sierras by way of the Gila River.

The early incidents of this final stage of his trip, Frémont has jotted down in his usual crisp English in the rough notes previously referred to: [22]

With 25 men all told and outfit renewed I resume journey, following down the Del Norte and intending to reach the Rio Grande by a route south of Gila River. The snows this season too heavy to insist on a direct route through the mountains. Engage a New Mexican for guide—spring weather in the valley—fruit trees in bloom—hospitality. Leave the river—open country—snowed on again—no wood and weather cold. Retreat into the Membres Mountains. Pleasant country, well wooded, resembling the oak region of the Sierra Nevada— color of soil—grass and water abundant. Travel along foot of mountains. Apaches around the camp—watch and watch—McGehee fired on—halt and have parley with chief—make friends. The Indians go to Membres River with us. Breakfast and presents. Indians direct us to watering place in the open country—appoint to meet us there —their war parties out in Chihuahua and Sonora. I push forward and avoid them.

The Apache visitor—Santa Cruz. The Mexican and the bunch of grass. Follow down the Santa Cruz River—Tucson. Spring on the Santa Cruz—peach orchard—the ruined missions. River lost in the sand. The grass field and water at foot of the hills. Reach the Gila River. The Pimah village (see Johnson's report)—Indian faces painted with black lead.

Follow the river around the bend. Meet large party of Sonorans going to California. Their pleasure in meeting us. Their fear of Indians. They urge me to travel with them. I consent. Many presents of fruit and provisions in various forms. Reach the Gila River. Determine position of the junction with the Rio Grande. Make bullboat—ferry women and children of the Sonorans across, with my party, and leave the bullboat for the men to complete their crossing.

Frémont was not merely undaunted; he believed that his fourth expedition had succeeded in its main object. "The survey has been uninterrupted up to this point," he wrote bravely from Taos to Jessie, "and I shall carry it on consecutively." Later, he publicly declared: "The result was entirely satis-

[22] Frémont MSS, Bancroft Library.

factory. It convinced me that neither the snow of winter nor the mountain ranges were obstacles in the way of the road, and furnished me with a far better line [for a railway] than any I had previously known." He had hopes that, if the continuance of his labors as an explorer proved to have been useful, President Zachary Taylor would take him back into government service for work upon the West coast.

For the rest, he looked forward to making a new home for Jessie, whose arrival he expected in March. The immediate prospect was that he would have to wage a legal battle before he could even claim the land upon which he had set his heart. When he gave Larkin $3,000, it was to purchase a chosen property on the hills some distance back of San Francisco. Its old orchards and vines and its atmosphere of peace and rest had appealed strongly to him, while its view over the sea recalled his Charleston boyhood. But by some error Larkin bought instead from Juan Alvarado a wild tract in the Sierra foothills, more than a hundred miles from the ocean and nearly that far from any settlement—the famous Mariposas tract, seventy square miles in area. Hostile Indians of the sturdy Cauchile tribe roamed the region in such numbers that it was impossible to reside there, or to pasture cattle, which would have been quickly destroyed. The land was apparently almost worthless. Frémont had felt outraged when, just before leaving California as Kearny's prisoner, he learned of this, and had told Larkin that he would return to demand a just settlement. He had consulted Senator Benton, whose long experience in land cases arising from the Louisiana Purchase had made his advice valuable, and had laid plans to institute a lawsuit. He meant to get either the property originally selected, or his $3,000.[23]

Despite such worries, he wrote in confident vein to Jessie. "I make frequent pleasant pictures," he told her, "of the

[23] Details of the legal history of this purchase are given in Bigelow, *Frémont*, pp. 379*ff*. It was bought under a Mexican title after California became a territory of the United States. Alvarado executed the deed to Frémont on February 10, 1847.

happy home we are to have, and oftenest and among the pleasantest of all I see our library with its bright fire in the rainy stormy days, and the large windows looking out upon the sea in the bright weather. I have it all planned in my own mind." But all his schemes for exploring, for a career at the bar, for developing a ranch, were suddenly forgotten when he learned the news which, coming from California during 1848, had electrified the civilized world.

XXIII

Golconda and the Senate

THE dramatic vicissitudes which make Frémont's life so romantic, the extraordinary alternations of disaster and good fortune which mark its course, were never better illustrated than now. Emerging from a humiliating court-martial, he had just been thrown into the jaws of death, and had escaped only after terrible suffering and loss. But already Fortune was spinning her wheel. She was about to toss into his lap a seat in the Federal Senate, and an estate of such wealth that within a few years it would be valued by cool-headed business men at ten million dollars.

The rough notes of Frémont's which we have just printed indicate the general course of his overland journey from Taos. At Santa Fé, he dined with the military governor of the territory, Colonel Washington, and at Socorro with the local commandant. Pursuing a general southwesterly line, he penetrated well into Mexico, touching Santa Cruz in that republic, and then turned northwest toward Tucson in what is now Arizona. From the point where he reached the Gila, his line of march was along its south bank. Here one blazing forenoon he descried in the distance a cloud of dust, in which vague figures drifted along the river margin. Hurrying on, he overtook a whole community on the move—Jessie Frémont says twelve hundred men, women, and children; babies crying, drivers hallooing, mules dragging lurching carts, and horses burdened with packs. Spurring up beside the rear guard, he asked, "Where are you going?" "Alta California," came the reply. "Why such a crowd of you?" demanded the puzzled Frémont. "Gold! Gold!" was the answer.

It was the first news Frémont had received of the discovery of gold on Sutter's property. Word had traveled most rapidly by sea; it had reached the ports of western Mexico—Guaymas, Mazatlan, Colima—before it penetrated to Tucson; and all Sonora was alive with the excitement which had emptied San Francisco and Monterey in a rush for the gold-fields. These Sonora Mexicans were on their way to the diggings. Frémont acted with characteristic impetuosity. Mariposa might be the best property after all. He leaped to the conclusion that gold would be found on his new lands, and promptly engaged twenty-eight Mexicans to work for him. He was to grubstake them, they were to contribute their muscle and skill, and the gold was to be equally divided.

Frémont, with his now impressive cavalcade, pressed on rapidly to Los Angeles and Monterey, where he expected Jessie to be already waiting for him. He little guessed what his wife had been through. She had crossed the Isthmus safely under the escort of her brother-in-law, Jacobs. It had been a horrible trip; she went up the Chagres River by slowly poled boats, burned by the sun, tormented by flies and mosquitoes, drinking dirty water, eating hastily cooked food, fearing the fever at every move; thence she crossed the rest of the way by mule train, sleeping at the camps of railway surveyors. Her brother-in-law marveled at her courage. "He judged, as we all do," she wrote later,[1] "by appearances. As there were no complaints or tears or visible breakdown, he gave me credit for high courage, while the fact was that the whole thing was so like a nightmare, that one took it as a bad dream—in helpless silence." When she arrived in Panama on the West coast, she was overtaken by "forty-niners" from New York, who brought word of the tragic fate of the fourth expedition; and here she also received Frémont's long letter from Taos, giving a full account of the disaster. At the same time, she learned that there was no boat to take her on north.

The vessel on which she had expected to proceed to Califor-

[1] Jessie Benton Frémont, *A Year of American Travel*, p. 56.

nia had not returned, for all its men had deserted to rush for
the mines, and the captain was fuming helplessly in San Francisco Bay. Steamer after steamer was arriving on the Atlantic
side of the Isthmus, and discharging thousands of eager gold
hunters, who hurried across to the Pacific—and then sat down
and swore. Fortunately, Jessie bore letters of introduction,
which soon rescued her from the intolerable heat, noise, and
dirt of the hotel. She went to the home of Mme. Arcé, a cul-
tivated widow, and, worn out by anxiety for Frémont and by
hardship, promptly collapsed. A friend named Mr. Gray one
morning brought her a newspaper containing a letter of her
father's describing the Frémont expedition, and in the evening,
when he returned with further news, found her sitting exactly
as he had left her, the paper in her hand and her forehead
purple from congestion of the brain. All Mme. Arcé's tender
nursing was needed.

As she was regaining her strength after a fever which had
almost brought her to a sudden grave, one night in the stillness
she heard the signal gun of a steamer far out at sea. There
was an instant uproar in the town. By scores, by hundreds,
the Americans rushed clattering and shouting down the streets
to the ramparts, while the excitable natives filled the streets
screaming *"El vapor!"* When the hubbub was at its height,
there suddenly came, from another quarter, a second signal
gun. Two steamers were in the offing. Wrapped in her dressing-
gown, and watching from a balcony, Jessie saw men weeping
and hugging one another as if they were Crusoes being taken
from some desert island. One ship, the *Panama,* had rounded
the Horn; the other, the *California,* had scraped together a
crew and come down from San Francisco. The next morning
Jessie was waited upon by the captain of the *Panama* and by
a naval officer, who told her she was to take their vessel. Among
her fellow-passengers were William M. Gwin and the handsome
young army officer later famous as "Fighting Joe" Hooker.
She went aboard still beset by fears for Frémont's safety, but
at San Diego was greeted by news that he had arrived before

her and had hurried on to San Francisco. "I think every man on the ship," she says, "came to tell me and say a choking word for joy for me." [2]

As her daughter Lilly relates the story, when the ship ran into San Diego, Jessie locked herself into her cabin, fearful of the tidings she might hear. The first men to board the vessel knocked at her door and called out: "The colonel's safe; riding up to San Francisco to meet you there; he didn't lose a leg— was only badly frostbitten!" [3]

Carried ashore through the surf to what is now the foot of Montgomery Street in San Francisco, Jessie found that Frémont had not yet arrived. She also found the region wild with excitement. San Francisco was a half-deserted town; deserted, that is, by its original inhabitants, and peopled mainly by new-comers counting the hours until they could get away to the interior. No servants could be had except half-trained Indians and Chinese. Mrs. Frémont was told that "time was worth fifty dollars a minute." The people lived as transients would be expected to live, in tents of dirty canvas, shanties knocked together with odd pieces of wood, or ragged shelters of blankets. The one really good private house in these first roaring "days of old, and days of gold, and the days of '49," was a two-story frame structure shipped out complete by a New Yorker, with furniture to fill it, at a cost said to reach ninety thousand dollars. It had been intended for a bride, and had witnessed her death a few weeks after it was erected. The only settled residents, besides a small corps of tradesmen who realized that the retail business was surer and richer than any placer venture they were likely to find, were the military officers, who stuck courageously to their posts. As there were no warehouses for the storage of goods, consignments were auctioned off as quickly as they arrived; and these auctions, advertised sometimes by brass bands, were a feature of the place. The hotels and lodging-houses being comfortless, at night almost the

2 Jessie Benton Frémont, *Souvenirs of My Time*, p. 188.
3 Elizabeth Benton Frémont MSS, Bancroft Library.

whole population betook itself to the saloons and gambling-dens. Within a few months, many of these places assumed the trappings of luxury: plate-glass mirrors, fine chandeliers, gaudy oil-paintings. Public improvements were conspicuously lacking: the streets were rivers of mud, which men tried to pave sometimes with bags of flour, bales of cotton, or other goods —for wood was not to be had. Water was one of the most precious of commodities, and laundry-work cost fabulous sums. With inadequate sanitary arrangements, cholera and fever were a grim menace, and the death-rate was high.[4]

Ships were now coming into the port in a steady stream, many of them fifty or sixty days from New York, some forty days from Australia, and some direct from Europe. As they discharged their cargoes and men, San Francisco underwent a swift change in appearance. High piers were hurriedly built out into the Bay. The ragged streets of shanties and tents, with the winds blowing furious clouds of dust down them, stretched farther and farther back over the hills. Everywhere arose buildings of all shapes and sizes, in all stages of construction. Many were mere canvas-covered sheds, open in front. Masses of merchandise were piled higgledly-piggledly in the open air, sometimes under a dirty tarpaulin, sometimes exposed. They displayed rudely painted signs in every European tongue and advertising every ware; while prominent among these "stores" rose several hotels—the Frémont Family Hotel, a two-story structure, the Parker House, the City Hotel, and others—all crammed to bursting.

Along the public ways, ankle-deep in mud or dust, crowded people of every nationality and description: Yankees nasal and electric, guttural Germans, nervous Frenchmen, burly Britons, Chinese with swinging pigtails, Californians wrapped in serapes, Chileans, Kanakas, and Malays with long creeses. Far back from the water-front lay the plaza (called Portsmouth Square after the warship which Frémont had found here in

---

[4] Stewart Edward White, *The Fortyniners*, Chs. 8, 9, and 10, picture early San Francisco.

'47), with a high flagpole marking the adobe customhouse. Military forces policed the town. The atmosphere was one of feverish activity. Everybody was talking of claims, of diggings, of town lots, of the new cities of Sacramento and Stockton; everybody hoped to get rich.[5]

The hurry, the wild new monetary standards, and the speculative spirit bewildered the newcomer. A porter who carried one's bags a few blocks demanded $2 in payment; an old New York newspaper sold at $1 a copy; and truckmen driving for merchants of the town made $15 or $20 a day. The sudden wealth had attracted an army of gamblers and saloon-keepers. At least $60,000 a year in rent was paid by the gamblers who at one time occupied most of the second story of the Parker House. A canvas tent near-by, called "Eldorado" by the faro and monte men who occupied it, only 15 by 20 feet in size, was rented for $40,000 a year. A wandering Easterner who wished to hang out his shingle as a lawyer was shown a cellar dug in the ground and told he could have it for $250 a month. All business was transacted with a rush, and men who tried to bargain were brushed impatiently aside.

If a customer entered a store, the owner eyed him with indifference, named the price he wanted for a given article, and turned away if the customer objected. Money in smaller amounts than a quarter-dollar did not pass current. The large-minded attitude toward financial affairs was seen at its best in the implicit trust which men were perforce compelled to place in one another's honesty. Loans were made without security, and repaid punctually. Yet the gambling spirit pervaded every group. Bayard Taylor, watching curiously one of the crowded "hells" where sperm-oil lamps lighted up the players' excited features, saw a boy of fifteen coolly pocket $500; one of his fellow-travelers from Panama lose $2,400; and a hard-bitten miner betting great piles of gold dust on a single throw, and finally losing his last hundred ounces at a stroke.

It was here that, ten days after Jessie landed, Frémont

[5] Bayard Taylor, *Eldorado, or Adventures in the Path of Empire*, p. 55.

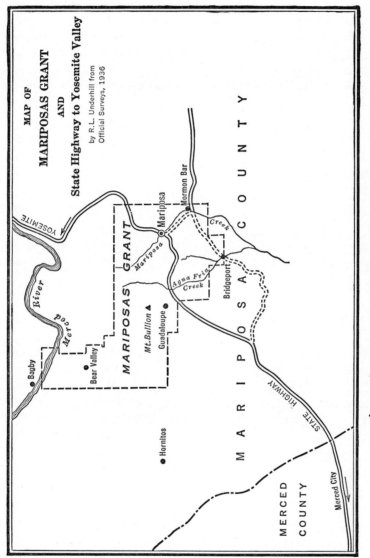

MAP OF
MARIPOSAS GRANT
AND
State Highway to Yosemite Valley

by R.L. Underhill from
Official Surveys, 1936

FRÉMONT'S MARIPOSA ESTATE AS FINALLY LAID OUT

arrived from Monterey. She was sitting in her cheerless room in the Parker House when she heard a shout from Portsmouth Square: "Your wife's inside the house, Colonel." A moment later her husband was kneeling by her chair; both of them too much overcome to utter a sound. She has described the scene with her usual feeling:

> Then we both spoke at once, each wanting the other to begin at the moment we had parted over a stirrup-cup of tea that morning on the Missouri. Suddenly he looked at me closely with fear in his eyes. "You have been ill, you are ill now, my darling." I was about to deny it when Lilly came in.... She looked at her father gravely as he knelt beside me. As he rose and hugged her, then drew a chair up close, and took her on his knee, she said bluntly: "You didn't come. Mother almost died. A lady downstairs says she will die."
>
> There was nothing to say in refutation, but I answered his stricken look: "In her innocence she is partly right. Being away from you is a kind of death. Only with you I am fully alive and well." [6]

When Frémont had exchanged with Jessie the history of the past eventful six months, the two looked earnestly for a home in this rushing beehive. The town changed with visible speed —men said that it grew daily by from fifteen to thirty houses. There was now an ebb-tide or backwash from the mines, as well as a tide setting steadily toward them. Broken-down, sick, and disheartened prospectors were returning from the diggings, and doing what they could to dampen the ardor of the new-comers. As the town leaped up to a population of six thousand its business and professional life increased in vigor. Here the Frémonts met well-known men: Major George H. Derby ("John Phoenix"), who had come on Jessie's ship and had organized theatricals to divert her; Edwin Bryant of Kentucky; the artist Osgood, who after three months in the hills had set up his easel as a portrait painter; and T. Butler King. For a time they lived in a house which had been occupied by the late vice-consul, Leidesdorff. But they could not make

[6] Catherine Coffin Phillips, *Jessie Benton Frémont*, pp. 142, 143.

themselves quite comfortable in San Francisco. The trade winds and fogs injured Jessie's lungs; moreover, it was too far from their new ranch, Mariposa. They therefore betook themselves south to Monterey, where they were only one hundred and twenty-five miles as the crow flies (about one hundred and forty miles by road) from the estate. A wing of the governor's house, the largest and best building in town, was thrown open to them, Mme. José Castro and her children occupying the other half.

For the next few months Jessie, rapidly recovering her health, enjoyed with characteristic zest her life in this long, low adobe house of red-tiled roof, with its spacious gardens and hedge of pink roses of Castile. They had Indian men for kitchen service, and she soon mastered the art of cookery with little meat, no fowls or eggs, no milk or butter, and not even potatoes—for the swarming gold-seekers had devoured all. She made friends with Mme. Castro, whose husband was still exiled in Mexico, but who felt no resentment for their lost position and fortune. Among the army officers then in Monterey, General Bennet Riley, General P. F. Smith, and young W. T. Sherman, who was thin and consumptive-looking, with a bad cough, she found congenial acquaintances. Frémont made a trip to San Francisco, and "with manlike prodigality, sent down what would have fitted up the whole large Castro House." They had bales of Chinese satins and French damasks to use for draperies and hangings, boxes of French and Chinese porcelain, bamboo couches and chairs, and wonderfully carved and inlaid Chinese furniture. Two English-china punchbowls served for wash basins. The house had a large fireplace, and Jessie threw down grizzly-bear skins to give warmth to the mat-covered floors, and to lend a cozy air to recesses between the satin-cushioned sofas and armchairs. Her Indian boys, Gregorio and Juan, shot doves and squirrels, and, broiling them upon sticks before the fire, would bring them at the most unusual hours. Jessie later wrote of the whole experience with enormous pleasure:[7]

[7] Jessie Benton Frémont MSS, Bancroft Library.

This was my first house and my first housekeeping—without any of what we consider indispensable necessities of servants, or usual supplies, but most comfortable and most charming. We had the luxuries of life, if not its necessities. Youth, health, and exultant happiness can do without commonplaces, though it is awkward to have only Indian men for kitchen service, and to study a cookery book and try to follow its directions with no staples. Whatever could be put up in glass or tins we had in quantity—and rice is a great reliance when you learn its many uses. ... Again, I was in the home-keeping domestic atmosphere of Spanish women, who offered me every help, though they could not give what they themselves did not have in this locust-like sweeping away of every green thing and no replanting, for Californians too were off to the placers, and speculators had bought up all attainable cattle and sheep for San Francisco. The expenses for army people were too great up there, so headquarters were at Monterey, and there General Riley planted cabbages and sweet women grew tired but laughed over their contrivances, and were hospitable and helping in spite of all drawbacks. General, then Major Canby, was stationed there, and his most amiable gentle wife was a center of helping good will. They had an excellent cook, a Mexican who had followed the general after the war, and who did not leave them now even to go to the placers. Mrs. Canby took pity on my tinned biscuit diet, and regularly her man came with the fragrant loaf of fresh bread wrapped in its delicate napkin and set on a plate of fine green enameled Chinese china. Who could need cream with tea, to make that a breakfast of delight to mind as well as palate? Mme. Castro, true to the gentle nature of Spanish women, sent daily a cup of milk for my little girl, for she had saved a cow for her children. This was another turn of the wheel. I had the name which represented to her total loss, for her husband had not returned from Mexico after we took her country, and yet her motherly feelings were stronger than the natural resentment for lost position and fortune. She had, though, the innate Spanish pride. A birthday among her children made the opportunity for giving a coral necklace they had admired on my child. The little Modesta brought it back with her soft-voice message. "My mamma says, if it is a present, yes; if it is pay for the milk, no."

Frémont was now spending all the time he could spare at the Mariposa ranch, which he found a singularly attractive place. From high up in the central Sierras, the Mariposa River flows west to join the San Joaquin. To the northeast, some forty miles away, lies the Yosemite; below, toward the Pacific, stretches the hot central valley. Covering a large segment of the Mariposa basin, the estate comprised the high eminence which they called Mount Bullion, in honor of Senator Benton—"Old Bullion"—picturesque wooded foothills of the Sierras, and broad green flats waving with grass. To reach it in summer from Monterey, the traveler had to ride across the scorching plains of the San Joaquin Valley, where the temperature often rose high above one hundred degrees, and ford a number of rushing streams like the Tuolumne. When, through clouds of suffocating dust, he came to slopes covered with the butterfly tulips which gave the ranch its name, and caught a breath of cooler air, he was nearing his destination. Farther up, where Frémont's estate lay, the sparkling atmosphere and the freshness and elasticity it gave every breath made the sun, still very hot, quite endurable. Bear Valley, in which the Colonel soon built a pleasant two-story frame house, was a little natural paradise. Pine trees, six or eight feet in diameter, towered two hundred feet into the air; the streams were full of salmon; the ground was covered with red clover; at night in summer, blankets were required. Not many years before, this spot had been the favorite hunting ground of the Cauchile Indians. The precise boundaries of the 43,000-acre estate, according to the frequent Mexican practice, were not fixed, and the grantee, as the government decided later, had the right of locating the land on any claim within a large area.[8]

Making Monterey his headquarters, Frémont led a life of incessant activity, and Jessie was much of the time at his side. They had a six-seated surrey, the only carriage in the territory, fitted with every convenience. Lilly recalls that for a time after

[8] John R. Howard, *Remembrance of Things Past*, Ch. 9; Bigelow, *Frémont*, p. 379*ff*.

mules were obtained for this vehicle they were perfect nomads, sleeping as much in the open as under a roof. Jessie would have the cushions drawn together in the surrey to form a mattress; the little girl would go to sleep in the boot; and Frémont and the other men would bunk in the open on their blankets or in hammocks strung to the trees. In time they obtained an Englishwoman, newly landed from Australia, as their housekeeper in Monterey, and Jessie writes that "she brought English comfort and thoroughness into everything about me."

Meanwhile, fortune smiled as never before. The Sonora miners had been sent to Mariposa without delay and were busy prospecting and extracting the gold from the river gravel. Bayard Taylor, riding into San José as a correspondent for the New York *Tribune,* happened upon Frémont as the explorer was returning from his first trip to the diggings. They shook hands upon the porch of a private house. The Colonel wore California garb, with sombrero and native-style jacket. Taylor was struck by his deep-set, hawklike eyes, bold aquiline nose, and thin, weather-beaten face; above all, by the compactness of his bodily build—"I have seen in no other man the qualities of lightness, activity, strength, and physical endurance in so perfect an equilibrium." His refinement of manner and polished address, unroughened by the camp life of months, also impressed the journalist. Frémont, despite his recent disasters, was now a man of greater note than ever; for the East, its curiosity aroused by the gold rush, was reading his reports on the West with insatiable appetite.

After a brief period in the old capital the Frémonts temporarily went back to San Francisco, where they established a home on some land which the Colonel had purchased, later (Jessie says) the site of the Palace Hotel. He bought and set up a ready-made Chinese-built house, which fitted together like a puzzle, the only nails being those which fastened the shingles to the roof. Walls and floors were grooved together, and doors and windows slid into their places like some exquisite piece of cabinet-work. The family slept on grass hammocks covered with navy-blue blankets. Since the house was small, Frémont often placed his own bunk in the carriage on the sand dunes outside. Some of the most interesting men of the booming new city rode over frequently when the day's work was done and in frontier fashion ate a hearty dinner with the Colonel. A house-man whom they had luckily kept served as cook; they had all the resources of the San Francisco markets for food; and they drank choice wines which had come out from France. In good weather the dinner was served outdoors, with the tables placed on the sand dunes, the blue sky overhead, the bay at their feet, and a strong touch of color added by the flowering lupines all about. Jessie relished the deference, amounting sometimes almost to worship, which was paid her, for women were rarities and men would walk many miles merely to see one. Among her friends were Joseph Hooker, later the Civil War general, then a slim young officer; a Dr. Bowie of Maryland; Samuel Ward of epicurean fame; and adventurers who had roved in India, South America, and all parts of the world. This interlude pleased them all, but it closed when the rainy season sent Jessie and the children to Monterey again.[9]

As soon as the news spread that Frémont's Sonoran helpers were washing out gold literally by the bucketful, crowds of other prospectors rushed to the region. Before long two or three thousand were on the ground. Under the Mexican law such a grant as Frémont had obtained gave no title to mineral rights, and public opinion regarded placer deposits, no matter on whose land, as general and unrestricted property. Frémont naturally made no effort to interfere with the army of prospectors swarming over his land. But the Sonorans, as the first comers, had an advantage over others. They washed out the gold in such quantities that it was sent down to his home in Monterey, so Jessie tells us, in hundred-pound buckskin sacks,

[9] Jessie Benton Frémont MSS, Bancroft Library.
[10] Jessie Benton Frémont, *A Year of American Travel*, p. 125.

worth not far from $25,000 each.[10] The quantity sounds like an exaggeration, but unquestionably enormous sums were taken out; the Frémonts kindly sent a Negro servant named Saunders, whose family were still in slavery, but who had been offered them by the owner for $1,700, up to Mariposa to dig enough gold for the purchase, and he soon obtained it. Unfortunately, the Sonorans did not get on well with the American newcomers. They left near Christmas for home; and as the Colonel was too busy with politics at the moment to go to Monterey and divide the gold, he sent the miners the keys to his store-room there. They made the division themselves, and took not a single ounce more than their just share.

To say that Frémont was busy with politics is to say merely that as one of the prominent citizens of California he was inevitably caught into the current of public affairs. With unexampled rapidity, a new state had been built out of an almost unpeopled land. In the year 1849 more than eighty thousand emigrants, three-fourths of them Americans, reached the Coast. The population at the end of the year was well above a hundred thousand, exclusive of Indians, and still growing by tremendous leaps. Already a convention of delegates, sitting at Monterey during September, had framed an anti-slavery constitution and applied for admission to the Union. Of this convention, one of the most picturesque bodies of its kind ever seen in America, Frémont was, rather strangely, not a member. The president was none other than the seven-foot Dr. Robert Semple, familiar to us as one of the leaders and, later, the Thucydides of the Bear Flag War; he was escorted to his seat by Captain Sutter and General Vallejo; the official reporter was that rhetorical journalist and traveler, J. Ross Browne; and the members chose as the first secretary of state Henry Wager Halleck, who was later to command the armies of the North in the Civil War. Bayard Taylor was an onlooker, and attended a gay dress ball in pantaloons lent him by an officer who weighed considerably more than two hundred pounds. It was a distinguished as well as an amusing assemblage (one member objected to trial by a jury of peers on the ground that only aristocratic England had a peerage), and Frémont should have been present.[11]

But he did use his influence, so far as it was needed, on behalf of free-soil principles. There proved to be surprisingly little opposition to the clause in the bill of rights prohibiting slavery forever in California, many even of the Southerners supporting it. Men realized that the climate and the whole social order were inimical to slavery; that, as one grizzled mountaineer put it in haranguing an election-day crowd, "in a country where every white man makes a slave of himself there is no use in keeping niggers." [12] The Frémonts themselves had resolutely treated slavery as a disgrace. A Texas gold-seeker offered to sell them a strong young mulatto woman, but Jessie indignantly refused. The Colonel was told by advocates of slavery that "You will be the richest man in the world if your mines are worked by slave labor," but he rejected the idea with scorn. Jessie informs us that fifteen members of the convention came in a body to hear from Thomas Hart Benton's daughter that under no circumstances would she consent to own or use a slave. She entertained largely as long as the convention lasted— Sutter was her first guest—and argued that the land her husband had called "the Italy of America" was an ideal place for moderate holdings, well-cultivated farms and orchards, and free institutions.

From the beginning of the agitation for statehood, Frémont's name was informally before the people of California as a candidate for the Senate. He was known to be a Democrat, and to belong nationally to the free-soil wing of that party. He and Jessie, influenced by their deepest instincts and by Senator Benton's views, had long been opposed to the extension of slavery into the territories. Already the California Democracy was showing signs of a decided split upon the question, and lines were being drawn which later resulted in the protracted political

---

[11] Bayard Taylor, *Eldorado,* Ch. 16; see J. Ross Browne, *Report of Debates in the Convention of California, passim.*
[12] New York *Tribune,* October 22, 1849.

duel between the slavery leader, William M. Gwin, and the free-soil leader, Broderick. To a politician who sent him a set of political questions, Frémont replied explicitly and at length. "By association, feeling, principle, and education," he wrote, "I am a Democrat." He believed in a central national railroad from the Mississippi to the Pacific, and would labor for its immediate location and construction. He defended his purchase of the Mariposa claim, and his financial transactions during his brief civil governorship in 1847.

That was in December, 1849. The same month, by a compromise between the anti-slavery and pro-slavery factions, the California legislature elected Frémont and William M. Gwin senators, and later, in drawing lots, Frémont received the short term. On the first ballot, he had received twenty-nine votes, Gwin twenty-two, Halleck twelve, and others scattering votes. Of course, the election had no validity until California was actually admitted to the Union. But Congress had already met; the question of bringing California and New Mexico in was the paramount issue before it, and it was believed that the famous explorer, with the influence of Benton to assist him, might prove a useful lobbyist in the national capital. He was expected to start for the East at once. It was further believed that, with his unequaled knowledge of the West, and his conviction that by his last exploring trip he had found the ideal route, he could do more than any one else to hasten the building of the Pacific railroad. Jessie tells us how characteristically Frémont responded to the new challenge:[13]

One evening of tremendous rain, when we were, as usual, around the fire, Mrs. McEvoy, with her table and lights, sewing at one side, myself by the other, explaining pictures from the *Illustrated Times* to my little girl, while the baby rolled about on the bearskin in front of the fire, suddenly Mr. Frémont came in upon us, dripping wet, as well he might be, for he had come through from San José— seventy miles on horseback through the heavy rain. He was so wet that we could hardly make him cross the pretty room; but...the

[13] *A Year of American Travel*, p. 159.

footmarks were all welcome, for they pointed home. He came to tell
me that he had been elected Senator, and that it was necessary we
should go to Washington on the steamer of the first of January.

At daybreak the next morning he was off again, having to be back
in San José. A young sorrel horse, of which Mr. Frémont was very
fond, brought him down and carried him back this 140 miles within
36 hours, without fatigue to either.

On New Year's night of 1850, with the rain pouring torrents
and every street in Monterey a stream, Frémont bore Jessie in
his arms down to the wharf and they embarked on the steamer
Oregon for New York via the Panama route. Among those
aboard were Gwin, Sam Ward, and T. Butler King; and the
vessel was estimated to be carrying three million dollars in gold
dust. The sudden return East meant an abandonment by the
Frémonts of many plans. Mariposa had to be left under the
oversight of California friends. Their hopes for a quiet life, a
cessation of struggle, had to be given up. They had meant to
stay seven years, "the world forgetting, by the world forgot,
our first object to live our lives in independence," but the gold
rush and statehood had made that impossible. It cost them
both a pang to leave the free outdoor life of the West. Jessie
had brought all her natural vivacity and gusto to the camping
excursions, when in some mountain glade they would eat veni-
son, drink claret, and afterward enjoy the camp-fire talk of old
Knight, the hunter, or the naval lieutenant, Edward F. Beale;
she had delighted in the gay, hospitable Californians, with their
families of twelve or fifteen children, their profuse hospitality,
their folk songs and serenades, their *guisada* and other dishes,
their three-day marriage feasts, their incomparable horseman-
ship, and their picturesque dress—the velvet jackets, gold em-
broidery, slashed trousers, and jingling bells of the men making
them look like figures out of an opera. She had enjoyed playing
the hostess herself, and during the progress of the constitutional
convention, when Frémont was fearful lest the slavery element
might prove strong, and when many of his old friends and

opponents, from Sutter to Castro, were in town, she had kept open house and laden her table with dainties.

Yet Frémont would have been more than human had he not felt a certain exultation in the changed circumstances of his return East. A year and a half earlier he had been traveling west on the Great Lakes, an impoverished young man of bleak prospects, just resigned under attack from the army. Now he was coming back a Senator-elect, his trunk full of buckskin bags of gold dust, with the title to one of the richest tracts on the Coast in his possession. What a transformation! An English man-of-war, at anchor off Mazatlan, fired a salute in his honor and that of Senator-elect Gwin, and lowered the captain's gig to put Frémont and Jessie ashore. He had even been gratified by an expression of Zachary Taylor's confidence in him. The President, no doubt partly to please Benton, had in June, 1849, appointed him a commissioner to run the boundary line with Mexico, and Frémont had accepted the place, resigning it, however, immediately afterward. No one in Washington would be able to sneer at him. Jessie, too, who was still ailing in health and had grown homesick, was glad to return with her small daughter to her father and invalid mother.

Before Frémont and his wife had reached Panama both were ill, Jessie with some unnamed malady which she says put her in danger of dying, and the Colonel with an attack of rheumatic fever in the leg which had been so badly frostbitten in the San Juan Mountains. They were taken to Mme. Arcé's home and nursed back to sufficient health to enable them to continue their travels. Lying on cots in her big ballroom, which was made the sick chamber because of its coolness, they were regularly visited by the explorer John L. Stephens, now vice-president of the Panama Railroad Company, who was also fever ridden, and who used to say, "I have come to take my chill with you." Running up from Colon to New York on the mail steamer *Georgia*, Jessie was again attacked and grew worse; a gale which buffeted the ship till she had to be lashed to a sofa made her so desperately ill that she was later told that by all the laws of medicine she should have died. Frémont himself had meanwhile been seized with "Chagres fever," and was in bed. But at last they were safe home; they went immediately to the Irving House, and the press announced: "Mrs. Frémont has entirely recovered from her illness. The colonel has been indisposed for some time past with intermittent fever, but is now convalescent."

On September 9, 1850, California was admitted to the Union, and shortly afterward Frémont took his seat as one of her Senators.

Still half-ill, he was actually in the Senate only twenty-one working days. In this time he introduced eighteen measures, the principal ones being a bill to regulate the working of the mines in California; a bill to grant the State public lands for educational purposes; a bill to grant it six townships to found a university; a bill to give it land for asylums for the deaf, dumb, blind, and insane; and a bill to open a wagon-road across the continent. He meanwhile distinguished himself for his anti-slavery temper. He voted for the suppression of the slave-trade in the District of Columbia, and against a measure which provided a heavy prison-sentence for any one who should entice a slave to run away. During the session he came into collision, in none too creditable a way, with Senator Foote of Mississippi. In debate the half-tipsy Foote angered Frémont by charging that his bill to regulate the operation of the mines in California was drafted for his own private advantage. A hot altercation in the antechamber followed. Thereupon the Colonel sent Foote a letter demanding a retraction of his language, to be signed in the presence of witnesses, and penned also a challenge to a duel if he refused. Foote, though declining to sign the retraction, wrote Frémont to disclaim any intention of giving offense in his language; and this satisfied every one, including Benton, to whom the explorer referred the matter. Meanwhile, the young Senator's stern anti-slavery temper gave offense in California, and the Southern forces there began to rally to prevent his reëlection.

Living again at Benton's house in Washington, Jessie and he enjoyed the social life of the capital. Mayor Seaton has sketched him for us as he appeared at a dinner party, a man of "arresting dignity," but looking worn and thin. "His black hair, heavily streaked with gray, gave distinction to his weather-worn features. His eyes shone youthfully as he answered questions as to the possibilities of the coast under a railway project." Often silent, he watched with frank admiration his wife, talking and laughing with the sparkle of a care-free girl. "When Jessie caught his glance upon her, there was an exchange which I can only describe as a mental wink, a flash of eye, a fleeting smile, discreet flirtation throughout the long dinner." [14] Gradually he gained strength. But when the Mississippi and Pacific Railroad Convention met in Philadelphia in the spring of 1851, a convention to which he sent a long letter urging the route between the thirty-eighth and thirty-ninth parallels for the railroad, he was still confined to his room by "Chagres fever."

[14] Catherine Coffin Phillips, *Jessie Benton Frémont*, p. 171.

XXIV

Managing the Mariposas

FRÉMONT had now risen to a pinnacle where his opportunities seemed far greater than ever before. He commanded wealth; he had held political office and power; he possessed a reputation as the foremost explorer of the West. He was a busy man of affairs, supervising his estate, laboring for the cause of free-soil democracy in Washington and California, answering scientific inquiries, and keeping abreast of geographical advances. His ambitions were increasingly complex, for he hoped to be one of the statesmen of the new West and one of her business entrepreneurs as well as the pathmarker who mapped her highways. Five years were to pass before he was to be widely discussed as a presidential candidate. How fruitfully was he to spend them?

Thus far his life had been shaped largely by personal forces —by Poinsett, Nicollet, Benton, Jessie, Stockton; now there enters the drama a powerful and on the whole sinister impersonal force, the Mariposa estate. For the next fifteen years this ten-league grant, rich in gold and grazing land, was to dominate all too much of Frémont's activities. Promising him wealth and happiness, it was to bring him in the end little but trouble and disappointment. Seeming a beneficent gift of luck, it was destined before it vanished—vanished as suddenly as a rainbow bubble—to appear rather like some malignant stroke of Fate. It did more to govern the central part of his career, and in the large view to warp it, than any other element; for it led him from the scientific pursuits for which he had been trained into the alien world of business.

To give Mariposa its true significance it must thus be treated

393

not as a mere mining enterprise, but as one of the great controlling influences upon Frémont's career. Its business history
is a thorny and profitless maze. From the outset the estate
proved to be a perfect Pandora's box of complications. Its
boundaries were undetermined; it was difficult to obtain an
American title, for Congress in 1851 passed an act refusing
confirmation to any California titles without absolute written
proof, and the papers of the Mexican administration were
nailed up in various repositories; while the region abounded in
land-jumpers. The state witnessed a half-dozen years of partial
chaos in landholding, many settlers taking up unauthorized
abodes wherever they pleased, and defending them with shot-
guns. Frémont's Sonoran workers, with the first flood of other
miners, shortly exhausted the rich placer deposits in the Mariposa area. There remained not merely its vast possibilities in
grain and cattle-growing, but plain evidences of gold-bearing
quartz—Alexis Godey picked up the first gold-veined rock—
which would pay well, but would first require a heavy capital
investment in mining tools and ore-crushing machinery.[1] Study
of these possibilities filled the sanguine Frémont with an un-

[1] News of this find was given in the California correspondence of the
Trenton, New Jersey, *Daily True American*, November 13, 1849: "But by far
the most magnificent discovery is that recently made upon the rancho of
Col. Frémont, on the Mariposas River. It is nothing less than a vein of
gold in the solid rock—a bona fide mine, the first which has been found in
California. I saw some specimens which were in Col. Frémont's possession.
The stone is a reddish quartz, filled with rich veins of gold, and far sur-
passing the specimens brought from North Carolina and Georgia. Some stones
picked up on the top of the quartz strata, without particular selection, yielded
two ounces of gold to every twenty-five pounds. Col. Frémont informed me
that the vein had been traced for more than a mile. The thickness on the
surface is two feet, gradually widening as it descends, and showing larger
particles of gold. The dip downward is only about twenty feet, so that the
mine can be worked with little expense. These are the particulars first given
me, when the discovery was announced. Still more astonishing facts have
just come to light.
"A geologist sent out to examine the place arrived here [San Francisco]
last night. He reports having traced the vein a distance of two leagues, with
an average breadth of 150 feet. At one extremity of the mine he found large
quantities of native silver, which he calculates will fully pay the expenses
of setting up machinery and working it.... This discovery has made a great
sensation throughout the country...."

fortunate conviction that he could be a highly successful business-man.

Within a year he began to learn that the Mariposa was a will-of-the-wisp, beckoning him forward with promises of stupendous wealth, sometimes placing small gifts within his grasp, and yet always cheating him. In June, 1850, he authorized an agent named David Hoffman to act for him in London and to organize mining companies upon the basis of leases. At the same time, he made out some other leases to Thomas Denny Sargent, who proceeded to California, duly located them on the property, obtained surveys and other necessary papers, and then going to London in the early spring of 1851, disposed of them in Great Britain at a large profit. Senator Benton was struck by Sargent's enterprise, and having received a power-of-attorney from Frémont, agreed with Sargent that he should take over the whole tract for a million dollars. Sargent seems to have made his first payment, to have proceeded to England, hustled about there, convinced capitalists of the value of the property, and concluded arrangements for its resale at a handsome price. Meanwhile, Hoffman had concluded important business arrangements of his own in London, and was filled with consternation to learn that the area had suddenly been whisked from beneath his feet. He protested, while Frémont declared that he had never authorized a sale. It was a very pretty and complicated quarrel till the Colonel cut through it in the fall of 1852 by ordering a temporary suspension of all transactions with regard to Mariposa.[2]

It was high time that he did so, for he was by no means certain that the government would recognize his claim to the land, and a long course of litigation, which finally landed him in the Supreme Court, was looming up ahead. His claim was duly filed before the Federal commissioners in the opening days of 1852, and by the autumn of 1853 was being fought out with

[2] David Hoffman, *The Frémont Estate: An Address to the British Public.* See also the anonymous pamphlet of 1856, *Who is Frémont? By One who has Known Him Socially, Financially, and Politically.*

Attorney-General Caleb Cushing in the Federal District Court. Even if Frémont got the land, he might well be refused title to the minerals. But the explorer was still exuberantly confident of becoming a millionaire, and had embarked upon efforts to develop the property with money of his own, and funds of the San Francisco banking house of Palmer, Cook & Co. This house, which was also interested in the defense, seems to have taken a certain part of the estate as security, and to have cut this part up into shares which were sold to certain other capitalists.[3]

Frémont had the more time for Mariposa in that his senatorial career had been brief, and his ambitions to succeed himself had proved abortive. The needs of the estate and his desire to campaign for reëlection took him hurriedly back to California in the fall of 1850. In San Francisco, after a long search, he finally bought an ugly but comfortable domicile high on Stockton Street, overlooking the Plaza. Here Frémont found that the pro-slavery wing of the Democratic party had grown in strength. Had his health been good, he might have done more to rally the free-soil element. But in December he was taken ill, and, as Senator Benton said in Congress, was chained to his bed "by sciatica, rheumatism, neuralgia," paying the penalty of his past exposures. Jessie hurried out from the East to nurse him. The legislative balloting came on in February, 1851; more than one hundred and forty votes were taken, and he was decisively defeated, though no choice was made. Nearly a year later, Colonel John B. Weller, of the now dominant slavery faction, was elected in his stead.

Frémont would have liked nothing better than to continue in the area of state and national politics, but the situation was unfavorable to a man of his temperament. The population of California was still rising like an irresistible tide, and the voters were a rough, heterogeneous lot who responded readily to the arts of the demagogue. The census of 1850 gave the state

[3] Montgomery Blair was retained as Frémont's attorney; W. E. Smith, *The Francis Preston Blair Family in Politics*, II, pp. 53, 54.

122,000 people. That summer the tide of emigration was so great that 9,270 wagons passed Fort Laramie on the California and Oregon Trail, and 42,000 persons registered with the commandant.[4] In 1852, the torrent overflowed all bounds. Before the close of May more than 2,600 wagons, more than 26,000 cattle, and some 11,000 men, women, and children had reached Fort Kearny on the way to the Coast. On the principal trails, the road showed almost a continuous line of covered wagons. San Francisco had sprung up into a great sprawling city, with many miles of graded streets, ambitious blocks of business buildings, and flimsy residences which proved food for a series of conflagrations. The majority of the new-comers were rude and illiterate frontier folk, or urban adventurers. They mingled in city and mining-camp with Mexicans, Chileans, swarms of Europeans, men from the British penal colonies, and Chinese. The French Government had taken deliberate measures for sending over a large part of the *Garde Mobile,* a turbulent body which Louis Napoleon had at one time found useful, but which had proved too troublesome to keep in Paris. But the convicts and ne'er-do-wells from Botany Bay and Sydney, who "escaped" to California in shiploads, were the most vicious of all; and they gave the English immigrants in general a bad name.

Racial antagonisms were intense; while the resentment which the landless squatters felt against the great estate owners like Frémont was strong. Disorder seemed to increase steadily. The electorate was easily played upon by such adept politicians of southern sympathies as Gwin, Weller, and the unprincipled Governor John Bigler,[5] but it was instinctively hostile to such a man as Frémont.

To Mariposa and other business, therefore, Frémont gave most of 1851. Always restless, always inclined to speculation, he did not confine himself, as common sense dictated, to his estate. His most impetuous venture was a contract for supply-

[4] John Bach McMaster, *History of the People of the United States,* VIII, p. 58.

[5] Compare Cardinal Goodwin, *Establishment of State Government in California, passim.*

ing beef to the Indians. The overrunning of the foothills and valleys by miners had driven many of the savages from their old hunting grounds; and pressed by hunger, they commenced killing live stock belonging to the whites. The settlers retaliated. There seemed danger of a general Indian war, which would wipe out isolated miners and prospectors, and Federal commissioners were hastily sent to treat with the tribes. These commissioners adopted the wise principle that it was better to feed the Indians than to fight them; but when they sought for beef they found that the ranchers were trying to take advantage of the emergency by demanding exorbitant prices. Frémont happened to have cattle interests, and he offered to furnish some $180,000 worth of beef at the usual rates; an offer which the commissioners accepted as "the lowest and best yet made by any responsible man." [6] The commissioners gave him drafts upon the Treasury, but they had heavily overdrawn their credit, and he met a great deal of trouble in getting his money. Special legislation by Congress was ultimately necessary to compensate the explorer for what was not merely a fair but a public-spirited transaction.[7] He had other irons in the fire at the same time. Leaving Jessie in San Francisco, where the disorders were growing dangerous and were resulting in incendiarism, he spent much time in the saddle or at Mariposa.

The first great San Francisco fire of 1851, that of May 4th, which destroyed at least seven million dollars' worth of property,[8] cost Jessie—who had given birth to another son two weeks earlier, and was confined to her bed at the time—a night of feverish excitement, but that was all. The Frémont home on Stockton Street, near the Plaza, was high up on the hillside, and her windows looked down into the sea of flames. At one time, it was necessary to hang soaking-wet carpets over the sides of the house to counteract the fierce heat; boxes of legal papers and silverware were taken to a friend's house on Russian

[6] MS Memoirs, Bancroft Library.
[7] See full history of the matter in Senator Weller's speech, *Congressional Globe*, August 11, 1856; *34th Cong., 1st Sess.*, p. 2022.
[8] J. S. Hittell, *History of San Francisco*, p. 168.

Hill; while the hammock and blankets in which she was to be carried away, if necessary, were placed ready beside her bed. But friendly fire-fighters, scorched and wet, ran in from time to time to reassure her. The second fire, occurring late in June while Frémont was at the Mariposas, proved much more dangerous.

This conflagration started at ten o'clock on a Sunday morning, and it was soon clear that it would sweep away the Frémont residence. Jessie and her baby were taken to the home of a hospitable South Carolinian on a safe elevation not far away. Other refugees were gathered there. One of them was a young Frenchwoman who had been very ill, and who took a large chair by a window overlooking the advancing fire. "Her wild fevered gaze was fixed on her burning home," writes Jessie. "Suddenly, with a crazy laugh, she rose and offered me her seat—'C'est votre tour, Madame; your house goes next,' she said. And after we had made her lie down and let wet cloths be applied to the poor fevered head, I in my turn watched from that window the burning of my home." Suffering from the shock, Jessie was transferred to one of the few houses available, a lonesome bare place, where she could do little more than camp out. Here, however, she met an unexpected piece of good fortune. Frémont had invested in a considerable tract of land in the city, and had leased it to an industrious, cleanly colony of English people, who had erected there a brewery and a number of cottages. They now came to the rescue in dramatic fashion:[9]

A procession of our English tenants came to me carrying parcels and bundles, and leading small carts over the uneven sand drives. A middle-aged man and his wife led them and spoke for the others. When the fire began on Sunday, they said, they thought it might take the direction of our house; assuring themselves of this, they at once started in force to offer their services, but I had already gone. Then they proceeded to save everything; working with such cool method that mirrors, china, and glass, several hundred books, fur-

[9] Jessie Benton Frémont MSS, Bancroft Library.

niture, even kitchen utensils, and all our clothing, were saved in good condition. The motherly woman apologized for having laundered the soiled clothing, but, she said, "I thought you might be so put about with the changing, the clothes would have long to wait." Then the man put down on the table a smaller but heavy parcel tied in a big red silk handkerchief. "We knew the master was from home," he said, "and there was a young babbie in the house, and we thought money might come in handy, so we brought a quarter's rent in advance"; untying the heavy red bundle and showing the heaps of silver and some gold. That made me cry—it was all so kind, so unexpected, and from people who were kept chilled by public ill-will.

When Frémont returned from Mariposa, he saw the sun shining on many acres—more then ten blocks—of smoking ashes. Of his own home, only a single shattered chimney remained. The city hospital had been burned; so had the office of the *Alta California,* the Jenny Lind Theatre, where the miners were entertained by rough and ready farces, and the "old adobe" on the Plaza, the last relic of the village of Yerba Buena. He learned that Mrs. Frémont and the children were somewhere upon the hill near Grace Church—that was all his informants could tell him. Thousands were utterly homeless, shivering amid the chaparral and sand beside what fragments of their household possessions they had been able to save. Standing near the church, Frémont gazed about and identified Jessie's temporary habitation by a set of upper windows where white muslin curtains with pink ribbons were fluttering in the fresh morning air; for, like her father, she insisted upon thorough ventilation. When he heard what the English tenants had done, he sent at once to thank them. They had previously asked him to sell them their home sites, and he had refused; but now he told them that as a mark of gratitude he would have deeds of sale prepared at once, at a low valuation. Decades later, Jessie could "remember clearly the dawning surprise and happiness lighting up the large-featured heavy faces, the hearty words of gratitude, and the large grip of the very big hands as they thanked us."

Jessie's health had been affected by the ordeal of the two fires. She frequently woke at night to find herself groping at the window or the door, with the sound of fire bells haunting her ears. Both she and her husband disliked the rough society of the state, where lynch law was now in full ascendancy, and a vigilance committee had just been organized in San Francisco as a last desperate means of stopping the disorder and violence. Moreover, he was badly in need of capital to develop the Mariposa mines, and it was only in Europe that he could obtain the funds to buy machinery and erect ore mills. One evening in December, 1851, he suddenly asked Jessie, "How would you like a trip to Paris as a New Year's gift?" She uttered some incredulous words about a trip to the moon being equally nice. Thereupon he took from his wallet brightly colored steamer tickets for passage to Chagres and thence to France. To her ecstatic exclamation that it would be his first vacation, he replied that it would also be hers: "The first rest since you spoke those fateful words, 'whither thou goest, I will go.'" [10]

What impression the history, the monuments, and the society of Europe made upon Frémont, who loved a lonely mountainscape better than a royal dinner party, we do not know; but the alert and social Jessie was in her element. Her pen has given us an animated record of the delights of transatlantic travel. Even the discomforts were remembered later with pleasure. Missing the European steamer at Chagres, they went to New York, stayed four days (March 6 to 10, 1852) at the Irving Hotel, and took the Cunard side-wheel steamer *Africa* for Liverpool, the bracing cold of the North Atlantic driving away their touch of the Isthmus fever. The roomy, rolling old vessel, where they were quartered in the ladies' parlor, with the ship's library and an open fire all the way over, was delightful. In London rooms had been prepared for them at the Clarendon Hotel by the Marchioness of Wellesley, who had been one of the three beautiful Misses Caton of Maryland, and who had long known Jessie; while Abbott Lawrence, the Amer-

[10] Catherine Coffin Phillips, *Jessie Benton Frémont*, p. 178.

ican minister, and his daughter, exerted themselves from the first day to make the newcomers welcome, and arranged what Mrs. Frémont called a terrifying program.

Jessie, it is clear, found every hour of the foreign sojourn enchanting. In her pages we find a description of meetings with the Duke of Wellington, stooped and abstracted in his old age; of dinners and teas at the important London houses; of an evening with Sir Roderick Murchison, president of the Royal Geographical Society; and of her presentation to Queen Victoria, who made an "impression of womanly goodness combined with a look of power." From London they went on to Paris early in May. Here they met a grand seigneur, the Comte de la Garde, who was connected by marriage with the Bonaparte family, and who was captivated by Jessie's vivacity and interest in life. He introduced them to the best Parisian society, and his talk and personality gave them glimpses into the most romantic and highly colored pages of French history. Later, when he died, he bequeathed Jessie a precious collection, chosen from among his treasures, to illustrate the topics of which they had often chatted: autographs, paintings by Isabey, water-colors of Queen Hortense, and so on. Through his kindness, they were allotted places on the official tribune to view the grand military parade before the Prince-President, Louis Napoleon, at which the imperial eagles were restored to the French standards—a symbol that the end of the Republic was near.[11]

To both Frémont and Jessie, Paris seemed very homelike: to him because his father had been French, to her because the city was only a splendid amplification of the old French St. Louis with which she had been so familiar. She surrounded herself with French servants, two of whom came back with her to America, where they remained fifteen and twenty years respectively in the Frémont household. They took a whole house to themselves, Lady Dundonald's mansion in the Italian style on the Champs Elysées, between the Place de l'Étoile and Rond

[11] See Jessie Benton Frémont, *Souvenirs of My Time*, Chs. 14-21 inclusive.

Point, and kept the children at home, with a governess to teach them. They kept a brougham and pair with an Irish coachman, had ponies for the youngsters, and every luxury that heart could desire. They drove out to Versailles, Fontainebleau, and other points near Paris, staying overnight. They saw Rachel at the Théâtre Française, and went to the opera. Frémont spent a good deal of time in fencing and in long walks. He made numerous friends in the scientific world, obtained an introduction to Arago, and entertained lavishly. It is plain that the Mariposa estate was furnishing, in spite of all financial and legal tangles, a handsome revenue. Jessie relates a revealing incident of her husband. He was fascinated, she says, by a magnificent Cedar of Lebanon which shaded part of the lawn of the Lauriston Hotel near by; in all his camp life he had never seen anything like its great layered boughs. Under this spell, he "opened negotiations for the purchase of the hotel when we were told it was for sale."

From the Tuileries, thanks to the Comte de la Garde, came cards to every fête, ball, or other court occasion. Many of these affairs were dreams of splendor to the Americans. Once, for example, they went to the dansant given by the Prince-President at St. Cloud, and found the magnificent rooms, the endless mirrors, and the brilliantly dressed company a delightful sight. "Far below the steep hill was the Seine, and the Bois du Boulogne lay between the river and the city four or five miles away. A full moon was shining on this, and made a perfect picture as we sat by one of the great open windows." Louis Napoleon, short, fat, dull-eyed, and yet impressive, entered, followed by a train of ladies and gentlemen in gay uniforms and lace and silk dresses; walked through the parted lines of guests, and seated himself above the diplomatic corps; and Jessie, who loved the theatrical, drew a sharp breath of admiration.

As a double climax, the Frémonts witnessed, in the closing days of 1852, the official entrance of Louis Napoleon as Emperor, and, in the first days of 1853, the pomp and pageantry which accompanied his marriage to Eugénie de Montijo. Jessie's house, with its balcony overlooking the Champs Elysées, was crowded with American friends and acquaintances when the new-made Emperor rode bowing through the avenue, twisting his long mustaches, and apparently quite unafraid—"alone, no troops, not a single officer within forty feet of him." From a different balcony, commanding a view of the Tuileries, they saw all the blare and pomp of the imperial wedding: the grenadiers, Cent Gardes, and cavalry, emerging from the Grand Court and pouring like a river into the streets, where they made a compact military order with tens of thousands of brightly dressed people pressing behind; the military escort; the Marshal de Loestine, representing the First Empire, riding alone; and then the bride and groom in their glass coach, surmounted by a gold crown and swung like some great bonbonnière between the front and rear wheels. The Emperor and Empress sat beside each other on white satin seats, the former stiff and upright in brilliantly decorated uniform, with half-shut eyes, the latter as pale as some waxen image, and as rigidly still, like some figure in a painful dream. A far cry, all this, from the deserts and forests of the West, the crudity of the California mining-camps!

As "Mariposa business" helped take Frémont to Europe, so now it and other financial perplexities quickly summoned him home. His title to the estate was still uncertain. His claim upon the Treasury for $180,000 upon the Indian beef contract was still unsettled. As yet the government had not paid the bills which he had incurred for the California Battalion, and he had received a sharp reminder that he might be held personally liable for them. In London, early in April, 1852, as he was stepping into a carriage with Jessie to go to a dinner, he was arrested by a party of Bow Street officers, who were accompanied by an insolent clerk from a solicitor's firm. The four constables hurried him off to prison, and, despite his protests, he was kept there until next day, when George Peabody furnished the necessary bail. This arrest was for the nonpayment of four drafts, amounting to $19,500 and interest, which he had drawn as governor of California upon Mr. Buchanan as Secretary of State, for supplies furnished to the Battalion by one F. Huttman.[12] Buchanan could not pay these drafts when they were presented, for Congress had made no appropriation. Since the government could not be sued, the holders of the notes concluded that the shortest way to get their money was to take the position that Frémont had acted upon his own responsibility in California. An expensive lawsuit against him at once began; and seeing that it might be followed by others, for amounts far beyond his ability to pay, Frémont hastily appealed to his friend Senator Gwin to press in Congress an old bill for payment of the claims arising from the conquest of California.[13]

While these affairs required his presence in America, Jessie had her own family reasons for returning. Benton had written her from St. Louis, in March, 1852, that her only brother Randolph was dead. A sudden illness had seized him just as he was about to enter St. Louis University. "His disease had all the violence of cholera, though bilious," wrote the Senator,[14] "and quickly set his bowels on fire with inflammation. On the second day he became delirious, not from fever but agony, and with three lucid intervals towards the last day, knew little but the torment he suffered." Deeply attached to her brother, Jessie was for a time almost prostrated, and her eyes were weakened by her constant weeping. Finally, as a decisive reason for hurrying home, Frémont learned that an important piece of government exploration was about to be carried out. He immediately determined to share in it, and Arago himself helped him select his scientific instruments.

The Pacific railway enterprise had taken another long stride ahead. Congress, early in 1852, had ordered several routes to be explored to the Pacific, to afford a wide choice for the site;

[12] New York *Tribune*, July 9, 1853. Ultimately Congress by act of March 3, 1854, paid the interest on the debt and the cost of the judgment against Frémont, amounting in all to $48,814. But the original $15,000 borrowed by Frémont was charged against him until he should prove that he had spent this money in the public service. He apparently never made any effective effort to do so. H. H. Bancroft, *History of California*, V, p. 465*ff*.

[13] *Congressional Globe*, April 28, 1852; *34th Cong., 1st Sess.*, p. 1205*ff*.

[14] In Jessie Benton Frémont MSS, Bancroft Library.

and it had apparently been understood by Benton that Frémont
should head one of the various parties. If this were so, the expectation was disappointed. Jefferson Davis, as Secretary of
War, designated five different lines to be explored, and five
different sets of men to do the work. One route, running along
the forty-seventh parallel through the Dakota and Montana
country, was assigned to Captain George B. McClellan and
Isaac I. Stevens; one running through Salt Lake City and the
Humboldt Valley, to Lieutenant E. J. Beckwith; one between
the thirty-eighth and thirty-ninth parallels, to Captain John W.
Gunnison; one along the thirty-fifth parallel, west of Fort Smith
in Arkansas, to Lieutenant A. W. Whipple; and the one farthest
south, running through El Paso and Yuma, to Captain John
Pope and others. Frémont was passed over.

Unquestionably the explorer felt a grievance in the fact, and
with some reason. His fourth expedition had been specifically
designed to blaze a path for a railway between the thirty-
seventh and thirty-eighth parallels, and he had given much publicity to his belief that he had found there the best possible
route. He had written the Philadelphia railroad convention in
1850 his reasons for the preference: it was direct, was cen-
trally situated, had marked advantages of wood, water, and
soil, was healthy, ran through an area fitted for general habitation, and had a much milder climate than any route running
farther north. Senator Benton had been the foremost advocate
in America of the transcontinental railway. No officer of the
army possessed so much practical experience of western exploration and surveying as Frémont; the name of none would
carry so much weight in any official recommendation. But
Jefferson Davis, a West Pointer who had been with the regular
army till 1835 and had fought in it again during the Mexican
War, felt that regular army officers were entitled to preference. Frémont could not even protest. But he was not to be
easily thwarted in his ambition to be a pathmarker for steam
transportation, as he had been for the wagon trains of the emigrants; and he prepared to set on foot an expedition of his own.

Jessie had given birth to a daughter, Anne Beverley, in Paris on February 1, 1853—a *petite Parisienne,* as the Comte said. They waited in France till mother and baby were able to travel, and then returned to Washington, where Jessie settled herself near her father. Frémont was busy with preparations for his western trip. For a time all went well. Then the heat of early summer affected the baby, and Jessie took her at once to the Francis Blair estate at Silver Springs, Maryland, just outside Washington. On July 12th, the child suddenly died in her arms. It was the second loss of the kind the family had sustained, and it helps explain the entry Jessie made in her family Bible after the list of births and deaths: "Care and sorrow and childbirth pain." Yet Frémont told Benton that she had shown more courage than he: "It was she who remained dry-eyed to comfort me, for I was unmanned over the cruelty of this bereavement. Her calm stoicism, so superior to mere resignation, soon shamed me into control." [15]

[15] Catherine Coffin Phillips, *op. cit.,* pp. 190, 191.

XXV

The Fifth Expedition

THE background of Frémont's fifth and last expedition was the now fully awakened rivalry of North and South over the route of the first transcontinental railroad. It was evident to every one acquainted with the West that the plains and mountains could be traversed by not merely one but numerous railways. But the nation was unlikely to give Federal aid to more than one at a time, and each section felt it important to prove that the most practicable and economical route lay westward from its own portals. Many Northerners were suspicious of the five surveys for which Congress had appropriated $150,000; they were not astonished when Secretary Jefferson Davis, after their completion, declared that the line along the thirty-second parallel—that is, the southernmost route—was clearly the best. It was to counteract the plans of the Southerners that Benton and other advocates of a central route encouraged Frémont, doubtless by financial assistance as well as applause, in his new expedition.[1]

Indeed, Benton believed that Southern interests had laid an elaborate plot to defeat a central railroad to the Pacific and build a line westward from Texas instead. In a letter to citizens

[1] As early as the spring of 1850 Benton's interest in a railroad to the Pacific was keen. He, Asa Whitney, and Robert J. Walker all had plans, and Benton obtained a good deal of newspaper publicity for his ideas. He proposed to build a railroad from St. Louis to San Francisco, with branches to the Columbia River, Salt Lake City, and Santa Fé; to apply the proceeds of public-land sales to the object; and to sell mortgage bonds in anticipation of this revenue. He wished the government to complete a wagon-road to the Pacific within a year, and a railroad within seven years. Like Frémont, he believed the line between the thirty-eighth and thirty-ninth parallels would furnish the best route. Indeed, he and Frémont were partners in supporting the consideration of this line. See New York *Tribune*, April 3, April 5, 1850.

of Green County, Missouri, early in the summer of 1853, he declared that the first plans "for a southern sectional route," had been devised six years earlier. A provision had been inserted in the treaty of peace with Mexico to make possible the construction of a road along the Gila, or within a marine league on either side. "With the design for the Gila road went the amputation of El Paso from New Mexico, and its surrender, with about 70,000 square miles of New Mexico, to Texas, all for the purpose of helping the Gila road." Now it was learned that the Gila route was impracticable, and Southern leaders were trying to find a new one. Benton was instrumental during the summer of 1853 in sending westward by the central route a party which included two active young men, Harris Heap and Lieutenant Edward F. Beale, and the aged Washington banker Riggs. Beyond doubt the Senator was one of the chief promoters of Frémont's expedition, which expected to cover the same route during the winter months. We find Benton writing in the *National Intelligencer* of September 6, 1853, on these parties:

I sent you two letters just received from Superintendent Beale and Mr. Harris Heap, and giving information of their having reached the Great Colorado of the West, and found the country good for a railway and for settlement all the way out to that river, which they reached in five days after crossing the divorce line of the waters... between the Atlantic and the Pacific, in the middle of that pass, Coo-che-topa, which Frémont went to find, which Leroux said was there, and which Beale's party had gone through. It is not merely a pass, but a valley between two mountains, with a distinct name of its own, Sah-wah-che Valley, some forty miles long, good for railways and settlements, and only wanting the hand of man to make it a perfect garden; and this in addition to the Valley of San Luis, which connects with it. So that problem is solved, at least so far as summer travel is concerned, and Frémont has gone out to solve it in *winter*....

These letters from Beale and Heap cover the only debatable ground on the Central Route. The whole route has now been seen (for Frémont knows the Grand River, and all beyond), and the passes traversed; and all found to be good for roads and settlements, and inviting the hand of the farmer to improve it. Nothing is now wanting but the *winter* exploration which Frémont has set out to give. He is not afraid of snows in the mountains where there are valleys and passes and wood.... He has been safe in his camp in a grove in a snowstorm which killed all animals on the prairies; witnessed the loss of about a thousand head of government oxen returning from New Mexico in 1848, while he, in the same snowstorm, sheltered by woods, lost not an animal, and his men amused themselves in hunting and killing buffalo.... He means to stand in the most elevated of these passes on the Central Route in January next. He will have with him Indians and mountainmen who are no more afraid of snow than himself.

The press told readers in July, 1853, that Frémont had arrived from England with the finest instruments that money could buy, and would do his utmost to demonstrate the superiority of the line crossing the Rockies at about the thirty-eighth parallel. "He proposes to start in November," remarked the St. Louis *Democrat*, "and thus to test the practicability of the route during the season of snows. This intelligence will be hailed with pleasure by the people of Missouri.... We understand that Colonel Frémont undertakes this survey without aid from the government, and if so, it gives him an additional claim to the gratitude of the whole country." The newspapers which carried this news also published an advertisement of a million dollar seven per cent bond issue which the Pacific Railroad of Missouri was selling. This company was already building from St. Louis to Independence, about two hundred and eighty miles, "on the line advocated by Colonel Benton as the central route to the Pacific"; it also proposed to construct a branch into southwestern Missouri, about three hundred miles. "Whichever route may be adopted for the national road," remarked the New York *Tribune*, "the Missouri company claims to be on the track."

The fifth expedition counted twenty-two members, ten being

Delaware Indians and two Mexicans. It included a topographer named Egloffstein, two other scientific assistants, and most interesting of all, an artist and daguerreotypist named Solomon N. Carvalho—the first official photographer ever attached to an exploring expedition.[2] Carvalho, who was of American birth despite his Portuguese name, had lived in Charleston in his early days, but was now owner of a daguerreotype studio in Baltimore. He had met Frémont in New York, and possessing no experience of life in the open, having never even saddled a horse, accepted the appointment on the spur of the moment, without consulting his family. It was the fascinating personality of the explorer which conquered him, he writes: "I know of no other man to whom I would have trusted my life under similar circumstances." [3] In thus hiring a photographer Frémont displayed no little enterprise; it was to be more than a year before the Englishman Roger Fenton joined the British forces in the Crimea as the first official war photographer. The daguerre process consisted essentially of exposing a highly polished silver plate to iodine vapor until the silver surface turned a bright golden yellow; the image from this exposed plate was then developed by subjecting it to the fumes from mercury heated in a saucer by a spirit lamp. Carvalho tells us that his friends asked how he could do all this on the summit of the Rockies, standing up to his waist in snow; but he successfully performed the feat. One W. H. Palmer joined the expedition as passenger. Preuss wished to go, but after his sufferings in 1849 his wife would not let him, and Jessie tells us that when he definitely saw that his glad free days in the open were over, he went into the woods near Washington and hanged himself.[4]

On the first part of this expedition Frémont was less a pathfinder than ever before. The route he had planned to travel

[2] See Charles Macnamara, The First Official Photographer, *Scientific Monthly*, January, 1936, XLII, pp. 68-74.

[3] S. N. Carvalho, *Incidents of Travel and Adventure in the Far West With Col. Frémont's Last Expedition*, pp. 17, 18.

[4] Jessie Benton Frémont MSS, Bancroft Library.

by Cochetopa Pass had just been covered not only by the Beale-Heap party, but by one of the men appointed by Jefferson Davis, Captain Gunnison. The latter this summer went up the Arkansas River, followed the Huerfano Valley, and crossed the Cochetopa Pass into the arid basin of the Uncompahgre. In October, just as Frémont was about to set out, Gunnison and seven of his men, including two who had been on the 1848 expedition, R. H. Kern and Creutzfeldt, were killed by Utes near Sevier Lake. But Frémont made no pretense to pathfinding. He had insisted ever since 1848 that the trail he had then partially blazed along the thirty-eighth parallel offered the best railroad route, and he believed that the Beale-Heap and Gunnison expeditions were simply proving his point. He would still further prove it by doing in winter what they did in summer.

The exploring party, which had no guide, was delayed in starting by the sudden illness of Frémont, who wrote Jessie that a wet saddle no longer made him a good pillow. He finally joined the camp on the Saline Fork of the Kansas on October 31st, and found it uneasily watching a great prairie fire approaching from the east. That night the fire jumped the Kansas. The next day on starting their "only escape was through the blazing grass; we dashed into it, Colonel Frémont at the head . . . passed through the fiery ordeal unscathed; made that day over fifteen miles, and camped that night on the dry bed of a creek, beyond the reach of the devouring element." [5] They crossed to the Arkansas and reached Bent's Fort on November 30th. From this point they traveled up the Arkansas and the Huerfano, finding the country hilly, well-watered, and abounding in grass and pine. Of the latter part of this journey Carvalho exuberantly exclaims: "If ever a railroad is built through this valley, I suggest that an equestrian statue of Col. J. C. Frémont be placed on the summit of Huerfano Butte; his right hand pointing to California, the land he conquered." On December 3rd they plunged into the mountains, and cross-

[5] Carvalho, *Incidents of Travel*, p. 51.

ing the divide between the Huerfano and the Rio Grande at Sand Hill or Williams Pass, proceeded to the Cochetopa Pass. This they surmounted on December 14th, finding only four inches of snow, and thus confirming Frémont's opinion that a railroad would be perfectly feasible.

From here they struck westward to the Uncompahgre River, and followed it, the Gunnison, and the Grand River till they arrived on the Green River in Utah. In part of this area he was again a true pathfinder; Dellenbaugh tells us that even on the War Department map of 1860 much of the region he traversed was a blank. Of the rest it is sufficient to say that his travels beyond the Green, through a difficult country of mountains and cañons, almost every league of it toilsome and dangerous, carried him across a great part of central Utah, and finally brought him out at the Mormon town of Parowan, in the southwest corner of the state, some sixty miles from the Nevada line. Long before they reached this isolated settlement, they were suffering terribly from want of food and proper clothing. They had to kill the animals for rations; the men lost heart and believed death was near; and at one time even Frémont's strength seemed utterly exhausted.

Carvalho's book on the expedition contains a vivid picture of Frémont as leader, and is warm in its tribute to his qualities of courage, endurance, and resourcefulness. Many of its pages illustrate the Colonel's incessant vigilance. In the after-midnight cold, when the sentries least expected it, he would suddenly appear, and the man who was caught napping had to expiate his offense by walking for a day or week while the others rode. Once his vigilance, when other watchers nodded, prevented a band of Cheyennes from stampeding the whole body of horses and mules, and thus leaving the expedition without transport, six hundred miles from the frontier, at the onset of bitter winter weather, with hostile Comanche, Pawnee, and Sioux Indians awaiting a chance to wipe them out. At every alarming incident the guards were doubled and guns examined; and any one who, like Carvalho on one occasion, let snow get into the barrel of his piece, was severely lectured.[6] Other pages in Carvalho's book illustrate Frémont's prudence and tact. He made it a strict rule never to give any Indian, in barter for food or horses, either firearms or ammunition. Once on the Grand River the camp was alarmed at supper by the approach of three-score mounted Utes, who, armed with rifles, bows, and knives, galloped at full speed upon the whites. Displaying their powderhorns and cartridges conspicuously, they demanded payment for a fat young horse which the party had recently killed for food, and for which they had already indemnified another band of savages. Frémont, as was his custom at such times, never showed himself, a fact which increased the respect of the savages for "the great Captain" and gave a mysterious impressiveness to the orders he issued from his tent.

In this instance Carvalho was much disturbed by the threatening demeanor of the Indians, but Frémont reassured him. He knew them thoroughly, he said; they were simply blustering and did not have powder enough to load a single rifle; "if they had any ammunition, they would have surrounded and massacred us, and stolen what they now demand and are parleying for." It proved true that their horns and cartridge-boxes were empty.

Carvalho makes it clear that the hardships and sufferings which rose in a seemingly interminable crescendo simply brought out Frémont's highest qualities. He never allowed himself or others to be discouraged. On one occasion when he felt himself collapsing, he simply pointed out a spot near by as an admirable situation for a camp, and ordered a stop there; the next morning he was able to go on, and he never mentioned his weakness to his subordinates. No matter how much he was suffering for want of food, no matter how intense the cold or stormy the weather, he kept up his astronomical observations, sometimes standing for hours in the deep snow taking his bearings. He never lost his temper; he never dropped his dignity or acted with excitement. Not once, amid vicissitudes

[6] *Ibid.*, pp. 89, 90.

which tried everybody's patience, and in the face of stupidly irritating mistakes by his men, did Frémont forget that he was a gentleman; not once was there an oath or a display of uncontrolled anger. He gave his orders calmly, and they were always obeyed. The starvation and cold would have rendered some of the party insubordinate had the men not been handled with great tact, but "in no instance was a slight request of his received with anything but the promptest obedience." So devoted were the Delaware Indians that they would have gone to certain death for him. He never asked an officer or man to undertake duties which he was not willing to share. And, says Carvalho: [7]

Although on the mountains and away from civilization, Col. Frémont's lodge was sacred from all and everything that was immodest, light, and trivial; each and all of us entertained the highest regard for him. The greatest etiquette and deference were always paid to him, although he never ostensibly required it. Yet his reserved and unexceptionable deportment demanded from us the same respect with which we were always treated, and which we ever took pleasure in reciprocating.

Only twice did Frémont betray in any fashion the strain under which he labored. In the worst days of starvation, he took his scanty meal of mule-gristle or horse-entrail soup alone in his tent. This he explained by saying that it brought back such vivid memories of the tragic experience of 1848-49 that he wished for solitude; but Carvalho thought that the actual reason was that he wished to allow his companions free speech during their meals. He knew that they would grumble over their hard fate, and to save his feelings from being hurt he retired to his lodge. Again, when the first horse was killed for food, Frémont called his men together and addressed them with evident emotion. After emphasizing the terrible necessities to which they were reduced, he recalled the suspicion that during his last expedition a party of men whom he sent out for succor

[7] *Ibid.,* pp. 133, 134.

had been guilty of eating one of their own number. He proposed that they should make a solemn compact that if they succumbed, they should die together like men, and he threatened to shoot the first person who hinted at cannibalism. It was a solemn and impressive sight, says Carvalho, to see this body of Americans, Indians, and Mexicans, on a snowy mountainside at night, the stars sparkling above in the cold sky, entering into their fervent agreement.

Evidently the idea of cannibalism preyed upon Frémont's mind as it did upon the hero of Joseph Conrad's *Falk*. Because, later, one or two disgruntled followers of Frémont spread malicious stories of his poor qualities as leader, Carvalho's testimony is important. We may pause here to note that it is supported by other men. A Captain Aram of Santa Clara, California, who had served with Frémont in the California Battalion, a little later, in a campaign speech of 1856, told an anecdote illustrative of his consideration for his men. He said:

On his march down the coast the supplies were furnished by a commissary named King, who, finding the stock of groceries running short, being enabled to procure a limited quantity along the route, concluded to use them only at the officers' mess. Frémont noticing some new articles on the table, inquired how they came there. Upon being informed, he immediately ordered a parade next morning. After the battalion was formed, Frémont ordered the commissary to give a history of the transaction, and his inquiry as to whether the rations had been distributed for the soldiers as well as officers being answered in the negative, he reprimanded Mr. King and informed him that upon a repetition of the offense he should be dismissed from the service.

To this testimony may be added that of Alexis Godey, who praised "his daring energy, his indomitable perseverance, and his goodness of heart": [8]

And now as to Frémont's private character, his tyranny, his arrogance, his exclusiveness, and others of like nature, as alleged against

[8] New York *Evening Post*, October 30, 1856.

him. No man who ever traveled with him but knows their falsity. Frémont, more than any other man I ever knew, possessed the respect and affection of his men; he ever lived on terms of familiarity with them. Yet never did commander possess more complete control. He ever partook of the same fare; underwent like hardships; rode when they rode—walked when they walked; and unhesitatingly exposed himself to every danger and privation.

In his private character he is a model; singularly temperate and abstemious in his habits, he never uses spirituous liquors; profane language is a stranger to his lips; and I never recollect to have heard, during my long intercourse with him, anything like blasphemy issue from his lips. I never knew him to have any difficulties with his men; disturbances were a stranger to his camp. He had a manner and a bearing toward his men which admitted of none of those petty altercations, or more serious occurrences, which are so common among parties beset with hardships and dangers, which are ever all-powerful to develop the most unfavorable features in the character of those composing them; and the truth of these things can be attested by all of the old companions of Frémont.

It was to Frémont's assiduity and skill that the expedition, when on its last legs, owed its final extrication. After one of his observations, apparently in Circle Valley, he told his associates that the Mormon hamlet Parowan, forty rods square, was just over the mountains in the Little Salt Lake Valley, and that he would reach it in three days.[9] The mountain ranges loomed tremendously ahead; the ascent was so steep and the snow so deep that the surviving animals could hardly be got up; and at the top of the first peaks the prospect seemed hopeless. "When I surveyed the distance," says Carvalho, "I saw nothing but continued ranges of the everlasting snow, and for the first time my heart failed me." But Frémont plunged con-

[9] Carvalho's account throws some light upon the endurance Frémont often showed in making his observations. "I selected a level spot on the snow, and prepared the artificial horizon. The thermometer indicated a very great degree of cold; and standing almost up to our middle in snow, Col. Frémont remained for hours making observations, first with one star, then with another, until the occultation took place. Our lantern was illuminated with a piece of sperm candle." *Incidents of Travel*, p. 129.

fidently onward; he took out his pocket compass, and pointing in a certain direction, began the descent. It led through a seemingly incomprehensible maze of defiles, slopes, cañons, and valleys. Thus they went on.

...and on the very day and hour previously indicated by Colonel Frémont, he conducted us to the small settlement of Parowan, which could not be distinguished two miles off, thus proving himself a most correct astronomer and geometrician. Here was no chance work—no guessing—for a deviation of one mile, either way, from the true course, would have plunged the whole party into certain destruction.

It was on February 8, 1854, that the four hundred people of Parowan welcomed Frémont's party, who had been for forty-eight hours without food of any kind. Every family took in one or several members. The kindness of these Mormons completely altered the explorer's views of the sect, and many years later he refused to introduce Kate Field in a hostile lecture in Los Angeles on the ground that "the Mormons saved me and mine from death by starvation in '54." One man, and one only, the assistant engineer Oliver Fuller of St. Louis, had died just before they reached safety.

Mrs. Frémont and her family always believed that she had a strange psychic revelation, precise to the day and hour, of her husband's emergence from the jaws of death.[10] She had been almost ill from anxiety during the last fortnight of the period of his perilous exposure. Then, she relates, on the very evening that he reached shelter her sister Susan and a young cousin came to spend the night with her. The fire needing fuel, she went to an adjoining room for some wood. As she stooped for it she felt a touch on her shoulder, and heard Frémont gaily whisper her name as he used to do when he meant to play some practical joke; and at once her heart grew light. Hurry-

[10] While Frémont states that he reached Parowan on the 8th, the *Deseret News* of March 16, 1854, contains a letter from J. C. L. Smith, who left Parowan on the 20th, saying that Frémont had arrived there on the 7th. This would overthrow Dellenbaugh's objections to the psychic communication story on the basis of time.

ing into the other room, she found Susie half-fainting from the sense of a mysterious presence. Whether some thought-transference had actually occurred or not, the incident completely revived Jessie's spirits.

Frémont left the hospitable Mormons on February 21, 1854. Two routes, he wrote later, suggested themselves for examination: one directly across the plateau between the thirty-seventh and thirty-eighth parallels, the other keeping south of the mountains, following for about two hundred miles the Virgin River, and thence running direct to the Tejon Pass at the head of the San Joaquin Valley. As the latter route had been examined by himself in 1844, he determined to take the more direct road. He struck west from the new Mormon settlement of Cedar City across the Escalante Desert into unknown territory; and passing the Utah boundary, crossed all of Nevada until his party met the California boundary at about the thirty-seventh parallel. West of this they found the Sierras blocked by deep snow. Frémont therefore turned southward, and crossed the range at the first favorable point, apparently a little south of Walker's Pass. The approach to the pass was so gradual and the terrain so smooth that he said later he could have set off in a buggy from a point fifteen miles east of the crest, and driven without difficulty to a point thirty-five miles west of it. Many of the party, indeed, would not believe that they had reached the summit.

On April 16, 1854, Frémont was in San Francisco, where the *Alta California* reported him "well, and so hearty that he is actually some fourteen pounds heavier than ever before." Declining a public dinner because he was eager to get back to the East, he was soon in New York again. Here he published in the press a long letter, setting forth the advantages of his easy central route to the Pacific. Though he called it central, actually its remoter section was a southwestern route. He declared against throwing a railroad across the high Sierras in the area later traversed by the Union Pacific-Central Pacific line, and in favor of "the low dry country, the long slope" to the southward, not far from the line subsequently used by the Santa Fé. The precise route which he advocated was never used, though some of his information, given by Jessie to the builders of the Santa Fé, was of value to them. Nor, unfortunately, did he find leisure to prepare a detailed account of his expedition. The daguerre plates taken by Carvalho were printed in the studio of the photographer Brady in Washington, and Jessie tells us that almost all of them were "beautifully clear." For a time Frémont planned to bring out the journals of all his expeditions under the imprint of George Childs of Philadelphia, as a companion-volume to the book of Elisha Kent Kane's Arctic travels, published by the same house. But first his business affairs and then his immersion in the Presidential campaign of 1856 forbade. The notes and plates alike were placed in a warehouse, where long years later they were destroyed by fire.

On the whole, the expedition was not much more fruitful than that of 1848-49. Its principal result was simply to encourage the general idea of a transcontinental railroad; and Frémont perhaps instinctively felt this when he penned the last sentence of his newspaper letter.

It seems a treason against mankind and the spirit of progress which marks the age to refuse to put this one completing link to our national prosperity and the civilization of the world. Europe still lies between Asia and America; build this railroad and things will have revolved about; America will lie between Asia and Europe—the golden vein which runs through the history of the world will follow the iron track to San Francisco.

XXVI

The Republican Nomination

WHILE Frémont had been dining in London and watching the pageantry of Versailles, while he was making his last invasion of the Rockies, while he was defending his property at Mariposa, the sectional antagonism of North and South had been rapidly rising. The Compromise of 1850 had proved but the briefest of truces. Before Clay was carried in 1852 to his grave at Lexington and Webster was laid by the sea at Marshfield, northern opposition to the new Fugitive Slave Act had excited a fierce southern resentment. The publication of *Uncle Tom's Cabin* converted hundreds of thousands to anti-slavery views. Extremists on both sides of the border, as the Pierce Administration proved subservient to the South, grew fiercer in their denunciation of each other. Then at the beginning of 1854 Douglas placed his Kansas-Nebraska Bill before an excited Congress, and a new and blacker storm began to arise. The intensity of the northern wrath over this repeal of the Missouri Compromise, opening the plains of Kansas to possible occupation by slaveholders, took Douglas and Pierce by surprise. From that moment the old Whig Party was doomed, and a new party dedicated to the exclusion of slavery from all the territories began to rise in its place. The bill passed Congress amid southern cheers and northern execration; and as Chase walked at dawn down the Capitol steps with the boom of exultant Democratic cannon in his ears, he truly said to Sumner, "They celebrate a present victory, but the echoes they awake shall never rest until slavery itself shall die."

The year 1855 opened with sectional tension at an alarming

pitch. The Fugitive Slave Act had now been proved impossible
of enforcement in many northern states; when the slave Burns
had been delivered to his master in Boston, it required the
force of the whole city police, the state militia, and the Federal
army and navy to carry him a few blocks through the aroused
populace. Men were organizing both North and South to gain
a secure grip upon Kansas. The first ebullition of violence in
that territory sent a tremor of foreboding throughout the
country. In the spring elections of 1855, some five thousand
boisterous pro-slavery Missourians, armed with revolvers,
bowie-knives, and guns, crowded over the boundary to vote.
Northern ministers were making pleas for money to equip
anti-slavery settlers with Sharp's rifles. Frémont had especial
reason to be aware of the rising passion of the day. In Missouri
the animosity had risen so high that his father-in-law Benton,
hated by many for his free-soil views, had been ejected in
1851 from the Senate seat he had so long and ably occupied.
But the indomitable old statesman refused to be silenced, and
promptly obtained a seat in the House. Benton was in fact one
of the men whom the crisis most deeply alarmed. He attacked
the Kansas-Nebraska Bill as a clumsy attempt to smuggle
slavery into the territories, and indeed throughout the whole
West up to the Canadian line. The year 1855 found him proclaiming on every side that the extension of slavery must be
opposed by all constitutional means; and even more fervently
proclaiming that the Union was in danger of dissolution, and
its friends must rally to its defense. Losing even his seat in
the House in the fall elections of 1854, he prepared to go on
the lecture platform to arouse the country to its danger. He
would be a new Peter the Hermit, he declared, and if the people
now called him mad, later they would admit that he had been
inspired. As the year 1855 piled the explosives higher in Kansas, other moderate leaders in both parties showed the same
anxiety.

The Frémonts in the spring of 1855 definitely gave up their
residence in Washington, where a succession of sorrows had

fallen upon Jessie's father. Mrs. Benton had died the previous September. On her last day she had asked Jessie to help her walk into the library, had gazed about the book-lined room, had fondly touched Benton's desk and chair, and then tottering back to her couch, had fallen into a sleep from which she did not awake. The following February, while Benton was at the Capitol and Jessie with her cousin Mrs. Preston, word came that the family home was on fire. Half the town hurried to watch, but the struggles of the firemen were useless; books, furniture, and papers, including the manuscript of the second volume of Benton's *Thirty Years' View*—which Jessie's older sister Eliza risked her life in trying to save—were lost. It was a severe shock to them all. President Pierce, who embraced Jessie and called her by her first name as in childhood days, asked the family to stay at the White House, but they declined. The rising political bitterness made Washington uncongenial to all of them. Jessie, who had borne another son, named Frank Preston, while the battle over the Kansas-Nebraska Bill was raging, has recorded her feeling: "Before my baby was a month old, the bitterness of the coming strife invaded even my guarded room. I felt the ground-swell—I felt I was no longer in my place—it was certainly too hard on Mr. Frémont, and as soon as I could be moved, New York became our city of refuge."

More squatter troubles at Mariposa again called Frémont to California; and while he was absent, Jessie took the children to spend the summer of 1855 at Siasconset, Nantucket. Here she was visited by Benton, who told her of his lecture-engagements in New York and Boston. Deeply depressed, he recalled John Quincy Adams's assertion in 1843: "I am satisfied slavery will not go down until it goes down in blood." By this time both great parties were looking anxiously to the campaign of 1856.

During the late summer or fall of 1855 the first clear intimation that he might be nominated for the Presidency came to Frémont from leaders of the Democratic Party. According to his daughter Elizabeth, her cousin William Preston, later Minister to Spain, brought the first proposals from that party. A writer in the Detroit *Tribune* the following year states that Frémont was about to sail for California in October, 1855, when John B. Floyd, recently governor of Virginia, came to offer the assistance of various Democratic leaders in obtaining the nomination, and that in two interviews the offer took explicit form. These two stories are not inharmonious. Floyd's wife had been Sally B. Preston of Virginia, a relative of William Preston and a member of Jessie's connection; and Floyd and Preston were doubtless working together. Their object was to have Frémont nominated as head of a Democratic-Know-Nothing combination. But Frémont in his manuscript *Memoirs* has told a fuller story.

He relates that in Washington he had become acquainted with Edward Carrington, a nephew of John B. Floyd and a relative of the Bentons, and through him was drawn into a number of discussions with southern leaders. That secret political order called the Native American or Know-Nothing Party was then rising to the height of its brief strength, having just swept Massachusetts and Delaware. Such leaders as Millard Fillmore and John B. Clayton thought that the new party might offer a strong haven from sectional strife. Frémont, impressed like many others by the disorderliness of the Irish in New York and other cities, felt some sympathy for its restrictionist aims. Though without prejudice against any nationality, he believed that America might be happier and better-governed if it granted citizenship less easily to a mass of ill-assimilated immigrants. His views interested those southerners who hoped for an alliance of the Native Americans and Democrats; and a group headed by John B. Floyd undertook to negotiate with him upon his possible nomination for the presidency. They wished an attractive and popular leader who was not connected in any way with the horrible Kansas struggle.

Finally, a conference lasting several days took place at the St. Nicholas Hotel in New York; at which place, writes Frémont, the southern agents offered to support him for the Democratic nomination if he would subscribe to stringent conditions. Frémont took to the conference Nathaniel P. Banks of Massachusetts, his friend and admirer since 1853, who held precisely his own political tenets; Banks was a former Democrat, who had been reëlected to Congress the previous fall as a Know-Nothing, but was now actually an ardent Free Soiler, and was soon to be the successful candidate of that group for Speaker. Both men objected vehemently to the proposal that Frémont should endorse the Kansas-Nebraska Act and Fugitive Slave Law, and Banks denounced these measures so violently that he broke up one conference. Jessie recalls that before her husband gave his final no, he came to Siasconset to consult her: [1]

One of them [the Democratic agents] said, "the Democratic party was sure to win, and no woman could refuse the Presidency." After tea Mr. Frémont said if I could walk as far as he wished me to with him to the Lighthouse Hill he had something to say to me without interruption. And so there and then he told me of the offered nomination, and of the conditions attached.

There was no shadow of doubt in our minds. At the foot of the bluff on which the lighthouse stood were the remains embedded in the sands of a ship, the seas washing into her ribs. Above, steady and brilliant, flashed out the recurring light. "It is the choice between a wreck of dishonor, or a kindly light that will go on its mission of doing good. You cannot give in to the execution of all the laws. [The fugitive slave law was specified.] And so his decision was made.

After Frémont had rebuffed the Democrats, certain leaders of the new Republican Party turned to him. Both Banks and Senator Henry Wilson of Massachusetts were intensely interested in the Republican organization, and they caught with enthusiasm at the suggestion that Frémont would make an ideal nominee. Joseph Palmer, head of Palmer, Cook & Co., was in the city in November, 1855, and at the Metropolitan Hotel

[1] Jessie Benton Frémont MSS, Bancroft Library.

conferred with Banks, Wilson, and Senator John P. Hale of New Hampshire, doing his utmost to persuade them that Frémont was their best candidate. He advised the explorer to stay and await developments. In consequence, instead of returning to California, Frémont took up his residence in the city. We find him writing Francis Lieber from 176 Second Avenue on November 18th that he regretted missing the latter:

The day after your departure I arrived here with my family with the intention of establishing ourselves for the winter. We have succeeded in doing this comfortably, and now in our temporary resting-place have leisure to look around and inquire how it fares with our friends and among the first of those who rise before us, is yourself. With some little amusement I am about to combine a good deal of labor in writing, and a kindred occupation naturally recalls you more to my mind.

He asked for Lieber's views on public affairs.[2]

During the winter the movement to make Frémont the Republican candidate gathered strength as rapidly as the new party itself. His boom fairly opened about Christmas, and moved forward with a simultaneous rush in Washington, New York, and Boston. At all three points Banks, later called by Boutwell the discoverer of Frémont as a presidential candidate, was the most active agent. Though engrossed during early December in his Speakership fight, he took some days at Christmas to work for his friend, visiting several cities. Carrying his message to influential newspapermen like John Bigelow of the New York *Evening Post* and Charles Congdon of the Boston *Atlas,* as well as politicians like ex-Representative Charles W. Upham, later one of Frémont's campaign workers and biographers, Banks told them that the free soil cause could make no headway till they had a man as well as a platform, and that Frémont was ideal; the others had been too active partisans to run well. Bigelow, Congdon, and Upham were all won over, and Bigelow began to convert his chief, William

2 Lieber Papers, Huntington Library.

Cullen Bryant. Then Frémont's old friend Francis P. Blair, the veteran Washington journalist, and his son Frank P. Blair of St. Louis, took up the cause. The snowball was growing.[3]

At the famous conference at Blair's Silver Spring estate late in December, 1855, called to lay plans for a national anti-slavery party, Frémont's name was discussed. According to one newspaper, the members—Blair, Banks, Preston King, Chase, Sumner, and others—decided that he would be the most suitable candidate. And there is no doubt that another conference summoned by John Bigelow in New York in the first days of 1856, with the elder Blair, Edwin D. Morgan, and some lesser politicians present, determined to back Frémont to the limit. Early in the year a strong machine was being set up. Capable men were obtained as organizers—Isaac Sherman of New York, Israel D. Andrews of Massachusetts, Colonel Charles James of Wisconsin, and others. Bigelow reported: "Thurlow Weed says he is contented with Frémont, and if so, of course Seward is."

Before spring fairly opened, a strong current of Frémont sentiment was manifest among Republicans all over the North. First various Massachusetts newspapers, such as the Worcester *Spy*, influenced by Banks, Wilson, and John R. Andrew, came out for the explorer. The Blair organ in St. Louis, the *Democrat*, echoed the demand, and Bryant's *Evening Post* took up the cry. The Cleveland *Herald* pronounced for Frémont in March; and "Frémont is very popular in Ohio," wrote the Cleveland correspondent of the New York *Tribune* on April 3rd. The *Herald of Freedom*, organ of the Emigrant Aid Society, had published a laudatory article in January, and at

[3] On this subject a main source of material is the Frémont MSS in the Bancroft Library. But see also A. W. Crandall, *Early History of the Republican Party*; R. J. Bartlett, *John C. Frémont and the Republican Party*; W. E. Smith, *The Francis Preston Blair Family in Politics*, Vol. I; Roy F. Nichols, "Some Problems of the First Republican Campaign," *American Historical Review*, XXVIII, pp. 492ff.; and Fred Harvey Harrington, "Frémont and the Nomination of 1856," *American Historical Review*, XXIX, p. 921ff. Mr. Reinhard H. Luthin has kindly furnished me transcripts from the Seward Papers in Auburn, New York, and the Thurlow Weed Papers at Rochester University.

the beginning of April placed his name at its masthead: "Our Candidate: John C. Frémont." Meanwhile, on February 2nd, the day Banks was elected Speaker, Ben: Perley Poore wrote the Boston *Journal* that the Republicans would undoubtedly nominate the explorer. New York organizers, abetted by Thurlow Weed, were earnestly at work, and Isaac Sherman told Banks early in February that he considered it settled that both the Republicans and Barnburners—the free-soil Democrats— desired Frémont as their candidate. By the time of the Pittsburgh Convention (February 22nd to 23rd), which officially organized the Republican party, his lead was established. An interesting feature of his strength was the support of German newspapers and such German leaders as Philip Dorsheimer of Buffalo, who believed him the least anti-foreign of the Republican aspirants.

As the spring advanced the argument of his "availability" rapidly became irresistible. Many Eastern Republicans would have preferred Seward, Chase, or some other leader who, as Bryant put it, bore the scars of long warfare against slavery. But it seemed clear that none of these veterans could win. Seward and Chase had taken too extreme a stand upon the slavery issue, both demanding the abolition of slavery in the District of Columbia and the repeal of the Fugitive Slave Act; both, and especially Seward, were repugnant to the Native Americans. A third possibility was John McLean of Ohio, associate justice of the Supreme Court, who had many adherents in Pennsylvania, New Jersey, and Illinois—among them Abraham Lincoln. But he was an old man, past seventy, and an uninspiring, colorless figure. Dana of the *Tribune* called him "an old fogy," "a marrowless old lawyer," and the younger and more aggressive Republicans turned away from him. To this element Frémont seemed by far the most effective candidate. He was just forty-three; he had no embarrassing record on the slavery question; a romantic aura hung about his name, and his activity and daring made him seem just the leader to typify a crusading new party. Such was his strength that certain supporters of Millard Fillmore, after his nomination this spring by the pro-slavery Know-Nothings, considered deserting him to support Frémont.

During May the race narrowed to a contest between McLean and Frémont, with the latter almost certain of the prize. Seward had been definitely withdrawn by Thurlow Weed, who believed that he should wait until 1860 for his chance. Chase was unacceptable, for it was now evident that the cry of Abolitionism would cost him tens of thousands of votes in southern Indiana and Illinois. Samuel Bowles wrote that the Frémont movement in the West was "going like a prairie fire"; Greeley, though noncommittal, was arguing that the paramount consideration was the ability to draw votes—and this meant Frémont. A letter of sympathy from the explorer to the free-soil governor of Kansas, Charles Robinson, published early in April, impressed all northern free-soilers. According to the Chicago correspondent of the New York *Tribune,* he was more frequently spoken of in Illinois than any other man. "A sort of intrusive feeling pervades the people that he will be nominated and elected. The same sentiment is extending over Iowa and spreading into Wisconsin. He seems to combine more elements of strength than any man who has yet been named."

But one great threat still menaced Frémont's ambitions, a threat from an extraordinary quarter. The anti-slavery Know-Nothings, who had tentatively parted from the pro-slavery wing during 1855, constituted a strong party; one which many observers as late as the fall of 1855 thought stronger than the Republicans. They were still a powerful factor in the situation when, in February, 1856, they cut entirely loose from the pro-slavery or Fillmore Know-Nothings to set up a national party of their own. Leaders in this party had no intention of making an independent fight, for that would mean certain defeat; but they wished to join the Republicans on equal terms, not to be swallowed by them. They felt that they would gain more by fusion if they had their own national committee and nominating convention; and they called this convention for

June 12th, five days before the Republicans were to meet. It was evident that they hoped to use it to dictate the choice of a candidate for both parties! This impaled the followers of Frémont upon the horns of a dilemma. If the anti-slavery Know-Nothings nominated McLean or Stockton, and the Republicans ratified the nomination, all would be lost. If the Know-Nothings nominated McLean and the Republicans Frémont, two anti-slavery tickets would divide the vote and make victory impossible. But if the Know-Nothings nominated Frémont on June 12th, then this action would weaken him with foreign-born voters, and might defeat him in the Republican Convention or afterwards. "I cannot solve the problem," Isaac Sherman despairingly wrote Banks; "it is out of my reach." Greeley was also deeply worried. "Our *real* trouble is the K.N. convention on the 12th," he declared.

It was while faced with this dilemma that Frémont prepared a letter to one of his supporters, Governor Ford, which was held in reserve for possible use. It was a stiff refusal to accept the Know-Nothing nominations on terms that might embarrass the Republican party. He spoke out plainly against racial or national prejudices: [4]

The people throughout the free States, with extraordinary unanimity and enthusiasm, appear to be rising in a simultaneous effort upon a single and great issue, regardless of the minor questions of party policy which in quieter times have sundered the north and nullified its power. On all sides there is a generous disposition to rise above all political animosities and all prejudices of birth and religion. With the feelings which are actuating the body of the people at this moment I take pleasure in saying that I am thoroughly imbued. I am hostile to slavery upon principle and feeling. While I feel myself inflexible in the belief that it ought not to be interfered with where it exists under the shield of state sovereignty, I am as inflexibly opposed to its extension on this continent beyond its present limits. Animated with these views, confident of their success, and earnestly disposed to do battle persistently in their behalf,

[4] Copy in Bigelow MSS, New York Public Library.

and having but little active sympathy with secondary questions, which are not involved in the great issue, I am naturally identified with the cause represented by the great Republican Convention about to assemble in Philadelphia. I could not therefore accept unconditionally the candidateship of the American party, inasmuch as I would feel bound by the decisions of that party with which I am identified.

But the problem was solved without issuance of such a drastic letter. Great numbers of Frémont men descended upon the Native American Convention in Philadelphia as its delegates gathered in early June. Thurlow Weed was busy buttonholing delegates; so were Preston King, E. D. Morgan, and other shrewd politicians. Money flowed freely, and one participant said later that the Frémont men spent $30,000 to control the gathering. With this to assist, agreement was easy. Isaac Sherman had broached a shrewd plan—a plan that the Know-Nothings should nominate Banks for President and some good Whig for Vice-President; and that as soon as the Republican Convention nominated Frémont, Banks should resign in his favor.

This plan was duly carried out. On June 16th the Know-Nothings nominated Banks and William F. Johnston of North Carolina, though a rump bolted in order to name Commodore Stockton of New Jersey and Kenneth Raynor of North Carolina. Next day the Republican Convention opened, and on the nineteenth nominated Frémont and William L. Dayton of New Jersey. Some of the Know-Nothings were offended that not even their vice-presidential candidate had been accepted, and threatened to kick over the traces. But the explorer's managers were determined and adroit. They took a group of the hesitant Native Americans to New York to call on Frémont at his Ninth Street home, and these men came away satisfied. The candidate, whose above-quoted letter to Ford would utterly have ruined him with the Nativists, gave such assurances as were necessary to satisfy his guests on points of principle. Moreover, he or the other Republican leaders promised that Dayton would be withdrawn in favor of Johnston. Next day, the 20th, the requisite program was carried through by the Know-Nothings. They let Banks withdraw, and substituted Frémont and Johnston. But as Johnston was persuaded to resign in favor of Dayton, the final ticket of both parties was Frémont and Dayton. Such were the virtuous circumstances amid which the Republican party, destined to so virtuous a career, entered upon its first race.

* * *

Upon some details of this first Republican National Convention we may well pause. Its delegates, nearly a thousand strong, met in the Musical Fund Hall of Philadelphia at eleven o'clock on the morning of June 17, 1856. Certain characteristics were strongly stamped upon it. It was a sectional gathering; only four slave states were represented, Delaware, Maryland, Virginia, and Kentucky, and they sent but a handful of members. All the free states and the territories of Kansas, Nebraska, and Minnesota had sent delegates. It was also a gathering in which the evangelical element—there were many vociferous ministers present—and the radical anti-slavery element, led by Wilmot, Lovejoy, and Giddings, were prominent. From the outset a camp-meeting fervor, a crusading enthusiasm such as was hardly known again in American politics till the Progressive Convention of 1912 in Chicago, marked the public proceedings. Most of the delegates believed that a great movement for free men, free speech, and free thought was being launched. They boasted that the moral elevation of the assemblage, its dignity and decorum, stood in bright contrast with the rowdy bar-room atmosphere of the Democratic Convention which had just named Buchanan at Cincinnati.

One name was plainly in the ascendancy—Frémont. Before the doors swung open, J. S. Pike wrote the *Tribune* that two days of investigation had satisfied him that Frémont's nomination was inevitable. The New York delegation, ruled by Thurlow Weed, was, he said, almost unanimously for the explorer; the majority of the Pennsylvania and New Jersey delegations were for McLean; Ohio's delegation was divided, some for Frémont, some for McLean, and most for Chase; a majority of the Illinois members were at least nominally for McLean; and the remainder of the country had generally chosen Frémont delegates. "The fact is not disguised," Pike concluded, "that as a general thing the outright, progressive-movement men are in favor of Frémont, while McLean is the candidate for the slow and hunkerish part of the convention. The general sentiment of all is conciliatory." But the "progressive" men were obviously in control, applauding every radical utterance and distributing such inflammatory literature as the House Committee Report on the assault of Brooks upon Sumner.[5]

The first important task was the platform. Edward D. Morgan called the Convention to order, and Robert Emmet of New York was made temporary chairman. With eighty-odd reporters scribbling like mad before him, and the delegates wild with enthusiasm, David Wilmot on the second morning read the platform. It was a brief document of nine "resolutions," which did not take ten minutes to recite. Each separate plank rang out like the report of a cannon and was followed by a salvo of applause. The denunciation of the Kansas atrocities was the signal for a tremendous demonstration. The band played and cheer followed cheer as Wilmot disclaimed that: "It is our fixed purpose to bring the perpetrators of these atrocious outrages, and their accomplices, to a sure and condign punishment hereafter." The platform upheld the Missouri Compromise, opposed the extension of slavery, demanded the admission of Kansas as a free state, denied the power of Congress or any local legislature to establish slavery within a territory, and declared that the Ostend Circular was "the highwayman's plea that 'might makes right.'" Mormon polygamy

[5] Upon the preference of the younger, more aggressive Republicans for Frémont see J. S. Pike, *First Blows of the Civil War*, p. 338.

and southern slavery were linked together as "twin relics of barbarism." [6]

On the third day came the balloting. Ex-Governor George W. Patterson of New Jersey formally withdrew the name of Seward; he was followed by Ex-Judge Rufus P. Spalding of Ohio, who by authority withdrew the name of McLean; and Thomas J. Mitchell of Ohio in the same way withdrew Chase. The convention, tense with excitement, expected Frémont's nomination to follow at once. Frank P. Blair, who had in his pocket a letter from Frémont authorizing him to do anything except permit the explorer to be named for Vice-President, felt that victory was within his grasp. At this moment, Thaddeus Stevens rose and begged for delay. One man only, he said, could carry Pennsylvania; that man, McLean, had been withdrawn; and it was necessary for the delegates from his state to consult on the situation. All the previous day Stevens, Wilmot, and other McLean men had done their best to make converts from the Frémont ranks, and had succeeded in winning over a number of Maine delegates. Now, during the recess, Stevens made a passionate appeal to the Pennsylvania delegation to stand fast for McLean; if Frémont were nominated, he told them, the Republicans would lose not only Pennsylvania but the whole election.

Stevens's effort was in vain, though immediately after the Convention reopened McLean was again put in nomination. An informal ballot at once showed that Frémont had 359 votes, McLean 196, Sumner 2, and Seward 1. David Wilmot then took the floor and made a plea for unanimity, after which the formal ballot resulted in Frémont's nomination with 529 votes against 37 for McLean. The usual scene of mass excitement ensued. The band blared forth, the floor and galleries were a sea of tossing hats and waving handkerchiefs, and as an American flag bearing Frémont's name was raised from the platform, and a broad pennant inscribed "John C. Frémont for President" was drawn the full width of the hall, the cheer-

[6] Charles W. Johnson, *First Three Republican National Conventions*, p. 35*ff*.

ing became deafening. Banners were flung from the windows, and applause from crowds in the streets mingled with that in the hall. "The enthusiasm is tremendous," Greeley wired his office while the demonstration still continued.

Then followed what Frémont thought the great error of the Convention—the nomination of W. L. Dayton for Vice-President. He had no personal objection to the man, but held that Simon Cameron should have been named instead, thus permitting a stronger fight against Buchanan in Pennsylvania. Frémont believed that Cameron would perhaps have received the nomination had not Francis P. Blair, whose antagonisms were always intense, sternly vetoed the suggestion. Thurlow Weed, who shared his view of Dayton, later placed the blame elsewhere. He wrote Cameron: [7] "The first, and as I still think fatal error, was in not taking a Vice-President in whose nomination the North Americans would have concurred cordially. The McLean men, aided by Greeley, threw us off the track."

* * *

The Republican press rallied to Frémont with unaffected liking and hope. Few editors knew much about him, but all that they did know seemed highly favorable. The *Tribune* declared that "having exhibited a singular force of character and a distinguished ability in every undertaking to which he applied himself," he had now been called to the difficult but glorious enterprise "of rescuing the government and the Union from the hands of a body of unprincipled politicians." Bryant asked what was the secret of his overwhelming popularity. "The times require in the chief magistrates of the nation an unshaken courage, perfect steadiness of purpose, and a ready command of resources. The times require a man who has something heroic in his character"; and the people believed that the Frémont who had so firmly surmounted western perils possessed these qualities. Raymond in the *Times* declared that the citi-

[7] Weed to Cameron, November 12, 1856, Cameron Papers, Library of Congress.

zens could not fail to elect him if they had "any admiration for high personal qualities, for perseverance, bravery, disinterested benevolence, generosity, heroism, for noble-mindedness, high attainments, and devotion to duty." The Frémont legend was approaching its rather absurd zenith. Republican writers and orators began to magnify the explorer into a figure

of heroic proportions, a combination of Lochinvar, Deerslayer, and William Pitt; and some newspapers even instituted a comparison between his achievements in his first forty years and the lesser feats of George Washington.

Frémont, waiting quietly at 56 Ninth Street, accepted his nomination in a serious spirit. Having been fairly certain of it, he had written Frank Blair several days earlier that he felt as men do who, after preliminary tremor of an earthquake,

are momentarily expecting the great shock. But my nerves seem to preserve their usual tranquillity, and I am well satisfied with myself.

From the anxious inquiries of friends for some days past it seems to have been expected that I should be ill, but I continue in rather better than ordinary health, which it will please you to know.

At once, friends crowded to congratulate him; he was overwhelmed with the usual mass of telegrams and letters; and, on June 25th, there was a great ratification meeting at the Tabernacle, with bands, speeches by Robert Emmet, Lyman Trumbull, and others, and an enthusiastic torch-light procession afterward up Broadway to the Colonel's home. Frémont spoke a few words, and Jessie was called forth to acknowledge a round of cheers. A fortnight later, on July 9th, his brief formal acceptance of the nomination was published. One passage, in which he declared against filibustering expeditions or aggressions upon the domain of other nations, attracted attention abroad and was warmly commended in London by *The Times*. But Americans were interested chiefly in his remarks upon slavery. He alined himself with the explicit declarations of the Republican platform:

Nothing is clearer in the history of our institutions than the design of the nation, in asserting its own independence and freedom, to avoid giving countenance to the extension of slavery. The influence of the small but compact and powerful class of men interested in slavery, who command one section of the country and wield a vast political control as a consequence in the other, is now directed to turn back the impulse of the Revolution and reverse its principles. The extension of slavery across the continent is the object of the power which now rules the government; and from this spirit have sprung those kindred wrongs of Kansas so truly portrayed in one of your resolutions, which prove that the elements of the most arbitrary governments have not been vanquished by the just theory of our own.

It would be out of place here to pledge myself to any particular policy that has been suggested to determine the sectional controversy engendered by political animosities, operating on a powerful class banded together by common interest. A practical remedy is the admission of Kansas into the Union as a free state. The South should, in my judgment, earnestly desire such a consummation. It would vindicate its good faith. It would correct the mistake of the repeal; and the North, having practically the benefit of the agreement between the two sections, would be satisfied and good feeling be restored.

With this acceptance—the first and last public utterance of any note by Frémont in the campaign—the battle of 1856 opened.

XXVII

The Campaign of 1856

ELEVATED thus suddenly to a conspicuous political pedestal, chosen by a powerful party as its leader in a great moral crusade, the unexperienced Frémont might have been pardoned some display of awkwardness, at least some tactical misstep. Fifteen years before he had been an obscure, impoverished army lieutenant, without resources or prospects. Now he was rich, famous, and admired, his name written large on the Golden West, the reputed conqueror of California, the dashing young marshal of a gallant cause. It illustrates his modesty and tact that his conduct was exemplary. Frémont had his faults, but lack of taste was never among them. The critical Gideon Welles, in a severe passage written some years after, did him the justice to remember that at this time his public demeanor was winning. "His bearing was very well so far as he appeared before the public. I saw that he was anxious to be elected but not offensively so; he was not obtrusive, but, on the contrary, reserved and retiring."[1] If his part in the campaign was open to criticism, it was on the ground that, with his public views and capacities still largely unknown, he kept too much in the background and made altogether too few statements. The nation was asked to accept this untrained man quite too completely on faith.

From the beginning of the campaign, Frémont and the other leaders had genuine hope of victory, which rapidly mounted as news of an increasing free-soil enthusiasm came in from many parts of the North and West. The strategic elements of the situation, as Greeley insisted, were simple. The Republicans

[1] Gideon Welles, *Diary*, II, p. 41.

were certain of 114 electoral votes—those of the New England
states, New York, Ohio, Michigan, Wisconsin, and Iowa. The
Democrats were certain of 108 electoral votes from the South
and the border states. The doubtful factors were Pennsylvania
with 27 electoral votes; Indiana with 13; Illinois with 11;
Maryland with 8; New Jersey with 7, and California with 4
—that is, 70 in all. Since 149 were sufficient to elect, the
Republicans needed only to carry Pennsylvania and Indiana,
or Pennsylvania and Illinois, to be victorious. Was this impossible? The best judges thought not.

Three tickets were in the field: Buchanan and Breckinridge
for the Democrats; Frémont and Dayton for the Republicans
and one section of Know-Nothings; and Millard Fillmore and
Donelson for the expiring Whigs and another section of Know-
Nothings. The great danger was that Fillmore would draw
enough votes from Frémont to defeat him; but, as the canvas
proceeded, the energy of the Republican organization surprised
even its members.

Throughout the North, indeed, the Republican campaign
awakened a fervor recalling the log-cabin campaign of 1840,
but possessing a moral character and a degree of statesman-
ship which the Harrison campaign had lacked. Mass meeting
followed mass meeting; torch-light procession, with red fire
and marching bands, followed torch-light procession. The nomination was immediately "ratified" by gatherings all over the
country. Then came a series of tremendous "rallies." Rock-
wood Hoar and Hannibal Hamlin spoke in Faneuil Hall;
Bryant, Franz Sigel, Friedrich Kapp, and Charles A. Dana
were heard in the Tabernacle in New York. Little preliminary
organization was needed in many parts of the North besides
that supplied by the existing Emigrant Aid Societies and other
agencies for the relief of Kansas, which already reached into
every county and almost every township. The gatherings
seemed to spring spontaneously from some pent-up popular
feeling. A Frémont demonstration of 25,000 people took place
at Massilon, Ohio, another of 30,000 at Kalamazoo, Michigan;

and a third of equal size at Beloit, Wisconsin, where the crowds cheered a procession six miles in length. Illinois was not behind her neighbors. Lincoln spoke to 10,000 at Princeton, and at Alton addressed an enormous concourse—some said 35,000 people—brought together by the State Fair; while at Jacksonville Lyman Trumbull reviewed a procession a mile and a quarter long. Perhaps most striking of all was the tremendous Frémont rally in Indianapolis in July, which attracted the most attention.

Here, while cannon roared all day, the procession took hours to pass a given point; a single delegation numbered almost 4,500 men; 50 blaring bands were in line; 25 marshals kept the ranks in order; uncounted gay floats rolled down the streets, the chief carrying 32 young women in white, one for each state, with a 33rd girl in black for bleeding Kansas; hundreds of banners and transparencies waved above the long line; and platoon after platoon of Germans, with their own flags, formed a special section of the pageant. At 5 different stands orators took turns exhorting the crowd to stand fast against slavery and polygamy, against border ruffians and Bully Brooks. That night a huge torch-light procession turned the streets into streams of fire, above which rose the voices of haranguing orators.

The West and North were rallying against slavery with a new ardor. An intense resentment had been aroused in the breasts of millions by the Kansas-Nebraska Act, and it was finding a sudden release in acclamation of Frémont and the Republican cause. Companies of Wide-Awakes, carrying torches and transparencies, sprang up everywhere. Fife and drum corps shrilled and rattled. Frémont glee clubs shook the village lyceum halls and opera houses. Long lines of gigs and wagons raised the dust on prairie roads as farming people streamed to Frémont picnics and rallies. A powerful array of Republican campaign speakers took the stump. In the East they included Banks, Chase, Greeley, Sumner, William M. Evarts, and John P. Hale, while even the aloof Emerson and the retiring Bryant made speeches. In the West, Schuyler Colfax of Indiana was active, Carl Schurz was busy addressing the Germans, and striplings like Whitelaw Reid were pressed into service. Lincoln, speaking ninety times in all, made some of the ablest addresses he had yet delivered. On every hand, newspapers which for years had been Whig or Democratic were turning to the new party.

Song, slogan, and picture lent their aid in the campaign. Banners were flung across village streets, emblazoned with such devices as "We Follow the Pathfinder"; "We Shall Be Redeemed From the Rule of Nigger Drivers"; "We Are Buck-Hunting"; or with a still bolder pun, "Jessie Bent-on Being Free." [2] The Democrats were taunted as Buchaneers. One slogan was repeated everywhere in Republican newspapers and on Republican posters: "Free Speech, Free Press, Free Soil, Free Men, Frémont and Victory." Jessie played only a slighter part in the campaign than her husband, and "Frémont and Jessie" seemed to constitute the Republican ticket rather than Frémont and Dayton. "We go for our country and Union, and for brave little Jessie forever," ran one ditty. A Philadelphia rally in June popularized a campaign song, chanted to the tune of "Camptown Races," which spread rapidly all over the North:

There's an old gray horse whose name is Buck; Du da, du da,
His dam was Folly and his sire Bad Luck; Du da, du da day.

Chorus:—We're bound to work all night,
We're bound to work all day,
I'll bet my money on the Mustang Colt,
Will anybody bet on the Gray?

The Mustang Colt is strong and young, Du da, du da,
His wind is sound and his knees not sprung, Du da, du da day.
The old gray horse when he tries to trot, Du da, du da,
Goes round and round in the same old spot, Du da, du da day.
The mustang goes a killing pace, Du da, du da,
He's bound to win in the four mile race, Du da, du da day.

[2] New York *Evening Post*, September 1, 1856.

The most powerful Northern newspapers supported Frémont. In New York he had the loyal assistance of not only the
Tribune, Evening Post, and *Times,* all possessing a national
circulation, but also of James Gordon Bennett's *Herald,* which
had long been Democratic and which four years later was
panic-stricken in its desire to let the South have its way. The
Philadelphia *North American,* edited by Morton McMichael,
took the Republican side; so did the Chicago *Tribune* of Medill
and Horace White. The German press did as valiant service
as the German speakers, who included Philip Dorsheimer,
Gustav Koerner, and Schurz. German songs were written, for
one of which, by E. V. Scherb, the poet-editor Bryant paid a
prize of $100:

> *Hurrah! Bald tönt der Jubelschrei!*
> *Kansas ist jetzt gerochen,*
> *Die Knechtschaft ist gebrochen,*
> *Frei ist Amerika!*
> *Frémont der Siegeskräftige,*
> *Er hat den Feind bezwungen,*
> *Drum jauchzen alle Zungen;*
> *Frémont! Victoria!*

Large lithographed portraits of Frémont, manufactured in
New York and retailed at a dollar each, blazed forth in shop-
windows and local headquarters. Two extended campaign
biographies were prepared, one by John Bigelow, with the aid
of Jessie Frémont, which Derby & Jackson of New York sold
in huge quantities at a dollar, and one by Charles Wentworth
Upham, published by Ticknor & Fields in Boston. The *Tribune*
also issued an excellent pamphlet life by Greeley. All the larger
newspapers made a special campaign price to summer sub-
scribers. John G. Whittier celebrated Frémont's achievements
in his poem, "The Pass of the Sierras," recalling the day when
the explorer bade his men press on "and look from Winter's
frozen throne on Summer's flowers and grass!" and urging him
now to lead the nation into the promised land; while such

minor poets as T. B. Read and the Cary sisters lent their pens. Above all, the women of the North enlisted under Frémont's banner as never before in politics, while most of the Protestant clergy of the section boldly used the pulpit to urge his election.

The Democrats were sufficiently shrewd enough to take the offensive, and their tactics embraced two main sets of operations. Although the Republicans made no attack upon the private character of Buchanan except to insinuate that a bachelor ought not to be President, the Democrats leveled scurrilous charges against Frémont. Their main accusation, made with ceaseless iteration for its effect upon the Know-Nothing vote, was that Frémont was secretly a Catholic. As "proofs," they declared that in his first western expedition he had carved a cross upon Rock Independence; that he and Jessie Benton had been married by a Catholic priest; that he had sent a ward and relative, his niece Nina, to a Catholic school; and that his father was a French Catholic. The New York *Express* fortified these allegations by a half-dozen absurd stories. It declared that he had been seen crossing himself in the Catholic cathedral in Washington, that he had once told a West Point professor that he was a Catholic, and that over a hotel table he had avowed the doctrine of transubstantiation! Of course John Bigelow and others had no difficulty in proving that Frémont was a good Episcopalian. A committee of Protestant clergymen, including several professors at the Union Theological Seminary, called upon Frémont and received proofs that he worshiped at Grace Episcopal Church; that Mrs. Frémont, reared as a Presbyterian, had united with the Episcopal Church on her marriage with him; and that the children had been baptized as Episcopalians.[3]

Nevertheless, these charges did Frémont substantial harm. Schuyler Colfax wrote Bigelow at the end of August that of hundreds of letters from the Northwest, "scarcely any omits a reference to the fact that the Catholic story injures us ma-

[3] Bigelow MSS, New York Public Library; compare the campaign pamphlet, *Col. Frémont's Religion;* also the pamphlet *Republican's Outfit, 1856.*

terially, both in keeping men in the Fillmore ranks who ought
to be with us, and in cooling many of our friends who fear
from Colonel Frémont's silence and the cloud of rumors on the
subject that there may be some truth in it." He added that
unfortunately they made nothing on the other side, the Cath-
olics being solidly against the Republicans.[4] So they were,
chiefly because they believed the Know-Nothings to be behind
Frémont; of nearly forty Catholic journals, not one in July
was found on the Republican side.[5]

At the height of the campaign, some forty Republican leaders, meeting at the Astor House, discussed the charge with
Frémont, and Thurlow Weed declared that he ought to make
a public disavowal. This the candidate declined to do. He took
the position that the main issue of the campaign was freedom,
intellectual as well as physical, that under the Constitution
no religious belief disqualified a man for office, and that he
would not ask for a single vote if in so doing he had to appeal
to the religious fanaticism which had long cursed certain nations of Europe. After the conference, he decided to consult
James Gordon Bennett. "What are your convictions?" asked
the editor, and Frémont told him. "Follow those convictions,
Colonel, and I will sustain you," was the reply.

A multitude of other charges, many of them silly, were
brought against the explorer. The most abstemious of men,
he was accused of being a hard drinker. It was said that he had
owned seventy-five slaves, whom he had hired to Colonel Brant
of St. Louis. The fact was, of course, that both Frémont and
Jessie had again and again declined to accept a single slave
from their southern relatives, though often pressed to do so
during their privations on the frontier; for both had an unconquerable aversion to slavery. The Democratic press made much
of Frémont's financial perplexities. He had signed a note for
$1,891, it said, due in a year, and when the brokers refused
to discount it, had offered it to Horace Greeley at 2 per cent

[4] Bigelow MSS, August 29, 1856.
[5] New York *Tribune*, July 21, 1856.

a month. Greeley angrily rejoined that in the first place he was not a note-shaver, and in the second everybody knew he did not have $1,891! Stories were printed that Frémont was ineligible to the presidency, having been born abroad, and a man came forward who recalled the very house in Montreal in which he had first seen the light! Most painful of all to Frémont's friends, the Democrats seized upon the whole dark story of his mother and her Anna Karenina elopement with a man of her own age, and magnified its unpleasant aspect.

Much more nearly legitimate were the attacks directed against Frémont's military and financial transactions in California. During the previous session of Congress, a foundation for these assaults had been laid by Senators Thompson of New Jersey and Bigler of Pennsylvania, who in bitterly partisan speeches raked over all Frémont's campaigns and California contracts. At the same time, the Los Angeles *Star* charged the explorer with cruelty and rapacity in his treatment of the native Californians during and after the Bear Flag War. So far as his share in the American acquisition of the Coast went, the Republicans had a sweeping answer ready. They simply quoted the testimony of Buchanan himself, in the British judicial inquiry into the suits against Frémont in 1852, that "his services were very valuable; he bore a conspicuous part in the conquest of California, and in my opinion is better entitled to be called the conqueror of California than any other man." The answer to the charges of cruelty was equally decisive. At Los Angeles and San José many native Californians, led by Don Pio Pico, signed statements denying them completely and appealing for the election of Frémont.[6] Thomas O. Larkin, former American consul, testified that Frémont had lived in his house for weeks or months at a time, from 1850 to 1854. Seeing the explorer at this close range, he had found him "of reserved and distant manners, active and industrious in his official duties, anxious to finish the business on hand and before him and to be on the march to accomplish more"; never coarse or profane;

[6] New York *Evening Post*, October 29, 1856.

always "polite, kind, and courteous." Larkin concluded with
an emphatic sentence: "I consider Mr. Frémont a just, correct, and moral man, abstemious, bold, and persevering."[7]

Nevertheless, in California especially, the history of Frémont's share in the Indian beef contract and his connection
with Palmer, Cook & Co., financial agents of the state of California and city of San Francisco, who had defaulted owing
those bodies $100,000, was so retold as to cost the explorer
heavily. Actually, he had performed a public service in forestalling a threatened Indian war. But his handling of the contract, his protracted siege of Congress to obtain payment, and
his negotiations with his creditors, were all interpreted in hostile manner. The San Francisco *Globe,* in a long and venomous
article, reviewed these business affairs and also accused Frémont of complicity with Palmer, Cook & Co., in trying to
swindle the public in exploiting the Mariposa mines. This
article was an adroit tissue of lies. Frémont and his friends did
everything in their power to disassociate his name from that
of the discredited banking firm, making it clear that he had
never been a partner or associate. But many Republicans on
the coast feared that there was some basis of truth for the
reports.

Dozens of "Bear Clubs" and similar organizations were
founded in California to support Frémont—sixteen in San
Francisco alone; six or seven newspapers vigorously defended
him. Nevertheless, a good deal of the mud stuck. The San Francisco *Bulletin,* James King of William's paper, was friendly
toward the Republican nominee. But it declared its firm conviction that "this disreputable firm has lost thousands of votes
for Frémont in this state," and that it had injured him more
than any other factor.[8]

The second main element in Democratic strategy lay in
systematic use of the bogey of secession as a consequence of

[7] Letter to Alpheus Hardy, August 2, 1856; Larkin Papers, Bancroft Library.
[8] San Francisco *Morning Globe,* August 19, 1856; San Francisco *Bulletin,*
November 5, December 2, 1856.

Frémont's election. Buchanan men declared that the Black Republicans, the party of "free soilers, Frémonters, free niggers, and freebooters," were the first sectional party in our history. Buchanan himself in his letter of acceptance recalled the warning of Washington against political organizations formed upon geographical lines. The Democratic platform repudiated "all sectional parties and platforms concerning domestic slavery," saying that they must eventuate in civil war and disunion. A multitude of patriotic men who disliked slavery as much as Frémont himself were converted to this point of view. One was Thomas Hart Benton, who with his usual high devotion to principle uncompromisingly opposed his son-in-law, and published an open letter attacking the proposed Frémont ticket in Missouri; the whole Republican movement, he said, was accentuating the hostility between the two sections. Denouncing any political party which tried to elect candidates from one part of the Union to rule over the whole of it, he asked if the people believed that the South would submit to such a President as Frémont? "We are treading," he said, "upon a volcano that is liable at any moment to burst forth and overwhelm the nation." [9]

Numerous Democratic newspapers, like the Washington *Union*, Richmond *Enquirer*, and Charleston *Mercury*, predicted disunion in emphatic terms if Frémont were elected. John Forsyth of Alabama wrote that "the South ought not to submit to it, and will not submit. The government of the United States will be at an end." Preston Brooks, the assailant of Sumner, fiercely addressed a great mass meeting at Ninety-Six, South Carolina. "I believe the only hope of the South," he said, "is in dissolving the bonds which connect us with the government—in separating the living body from the dead carcass." If Frémont were actually chosen, he added, the news should be the signal for an instant southern march upon Washington, for it would be a patriotic duty to "lay the strong arm of Southern freemen upon the treasury and archives of the gov-

[9] New York *Tribune*, August 18, 1856.

ernment." [10] Senator Slidell asserted that if the Republicans triumphed, "the Union cannot and ought not to be preserved." Senator Mason declared that only one course would be open— "immediate, absolute, eternal separation." The editor of the Charleston *Mercury* believed that such an event "will be and ought to be the knell of the Union." When John Minor Botts defended the idea of an indissoluble Union, the Richmond *Enquirer* called him a traitor and threatened him with lynching. That the threat of secession was real is evident from a letter that a Southerner, T. Turner, wrote Hamilton Fish in September: [11]

I live farther South, see more and know more of Southern people than you do. Last evening was with Cobb of Ga. and Judge Stuart of Maryland—if I am wrong, they are wrong—they both emphatically declare, and with great calmness, that if Frémont is elected, secession follows fast as soon as they can receive the news. Cobb told me that Georgia has already taken the first step, in anticipation of this crisis, by the enactment of a law by the last Legislature empowering the Gov. to call a state convention, as soon as he might deem it necessary. I saw other Southern gentlemen—who talk precisely in the same way.

While many Republican newspapers and speakers affected to scoff, these secessionist utterances awakened a profound dread among conservative Northerners. Bryant's *Evening Post* felt it necessary to publish long editorials assuring the nation that Frémont was not a radical, and would not countenance Sumner in his denunciation of the South, or Seward in his insistence upon repeal of the Fugitive Slave Act. An impressive list of northern Whigs were so affected by the southern threats that they alined themselves with Buchanan, and appealed to the voters to take the same position. Rufus Choate, in a long public letter, well reasoned and well written, declared that it was the first duty of Whigs "to defeat and dissolve the new

[10] New York *Evening Post*, October 9, 1856.
[11] Fish MSS, Library of Congress.

geographical party," and that in these circumstances he would vote for Buchanan.[12] Webster's son Fletcher violently assailed the new party, and so did James B. Clay, son of Henry Clay. Such other old-time Whigs as Caleb Cushing, Robert Winthrop, and Amos A. Lawrence, all influential, took their stand by Choate to "prevent the madness of the times from working its maddest act." Meanwhile, Wendell Phillips gloried in the sectional nature of the new party, and asked why the North had never before dared to assert its sectional convictions.

It was one of the paradoxes of the campaign that while the South was thus fulminating against the "Black Republicans" for their hostility to slavery, the Abolitionists were assailing them for their tolerance of the institution. William Lloyd Garrison abused the Republican organization as feeble and indefinite, and sneered at the leaders for reassuring men of moderate views in order to poll a large vote at the election. An abolitionist ticket was placed in the field, with Gerrit Smith as its candidate, and its mouthpiece, the *Radical Abolitionist*, attacked Frémont in every issue as a leader who would compromise with a great evil.[13]

As the campaign drew toward its close, Frémont continued to play a rôle of dignified aloofness. He greeted the curious and for the most part friendly crowds of people who came to his Ninth Street home, made brief and perfunctory speeches to various delegations, and carried on a wide correspondence. He maintained his health by fencing every morning and taking long walks after dark, while in the middle of October he made a brief run into Vermont. The actual management of the campaign was in the hands of E. D. Morgan, Francis P. Blair, John Bigelow, Isaac Sherman (who took New York for his special province), a Charles James, and Thurlow Weed, men in whom Frémont had full confidence. Bigelow, James, and

[12] S. G. Brown, *Life of Rufus Choate*, p. 321; New York *Times*, August 15, 1856.
[13] W. P. and F. J. Garrison, *William Lloyd Garrison*, IV, p. 442ff.

Sherman made up a private committee which, together with Mrs. Frémont, handled the mail.

The most painful aspect of the campaign was the growing intensity of the personal and sectional animosity which accompanied it. A fair illustration of the vituperation which Southerners of the Rhett and Brooks type poured forth is furnished by a speech of Henry A. Wise in Richmond:

Frémont is nothing. (Cheers.) He is less than nothing in my estimation. (Enthusiastic cheering.) He is but a mere personification of Black Republicanism, the bearer of the black flag. (Cheers.) The question will not be, shall Frémont reign over you and me? but it will be, shall the black flag be erected, shall the higher law be executed by the President of the United States over the reign of the Constitution and the laws? Shall property be invaded with impunity? Yes, you will find hundreds that will say—they begin already to say—"O, wait, wait for some overt act!—wait for him to do some wrong!" Tell me, will any person entertaining feeling of self-respect, having the spirit and courage of a man, wait to prepare for war while its cloud is on the horizon until after the declaration of war is made?

Tell me, if the hoisting of the Black Republican flag in the hands of an adventurer, born illegitimately in a neighboring State, if not ill-begotten in this very city—tell me, if the hoisting of the black flag over you by a Frenchman's bastard, while the arms of civil war are already clashing, is not to be deemed an overt act and declaration of war?

One southern friend and relative after another, both of Frémont and his wife, now renounced them forever. From a former comrade, later a distinguished soldier and historian— Edward McCrady—with whom Frémont had grown up in Charleston, and for whom he had named a stream in the Far West, he received a note in explanation of the unauthorized publication of a private letter; and McCrady closed thus:[14]

Mrs. Johnson and myself keenly feel the gross outrage committed upon us, by this most unwarranted reference to our private. cor-

[14] Frémont, MS *Memoirs*, Bancroft Library.

respondence. After your course in reference to the Presidential election, any correspondence with you is painful to me, and nothing but the necessity of vindicating myself and family from a suspicion of such gross indelicacy as is implied in that reference, could have induced me again to address you.

The chief compensating feature of the campaign was the enthusiasm with which the youth, the womanhood, the clergy, the cultural and intellectual leaders of the North, united in what seemed to them a great moral crusade. The universities, with such spokesmen as Felton of Harvard and Silliman of Yale, were almost unanimously for Frémont. The literary leaders of New England and New York had actively espoused his candidacy—Emerson, Longfellow, Bryant, Whittier, Bayard Taylor, and even the venerable Washington Irving. One of George W. Curtis's campaign utterances, a felicitous address to the students of Wesleyan University in Connecticut, at once became a classic of American politics—"The Duty of the American Scholar." The religious press rallied under the leadership of Henry Ward Beecher, whose pen in the pages of the *Independent* was only less effective than Greeley's in the *Tribune*. On the Sunday preceding the election, most of the New England ministers preached and prayed for the defeat of Buchanan, and the pulpits of the Middle West poured forth a thousand pleas for the Republican cause.

The critical event of the early autumn was Pennsylvania's state election of October 14th, which was universally expected to show how her twenty-seven electoral votes would be cast. Both sides girded up their loins. Two state parties were in the field, one the Democratic and the other the Union, the latter supposedly comprising the Republicans, Whigs, and Native Americans. At the beginning of the battle, all Republican strategists had pointed to Pennsylvania as the crucial ground and urged that money be poured into it. Unfortunately, the party was straitened for funds, while its state organization was weak and defective. It was said later that the Democrats had spent nearly $500,000 in Pennsylvania, and it is certain that

John W. Forney and others came to New York, demanded large sums from merchants in the southern trade, and used the funds to subsidize not merely the Democratic but also the Native American party. August Belmont was reported to have given $50,000, and other Wall Street bankers and brokers $100,000 more. The Republicans loudly lamented their poverty. "When Frémont was nominated," Russell Errett wrote reproachfully from Pittsburgh to Salmon P. Chase, "our friends in New York, and Ohio, and everywhere, assured us that we could and should have whatever aid we needed, both in money and speakers, to carry the State; yet, so far ... we have failed to get either." "We Frémonters of this town," Greeley wrote from New York, "have not one dollar where the Fillmoreans and Buchanans have ten each, and we have Pennsylvania and New Jersey both on our shoulders. Each State is utterly miserable, so far as money is concerned." [15]

The Republicans placed a brigade of speakers in the field in the closing days of the fight, Charles A. Dana writing jubilantly, "I suppose there are about two hundred orators, great and small, now stumping Pennsylvania for Frémont"; but they included few men of national renown. The ablest campaigners were Robert Collyer, the great-hearted Yorkshire workingman and minister, whose rugged eloquence went straight to the hearts of the laborers, David Wilmot, and Hannibal Hamlin. State affection for Buchanan, as a favorite son,

[15] C. B. Going, *David Wilmot, Free Soiler,* p. 493; J. S. Pike, *First Blows of the Civil War,* p. 346. The Gideon Welles Papers in the Library of Congress contain several letters from Chairman E. D. Morgan to Welles on money matters. He writes September 30th: "It rained hard last night, and yet I succeeded in getting 38 to 40 pretty good men, and got subscribed $8,000. If it had been pleasant we would have got from $12,000 to $15,000, which we will get, but with more effort." On October 8th: "We are still at work for Pennsylvania....I have raised something near $15,000, and have appropriated it, since which under the arrangement with Ford he has turned up suddenly with a list of 15 or 18 persons in Pa. and drafts on Howard for $8,000." On October 22nd: "We have been and are now exerting ourselves to raise money for Pa. I authorized a draft on me yesterday for $8,000—and for $25,000 in event of Frémont's election. At Boston the true men meet at three o'clock today for the same purpose. At Philadelphia Mr. Lindley Smith, a merchant, is at the same thing."

counted for a great deal; the Republican press, outside of Philadelphia, counted for little. Moreover, the Union leadership was weak and divided. Simon Cameron wrote Thurlow Weed later: "From the first I saw little hopes of Pennsylvania. I saw the error committed in placing the movement in the hands of ignorant and conceited men. The Whigs of this State cannot control a campaign; and they would not permit Democrats to advise or help them." [16] But perhaps the decisive factor was the fear of the conservative, peace-loving "Pennsylvania Dutch" that Frémont's election would produce a costly upheaval, and their consequent decision to cling to the older parties.

Election day in Pennsylvania dawned with party feeling so intense that sober men were glad to find the weather raw and drizzling, for they feared a clash of turbulent crowds. The streets of Philadelphia that night were jammed with people eager to hear the news. Two days elapsed before it was certain that the Buchanan state ticket was elected, and a still longer period before it was known that its majority fell short of 3,000. A change of 1,500 votes would have given Frémont's Union party the victory. Yet this close result was decisive; it was at once seen that if the free-soil forces, uniting Whigs, Know-Nothings, and Republicans under one banner, could not carry Pennsylvania, the Republicans single-handed could not do so. The same day also witnessed elections in Ohio and Indiana, and although Ohio went Republican, Indiana proved safely Democratic. Buchanan's election thus seemed doubly sure. Young Rutherford B. Hayes expressed the opinion of a host of Republicans. "Before the October elections in Pennsylvania and Indiana," he wrote, "I was confident Colonel Frémont would be elected. But the disastrous results in those states indicate and will probably do much to produce his defeat. The majori-

---

[16] November 9, 1856, Weed Papers, University of Rochester. Cameron added that he believed that if he and Weed had met in July and laid complete plans for Pennsylvania they could have carried the state. Weed replied on the twelfth: "Our organization in your State was sadly neglected. We had feeble men in Philadelphia."

ties are small—very small—but they discourage our side." [17]

More than a fortnight before the final election, therefore, Republican leaders knew that they were virtually beaten. They still affected to look forward confidently to the result, but their hopes were gone. To the end of his life, Frémont believed that if his wishes had been followed in the selection of Simon Cameron as running mate, and an organization developed in Pennsylvania sufficient to prevent Democratic corruption of the voters, he would have carried the state in both October and November, and the resulting prestige of the Republicans would have swept Indiana or Illinois into line. This is doubtful, for even had Frémont won the state election, Buchanan's chances for carrying Pennsylvania in November would have remained good; the Whig supporters of Fillmore, who in Philadelphia outnumbered the Republicans three to one, would have voted almost *en masse* against Frémont. But it is interesting to note that Cameron believed that if he and Thurlow Weed had been able to organize the state fully in July, victory would have been certain.

The complete returns were just what the shrewder politicians expected. Of the thirty-one states, Buchanan carried nineteen, Frémont eleven, and Fillmore one; Buchanan had 174 electoral votes, Frémont 114, and Fillmore 8. No fewer than 1,341,264 votes were polled by Frémont, about a half-million fewer than those received by Buchanan, and a half-million more than those cast for Fillmore. New York was safely in the Frémont column, for his vote outside of the Democratic metropolis was prodigious; so were Ohio, Michigan, Wisconsin, and Iowa. The principal disappointments, aside from Pennsylvania, were Illinois and Indiana. A broad view of the election showed that the Republicans had been beaten by the Whig votes cast for Buchanan and Fillmore. Fillmore alone received the support of almost 900,000 Whigs and Native Americans, a third of them in the North; they were cast against a sectional party and to avert the threat of civil war, and not against Frémont.

[17] C. R. Williams, *Life of Rutherford B. Hayes,* I, pp. 105, 107.

Frémont took his defeat philosophically, and Mrs. Frémont accepted it with a surprising restraint of emotion. They had spent election night at headquarters, and then returned at dawn with old Francis P. Blair to their home for breakfast. When they spoke of the Missouri result Jessie remarked brightly: "Colonel Benton, I perceive, has the best of the family argument." Frémont smiled, but Blair's voice choked and tears rolled down his cheeks as he declared: "Tom Benton's stubborn stand cost us many a vote outside Missouri." At this Lilly, who had set her heart on the White House as a delightful place of residence, broke into loud weeping. Jessie forthwith sent her for a long walk, and as she rebuked the little girl Blair blew his nose and said contritely: "That will do for me too, Jessie Anne. Come, Colonel, let's go to headquarters." [18]

As they looked about after election day, the Republicans had much with which to console themselves. The Whig party was dead; it was now evident that Millard Fillmore's campaign represented its expiring throes, and that it would never again figure in a presidential campaign. Such northern Democrats as President Pierce, Lewis Cass, and John A. Dix, detested by many free-soilers because of their complaisance toward slavery, had been stingingly rebuked by their states; so had such New England Whigs as Choate and Caleb Cushing. In the brief space of six months the Republican party had succeeded in crystallizing public sentiment throughout the North and establishing itself in that section as the dominant party. The *Tribune* rejoiced that the future success of the Republicans seemed certain, the *Herald* proposed that Frémont should be at once renominated for the campaign of 1860, and, in the *Evening Post,* Bryant proclaimed that the tide was becoming irresistible:

In those States of the Union which have now given such large majorities for Frémont, pubic opinion, which till lately has been shuffling and undecided in regard to the slavery question, is now clear,

[18] I. T. Martin, *Recollections of Elizabeth Benton Frémont,* pp. 79, 80.

fixed, and resolute. If we look back to 1848, when we conducted a Presidential election on this very ground of opposition to the spread of slavery, we shall see that we have made immense strides towards the ascendancy which, if there be any grounds to hope for the perpetuity of free institutions, is yet to be ours. We were then comparatively weak, we are now strong; we then counted our thousands, we now count our millions; we could then point to our respectable minorities in a few States, we now point to State after State.... The cause is not going back—it is going rapidly forward; the Free Soil party of 1848 is the nucleus of the Republican party of 1856; but with what accessions of numbers, of moral power, of influence, not merely in public assemblies, but at the domestic fireside!

For Frémont himself the outlook was of less roseate character. True, he had borne himself through a heated and abusive campaign with notable dignity and poise, and had emerged from it with no lessening of public esteem. The Republican party would have pursued a more courageous course had it nominated some veteran of the free-soil struggle, some man of greater public experience. But parties have to think of expediency; and the Republicans owed Frémont a good deal, for his gallant record and attractive personality had served them well in their first national campaign. Neither Chase nor McLean would have obtained more votes, and Seward would probably have polled fewer. At the same time, his political career was now plainly ended. He had neither the gifts nor training that a politician needs; he had failed to make any public utterances that impressed the country with his intellectual powers or force of character. He must turn back to private life—to the vexatious business affairs he had dropped the previous fall.

Historians of the period, almost without exception, have declared it fortunate that Frémont was not elected and that the United States did not have to face the possible ordeal of civil war under a head so inexperienced, so rash and impetuous, so brilliantly erratic. Assuming that secession would have followed a Republican victory, they are unquestionably right.

At no stage of his career did Frémont exhibit the qualities indispensable to the head of a nation racked by civil strife; he held in reserve none of these powers which Lincoln, coming to Washington in 1861 and seeming to many easterners totally incapable of meeting the crisis, possessed. Had there been no secession, Frémont might have made a far better President than Buchanan. He would have shown none of the feeble pliancy of that Executive, and while doing his best to conciliate the South, would have capitulated to it in no essential point. Frémont always believed that, had he been elected, the influence of his and Mrs. Frémont's large family connections in the South, and of Benton's name, would have done much to prevent for all time a resort to arms. During the campaign he had given attention to a plan, one which later commended itself to Lincoln, for the gradual abolition of slavery with Federal compensation, and had spent some time with Jeremiah S. Black, the able Pennsylvanian who became Attorney-General and Secretary of State under Buchanan, in discussing its details.[19] But the danger of secession was too real to be trifled with. It was well for the country that Frémont was not placed in the White House.

[19] Frémont, MS Memoirs, Bancroft Library.

XXVIII

New Mariposa Troubles

WITHIN eighteen months after Frémont's defeat for the presidency, the last heroic chapter in the career of Thomas Hart Benton—never more Roman than in the shadow of death—was written. In his departure the Frémonts lost a greater pillar of strength than they realized.

In the spring of 1857 Frémont went to California to look after his properties, while Jessie took the children, two of whom had been seriously ill, to Paris for change and rest. Her sister Susan had married Baron Gauldrée Boileau, formerly in the French legation in Washington; and as an accomplished pianiste, whom Rossini liked to have at his Sunday musicales, she had made herself a place in Paris society. She and the Comte de la Garde saw to it that Jessie was again widely entertained. A quaint little house was found at St. Germain-en-Laye, and the children were enjoying the forest, the donkey-ride, and the peasants when news came by a friend that Benton was seriously ill. He had written Jessie that he was troubled by a slight fistula, when actually he was painfully dying from cancer. She at once caught a steamer home, while at the same time Frémont returned from the West. During the winter of 1857-58 they occupied a furnished house in Washington near the venerable Senator, now thin, pallid, and in constant pain. He was laboring with iron determination upon his final literary task, the compilation of his *Digest of Congressional Debates;* and he resolutely kept up a show of good spirits even when he could gain sleep only by the use of opiates.

Though even yet they hardly realized how ill he was, the Frémonts would have liked to stay with him. But Mariposa dfficulties called the explorer back to the Coast, and in February Jessie left with him on the Panama route. Benton made a last grim effort of will to maintain a cheerful mien as they said good-by; and on the day they sailed took to his bed, never again to leave it.

Jessie records that during part of the outward voyage a dull, haunting depression gripped her, and that early in April she broke down completely, unable to eat or sleep and submerged in gloom. The attack departed as quickly as it had come, and at the Mariposas she wholly recovered her spirits. Here she was extremely busy fitting up her new home. She and Frémont bought household furnishings in San Francisco, took them by river steamboat to Sacramento and thence by wagon across the Sierra foothills into Bear Valley, and deposited them in the wooden cottage they were to occupy on a hillside above the little mining village. The bare, comfortless little house would have depressed a less resourceful woman, but Jessie soon made it cheerful. Enlisting a lanky Pennsylvanian named Biddle Boggs, she built a fireplace in the living-room, added a lean-to kitchen at the rear, covered the canvas partitions with bright wallpaper, and threw rugs and skins on the floor. Giving the cottage a gleaming coat of whitewash, she christened it the "White House," to Frémont's delight and the mystification of Boggs, who grumbled: "Anybody can *see* it's white!" But while she was lending the place its final touches, one day Frémont's lawyer and his wife rode out to the estate. Jessie relates what followed:

He left her sitting on her horse outside the gate, and I went to her to say some polite word. She surprised me by saying that she was glad to see me in colors, and cheerful again.

"Why not?" I answered. "I am very well now."

"O, so soon after your father's death—" Her husband sprang over the fence and seizing her bridle tore off with her heedless of bushes and every obstacle.

Mr. Frémont was by me at once. "Is my father dead?" I asked.

For answer he gathered me in his arms, and as I asked "When?" I saw his tears....

April the tenth the soul was freed.

When he was gone, Missouri, which had discharged him from Congress, realized that it had lost by far its greatest leader. Twenty-five thousand people viewed the body as it lay in state in St. Louis; on the day of the funeral the entire population of the region seemed to gather in the city; the cortège was two miles in length, and as it passed every head was bare. The border states and the Union, their darkest hour just ahead, lost much. But the Frémonts lost more; Benton's calm sagacity, his weight of judgment, had been invaluable, and the impetuous explorer and his enthusiastic wife were henceforth without them. Had Benton survived till 1861, Frémont's wartime task in Missouri would have been far easier.

The Frémonts made themselves at home on the Mariposa estate for what was to prove an exciting summer. Their cottage, three miles from the quartz mines and half a mile from the hamlet Bear Valley, had delightful surroundings; it stood in an oak-studded glade of the foothills with pleasant walks and views. The agent who had occupied it before them had left a good collection of English and French books. Their household numbered seven, for in addition to the parents, Lilly, and the two boys, it included an attractive English lad, Charles Douglas Fox, who wanted practical mining experience, and Frémont's niece Nina, a graceful, vivacious girl of nineteen. As frequent guests they had Frémont's business associate John Howard of Brooklyn, who had been an active and generous supporter in the campaign of 1856; his son; and a mining engineer named Dr. Festus Adelbery. All these made up a lively group.

Indeed, for a brief period every prospect was hopeful—especially to Jessie, who knew nothing of business accounts and of squatter turbulence. Money seemed pouring in, for the ore-mills whose stamps filled the valley with a continuous clamor furnished a weekly revenue of $2,600 in the spring of 1858, and the output steadily increased; it was not so evident that money was also pouring out. The young people made free use of the stable, including the Colonel's own spirited mount. During the day the family read, wrote, and chatted indoors; but when the sun sank behind the western hills they would climb the slopes or gallop down the valleys. For the hottest weather a camp had been established atop a neighboring mountain, where the high air was always crisp, and whence they could look northeast over the wonderful panorama of the Yosemite Valley, the far-off silver falls, and the heights surrounding them. The Irish cook provided good food, and after dinner at night the whole group sang to the accompaniment of violin and guitar. Usually Frémont was at the estate, rising almost before dawn to ride off to the mines; sometimes, in company with his attorney and the elder Howard, he went to San Francisco or Monterey on business. As summer came on Jessie was told nothing of the excitement and danger gathering about them. In consequence, she was not alarmed when one morning she heard a heavy knock on the window of the beddoom she and Frémont used, and a voice announced:

"Colonel, the Hornitas League has jumped the Black Drift!"

"What does that mean?" she asked.

"Only mining work," Frémont answered. "You had best go to sleep again."

And in the refreshing coolness of the dawn she did sink back to sleep.

The Supreme Court, in a historic opinion written by Chief Justice Taney, and of great importance as a precedent on Mexican land grants, had duly confirmed Frémont's title to the Mariposa estates during 1855.[1] This decision followed a brilliant legal duel between Attorney-General Caleb Cushing for the government, and John J. Crittenden and Montgomery Blair for Frémont. Mr. Crittenden, we are told,

[1] Howard, *Supreme Court Reports*, XVII, p. 564ff.; Charles Warren, *History of the Supreme Court* (two-vol. ed.), II, p. 350.

brought into the argument not only legal acumen and research, but all the impassioned eloquence that has distinguished his most powerful efforts, whether in the Senate or before judicial forums, and was listened to with marked attention by a crowded audience of the beauty and intellect at present congregated in the city. We presume from all we have heard that the eloquent Kentuckian equaled, if he did not surpass, any previous effort, forensic or senatorial." [2]

But this victory had proved only the beginning of fresh difficulties.

On the basis of his Federal patent, the Colonel had requested the state authorities to measure off seventy square miles along both banks of the Merced River in a long, irregular strip. They quite properly refused, holding that in the interests of the public the grant must be compact; whereupon Frémont, who under the vague terms of the grant had a wide latitude of choice, caused his estate to be so defined as to include valuable mining claims theretofore in the possession of others. The length of this property was seventeen miles, and its width varied greatly. His action was perfectly legal—doubtless also perfectly equitable—but in the eyes of a good many miners it seemed unjust, and aroused their angry resentment. It would have been impossible for him to "locate" his estate in any fashion whatever without awakening the jealousy and ill-will of men who had swarmed over that region for gold. The whole tract—on which Frémont ultimately found twenty-nine different gold-bearing veins—had been overrun by prospectors who had cut up its fields, chopped down its timber, and used its grass at will, leaving him the privilege of paying the taxes, which shortly reached sixteen thousand dollars a year. A suit at law was now brought against him by the Merced Mining Company, which operated one of the mines included in his new limits, and armed violence was threatened against him and his

[2] Washington *National Intelligencer*, February 26, 1855. Frémont's grant had originally been confirmed in December, 1852, by the Commissioners appointed to settle the private land claims in the State of California. The Attorney-General in September, 1853, filed an appeal; the District Court decided against Frémont; but now the Supreme Court sustained him.

property by irresponsible men, some of them under the Company's influence.

The news that the Hornitas League had seized the Black Drift meant that a body of aggrieved miners and hired thugs, variously estimated at from seventy-five to one hundred and twenty in number, had taken possession of one of Frémont's richest shafts. A recent decision by Chief Justice Terry of the State Supreme Court had interpreted the California law as giving all persons the right to enter and hold any "unoccupied" claim or mine. The Merced Company had bribed the night watchman of the Black Drift mine to leave his shaft open to them, and had at once entered and fortified it. Fortunately for Frémont, one of two neighboring shafts which the League wished to capture was occupied by six men still working there, so that the invaders could lay siege to them only at the entrance. All three mines opened high on the mountain side upon a small leveled plateau just large enough to enable the ox teams to take wagon-loads of ore from the shafts and turn them easily; it was reached only by a single narrow road cut into the face of the mountain. The rocky slope fell almost perpendicularly below this road sixteen hundred feet to a ravine opening to the Merced River. This plateau and slope were now the scene of a stubborn contest of armed forces. The six besieged miners entrenched themselves behind rocks, machinery, and powder kegs; the Hornitas League lay on its arms about them and devised plans to capture the whole property; while farther down the road Frémont's hastily rallied force of some twenty men tried to cut off the League from reinforcements. A single shot, fired by chance, might be the signal for a bloody affray.[3]

It is unnecessary to relate in detail the steps by which the attack was foiled. How the seventeen-year-old English boy, Douglas Fox, saddled Lilly Frémont's horse Ayah; how, knowing that all the roads and trails were guarded, he led it up a hidden mountain path and over the summit; how he dashed

[3] John R. Howard, *Remembrance of Things Past*, Ch. 9.

along the banks of the Merced into the town of Coultersville;
how messengers were thence hurried off to Stockton, eighty
miles distant; and how the Governor at once ordered five
hundred militia to the Mariposas, promising to follow himself
if necessary. The troops came in good season, for not a shot
had been fired by the forces glowering at each other about the
mines. Jessie's relief was enormous. She had been threatened
with personal injury if the Leaguers captured her, and her
servants had been instructed to shoot her rather than let her
fall into their hands. One of the Hornitas leaders immediately
deserted to Frémont's side, saying: "When I go gunning next
time I'll make sure first if we are after wild duck or tame
duck"; and thereafter such troubles as Frémont had with the
Mariposa property were confined to the courts and counting
rooms.

The Colonel now rapidly pushed forward the physical development of the estate. His works were of the most ambitious
character. A storage dam was built on the Merced and gave
them water power in place of the steam power which had been
denuding the mountain sides; apparently this was the first
power dam constructed in California. New and better ore-
crushing apparatus—"the Benton Mills"—was installed on the
river. With the aid of hundreds of Chinese workmen, a railroad
more than three miles in length—the first railroad in the state
—was built, winding along the steep slopes with connecting
links of trestlework. Smelting works were erected in the village. Honest shopkeepers were brought in; a Viennese baker
and an Italian restaurant keeper were installed to prepare food
for the men who had no wives; and to maintain order, Frémont
required that his employees must neither drink nor carry
weapons. The village was as peaceful as a New England mill
town.

It need not be said that Frémont was now, through his
wealth and renown, one of the first citizens of California. The
country was full of colonels; but when men spoke of "the
Colonel," as Richard Henry Dana said, they meant Frémont.

When Horace Greeley visited the Pacific slope early in 1859 he spent some days with the Frémonts at Mariposa, and wrote a glowing letter to the *Tribune* upon the prosperity of the settlement and the orderliness and productiveness of the estate. Frémont told him that his aggregate liabilities from taxes, litigation, and the costs of development had mounted, when he returned to California in 1857, to at least $500,000. He had set to work resolved to extricate his great property. "In the spirit of that determination," wrote Greeley, "he has since lived and labored, rising with the lark and striving to obtain a complete knowledge and mastery of the entire business, taking more and more labor and responsibility upon his own shoulders as he felt able to bear them, until he is now manager, chief engineer, cashier, accountant, and at the head of every other department but law, for which he finds it necessary still to rely upon professional aid." The editor thought that his mines were at length becoming profitable. The steam mill near his home ran eight stamps a day and night to crush the ore, while his water mill on the Merced operated twelve stamps. The two, Greeley declared, "are producing gold at the rate of at least $250,000 per annum at an absolute cost, I am confident, of not more than $150,000." Always sanguine, Frémont was talking of a hundred stamps in constant operation before the close of 1860; and with that number, expected to clear at least $10,000 a week, which would soon relieve him of his burden of indebtedness.[4]

The editor was surprised by the luxury in which Jessie seemed to live, and inquiring how she managed to provide herself with beautifully ruffled muslin gowns and French cooking, ejaculated: "Well, you have executive faculty—my poor wife has none." He did not know that Jessie, with only three days' warning of Greeley's arrival, had cut up two well-worn cashmere dresses to make a new one, had turned some white jaconet undershirts into new frocks for Lilly and Nina, and

4 Horace Greeley, *An Overland Journey from New York to San Francisco*, p. 316*ff*.

had cut down a linen dress-shirt of Frémont's for Charley. R. H. Dana, Jr., visiting them at about the same time, was charmed equally by the beauty of the spot and the attractiveness and comfort with which the house had been fitted up. He had been in California or off its coast, collecting the experiences described in *Two Years Before the Mast,* in 1835-36, and he and the explorer drew many contrasts between the past and the present. Dana told the Colonel he was "especially glad to have met you coming out of your mine on a mountain, and not in a parlor."

To escape the hot summer and withering dry air, in the spring of 1859 Jessie returned to San Francisco to find a delightful surprise which Frémont had made ready for her—a new home. She was entranced when she saw it: a little promontory, jutting into the channel entrance of San Francisco harbor directly opposite Alcatraz Island, and bearing the name "Black Point" from its thick covering of mountain laurel. Standing on this hundred-foot bluff, a sweeping glance embraced to the west the Golden Gate and the blue Pacific between its portals; far away over miles of water to the east the Contra Costa Mountains; and, beyond Alcatraz, more high hills. It had historic associations, for near by Frémont had rowed across the Bay and spiked the old brass Spanish guns. He was able to buy the twelve acres and house from the banker Mark Brumagin for $42,000. Once ensconced in the cottage here, isolated and yet within the city limits, Jessie found that all desire to return East left her. "At last," she wrote, "after many wanderings, many separations, and many strange experiences, we saw a home of congenial beauty and repose—a home which time would make a fortune to our children as holders of this little property; its thirteen acres were more dear to me than the many miles and mines of the Mariposa." Unfortunately, the title to the property was clouded, and during the Civil War the Government was to order the seizure of the whole peninsula for military purposes.

Black Point soon became the center of a small but congenial

group of friends. One was Thomas Starr King, the slight, eloquent Unitarian minister and patriot who a little later did so much to save California to the Union; he arrived from Boston in the spring of 1860, and was promptly writing east of dinners at Black Point with such other guests as Colonel Edward D. Baker, the new senator from Oregon. Another was Bret Harte, whose genius Jessie perceived in his newspaper writings before she knew his name. She insisted that the shy, proud, unhappy young journalist should visit her, and for more than a year he dined with the Frémonts every Sunday, bringing his manuscripts and listening to their praise and criticism. Mrs. Frémont encouraged him to send the *Atlantic Monthly* the sketch called *The Legend of Monte del Diablo,* and did him a still larger service when, through General Fitzhugh Beale, now head of the Coast Survey, she obtained him a government appointment. "I shall no longer disquiet myself," he wrote, "about changes in residence or anything else, for I believe that if I were cast upon a desert island, a savage would come to me next morning and hand me a three-cornered note to say that I had been appointed governor at Mrs. Frémont's request, at $2,400 a year." He always spoke of Jessie as his "fairy godmother." [5]

This free outdoor life in California, this management of one of the great American mines, would have suited Frémont's restless, adventurous, sanguine temperament precisely if only the estate had been more profitable. But even as gold-production increased, Mariposa ran into deeper difficulties. He was learning the truth of the Spanish proverb that "it takes a mine to work a mine." At a later date he computed the value of the whole output from 1850 to 1862 at about $3,000,000. But his

[5] C. H. Wendte, *Thomas Starr King,* p. 90*ff.*; Henry C. Merwin, *Life of Bret Harte,* pp. 34, 35. "Mrs. Frémont," writes Merwin, "was an extremely clever, kind-hearted woman, who assisted Bret Harte greatly by her advice and criticism, still more by her sympathy and encouragement. Bret Harte was always inclined to underrate his own powers, and to be despondent as to his literary future." Harte named Lilly Frémont's pony "Chiquita," after the mare in his poem of that name. Many letters which he wrote the Frémonts were later lost in a fire in New York.

ambitious works had cost large sums, and California interest rates were cruelly high—2 per cent a month or more, compounded monthly. Frémont's letters of 1858-60 indicate constant embarrassment. One written on June 6, 1858, from Bear Valley, reads: "Last week the sheriff attached all moneys, etc., which might be in my hands and belonging to or due from me to Mr. Hammett. Will you be kind enough to refer to the books so as to ascertain what is the condition of his account and transmit accordingly a statement to the sheriff at Mariposas by today's mail and oblige yours truly, J. C. Frémont." A series of letters in the spring of 1860 exhibit heavy pecuniary pressure. Dated at Black Point, they are addressed to the Bear Valley manager, Hopper: [6]

(June 2): As no boat leaves tomorrow I write to acknowledge yours of the 31st, and to say that I continue yet unwell. I hope by next mail to be able to write at length. Let Mr. Williams know that I will write to him next week. In regard to the men whose wages we wished to reduce at the mines, and Mr. Davenport's action in regard to them, I think that it will be well as much as possible to let it stand until I get back. I would very much regret any difficulty just now, and intend to rely upon your prudence and good judgment to see that none does take place....

(June 5): I am still quite unwell, with the usual feeling of mental indolence belonging to the condition, and came in only to get your letter. Dr. Raymond called on me at Black Point this morning with a letter from Mr. Charter, giving a statement of your conversation with him. Manage affairs along so as to keep everything quiet until I get back—meanwhile I will talk over the whole matter with Dr. Raymond. I have seen very little of him since I came here and he knows nothing whatever of my affairs. In regard to the mines, have a friendly conversation with Ketton and Davenport about the pay of the men and let it rest until I come back. I think you will find them disposed to do all that they can for our interest....

(June 13): I have finally succeeded in making arrangements for putting the estate, or rather its operations, upon a cash basis, but the large amount of money which would have been required under

[6] Copies furnished me from various private sources.

the operation of the new attachment law has obliged me to make these arrangements in a manner entirely different from what I had proposed when I left Bear Valley. But the great object, which is the uninterrupted carrying on of the works and the security and continuous improvement of the estate, will be quite as fully accomplished in this way. Mr. Park will be in Bear Valley on Saturday night or Thursday morning, and you should be there to meet him. He will give you all necessary information....

But despite the hopeful tone of this last letter, his mining operations continued to bring him heavy financial perplexities.

For the Republican nomination in 1860 Frémont was, of course, not seriously considered. An unsuccessful candidate for the Presidency is almost never named again; and Frémont had done nothing to improve his political standing, while other aspirants had come steadily forward. When Gideon Welles made inquiries of friends as to the complete dropping of Frémont, he heard various gossipy explanations which—recorded in the Welles papers—are of no value save as they indicate that John Bigelow had become extremely dubious of Frémont's stability, while the Blair family had grown actively critical. Old Francis P. Blair spoke of the explorer with positive dislike. The ground had been laid for the subsequent breach between the two men. Yet some talk of Frémont persisted till the very eve of the convention. The explorer thought it worth while to authorize a California friend to withdraw his name if presented, saying he would not stand against any man acceptable on general grounds, and as zealous as himself for building a Pacific railroad from the Middle West. Edward Bates of Missouri helped spread the news of this position among delegates to the convention.

Following Lincoln's election, Frémont late in 1860 received a visit from Senator Baker, who had been campaigning in the East and who brought him a strong intimation that he would be offered either a Cabinet position or one of the principal diplomatic posts. We know from other sources that Seward had suggested that he be made Secretary of War, while Lincoln had thought of him for Minister to France. At the moment his eternal "Mariposa business" had developed a new crisis. Needing funds for development and for discharging his debts, he had resolved to go to Europe, form a company, and sell enough shares for his purposes. He asked Baker to tell Lincoln that his hands were tied for the moment, while he would prefer, if civil war began, to take command of an army in the field. As state after state seceded, he and Starr King agreed that hostilities were inevitable. During the fall of 1860 careful data were assembled on the resources of Mariposa, and a series of costly photographs (now in the Bancroft Library) were taken of all the works. With this material, Frémont and his lawyer Frederick K. Billings sailed in January, 1861, for Europe. Jessie, who had suffered a bad carriage accident, was left behind, with instructions to join him in New York if he was given a military command; and affairs at Mariposa were placed in rough shape for a protracted absence. Little did either think that they would never again set foot on their famous estate as its owners.

Staying for a few days in New York in the middle of February, Frémont had a brief and cordial interview at the Astor House with Lincoln, who was on his way to Washington. He found the President-elect still outwardly strong in his hope that peace would be preserved, but all his own convictions were that fighting was inevitable. He wrote Jessie: "With the inflammatory press and inflammatory conversations on every hand, I am convinced that actual war is not far off." Sailing at once for France, he soon found that the threat of civil war made it impossible to raise money for Mariposa on any acceptable terms. He was still in Europe when news of the firing upon Fort Sumter reached him; and, having already written to Washington to offer his services, he was there notified that his abilities and experience had been recognized by appointment as one of the ranking Union generals. He at once sent word to Jessie to join him in the East. Doubtless he was proud and elated that he was to have a new opportunity to serve his country; certainly his wife was so, for she expressed her feelings with characteristic frankness in a letter to the estate-manager, Hopper:

Mr. Frémont has written to us to join him at once at New York, where he was to be about the 30th of May. We shall leave in the next steamer, the 21st. I wish it could have been on that of to-day, but we got our orders too late for that.

Mr. Frémont's last letters were to noon of May 10th, London. Mr. Billings was to remain, but Mr. Frémont was called to his old first love and duty, and I have not been so happy in years for him as now—

> What if the storm clouds blow?
> What if the green leaves fall?
> Better the crashing tempest's throe
> Than the army of worries
> That gnawed below.

An army of cares has been boring into our lives these few years past, and I thank heaven for this noble chance in a great cause, which has come to Mr. Frémont now. He promised me other and fuller letters before his leaving Europe, which was fixed for the 21st May. We leave certainly on the 21st, so that you will only have time to let me know this has reached you. I take your picture of Bear Valley cottage with us, and it will always remind me of the many times you helped to smooth worries away from Mr. Frémont. I am so glad I am going into an atmosphere where dollars and cents are not the first object. The noble and beautiful side of the nation is now apparent, and it will be a comfort to feel its influence.

XXIX

Civil War in the West

JULY of 1861 found Frémont commander of the Department of the West—the great military area comprising Illinois and all the states and territories between the Mississippi and the Rockies—with his headquarters in St. Louis.

A St. Louis how changed! Once the most hospitable and cordial of towns to all who bore the name Frémont or Benton, now it was a shuttered, sullen, and hostile city. The hot July sun beat down upon a river that stretched empty from shore to shore—the steamboats laid up at their wharves with fires out and crews gone. The streets were half deserted, with knots of unemployed men glowering resentfully at the soldiers who patrolled the corners, with curtains drawn in the shop windows, and with the wheels of the few vehicles echoing loudly against empty warehouses. Of the 160,000 people, a majority seemed definitely alined against the Union. Hardly an American flag was flying; but in its stead the secession banner hung over the buildings in which recruiting for the Confederate armies was being publicly carried on, while in the best residential sections the Stars and Bars were lavishly displayed. Army officers, intimidated and few in number, dared not venture far from the arsenal, the barracks, and the center of the city. At night bands of ruffians, armed or unarmed, marched through the streets hurrahing for Jeff Davis and the rebel cause. This was the disaffected town, the metropolis of a half-disaffected state, in which Frémont arrived from New York on the morning of July 25, 1861.[1]

---

[1] Jessie Benton Frémont, *Souvenirs of My Time,* p. 166ff.

The previous two months had been full of labor and anxiety. Overtaken in Europe by the news of war, and knowing how destitute of arms the government was, he had instantly dropped his private affairs and begun examining field-guns, rifles, and ammunition in both France and England. It was a characteristically impetuous enterprise, for he had no authority from the government, no certainty of a cent of money, and no knowledge even of how serious the war might be. But it was patriotic and timely. By the end of May, Confederate agents were on the ground, but no Federal emissary; and Frémont stepped into the breach. We find him writing from the Athenaeum Club in London on May 24th to Francis P. Blair.[2]

I had fully intended to sail for New York in the *Asia* to-morrow but under all the information that I can obtain I judge that a supply of efficient arms would be valuable to our cause just now and I have decided to remain a short time longer with the object of bringing them with me. I have succeeded in producing the control of funds sufficient to purchase three or four batteries of guns fully equipped for the field and perhaps 10,000 rifles. The guns will be of the most approved construction, and will be accompanied with carriages, shot, shell, etc. The difficulty was first, to obtain the means, and now that the means are obtained the difficulty is in having the guns cast, ammunition got ready, etc., within the few weeks that I can bring myself to remain over here. I shall have an answer from foundries and factories before night and if I get them in time will advise you. I trust that you have already offered my services to the President. If not, pray do so, and in either case explain to him the cause of my delay. I think that this delay is justifiable if it enables me to come prepared with an equipment of all arms and of the most efficient kind, sufficient to put a force of ten thousand men directly in the face of the enemy. Pray don't let these few weeks operate prejudicially to me. My great desire is to serve the country in the most direct and effective way that possibly I can. From all that I can see I judge that there will be need for our best services. The agents for the Seceders are very active here. The last steamer brought them an accession of credit, and they completed yesterday the purchase of

2 Letter in my possession.

two screw steamers (one for £75,000) and are contracting for more. These steamers are to sail from Liverpool and are to endeavor to enter the port of Charleston. They are to be under English colors, are not to carry any contraband of war, and will probably be underwritten here. The former owners were yesterday endeavoring to obtain underwriters. I will try to let you know the names, captains, underwriters, when to sail, etc., etc. Meanwhile I will let Sanford (Belgium) who is here know of this, and also Mr. Adams, if I see him to-day. Mr. Sanford is an admirable representative, and Mr. Adams in this respect more than justifies his good old name.

Our minister to France hesitated to support him, but in England Charles Francis Adams had the courage to do so. In the end, Frémont contracted for $75,000 worth of cannon and shells in England, and for 10,000 rifles in France, to be shipped at his personal charge if necessary; and Adams boldly drew on the government to pay for them.[3] Then Frémont, notified that he had been appointed one of the first four major-generals authorized by Congress, had caught a fast ship, arrived in Boston on June 27th, and at once reported to the President in Washington.

He found the government eager for his services. He and Postmaster-General Montgomery Blair held several conferences with Lincoln upon the command to which he should be assigned; and he tells us that although the military authorities suggested eastern positions, he insisted upon the West. This suited the views of Montgomery Blair. For the command in Missouri, the Blair family would have preferred their favorite, Nathaniel Lyon, but the conservative Unionists of that state, led by Attorney-General Edward Bates, would not hear of him. Frémont made an admirable compromise. Early in July the Western Department was created, with the understanding that it should include not only the loyal prairie region, but the wavering state of Kentucky as soon as Frémont had raised and organized a sufficient force to descend the Mississippi. He

---

[3] J. B. McMaster, *United States During Lincoln's Administration,* p. 190; Frémont, MS. *Memoirs.*

immediately took up the task of creating an army—finding out what troops were available, how he could concentrate and drill them, and how he could get them armed and supplied.

Not one labor but a myriad; in these hot July days he had suddenly a million things to do. Frémont has been harshly criticized by Nicolay and Hay, chiefly upon the basis of statements which Montgomery Blair made after he became the General's enemy, for his delay in reaching St. Louis. But this criticism is unjustified. He stayed in the East just three weeks, and would have left sooner—in fact, would have left on July 16th or 17th—had he not been told that General Winfield Scott had further instructions for him. He remained principally because his Department was destitute of munitions of all kinds, and he could best procure them from New York and Washington. The troops being enlisted in Illinois, Iowa, Missouri, and other states were wretchedly supplied with blankets, shoes, tents, uniforms, and firearms. Governor Richard Yates of Illinois, who was in Washington, declared that their condition was a public scandal. After obtaining the personal intervention of President Lincoln, Frémont received an order for only 17,000 stands of arms from the government arsenals, the number later being reduced to 5,000. In desperation, he examined various supplies of arms in the hands of private owners, and was on the point of having 25,000 carbines sent to the West; but finding that they were not rifled, left the transaction uncompleted. The main object of the Administration at the moment was to equip the armies in Virginia, and it was difficult to interest the War Department in Missouri.

In these three weeks, Frémont was also assembling his aides and sketching the outlines of a plan of campaign. As chief of staff he appointed General Alexander S. Asboth, a Hungarian who had served with distinction under Kossuth in the great revolt of 1848-49 and who had come to the United States with his chief in 1851. Asboth was destined to do good service throughout the Civil War, to be brevetted a major-general, and to die minister to the Argentine. As chief topographical engineer Frémont appointed another Hungarian, Colonel John Fiala. From Cincinnati he summoned a lawyer of distinction, R. R. Corwine, to be judge-advocate of the Department. A multitude of other details had to be attended to. As for the plan of campaign, Frémont later told the Committee on the Conduct of the War that the government had given him none whatever. General discussions with Scott and others resulted in an understanding that the great object in view was the descent of the Mississippi, and that when his army was ready for this he was to let the President know. He himself devised a scheme whose main features were the clearance of all rebels from Missouri, and a movement down the Mississippi upon Memphis; and he tells us that he consulted Lincoln upon it: [4]

The President had gone carefully over with me the subject of my intended campaign, and this with the single desire to find out what was best to do and how to do it. This he did in the unpretentious and kindly manner which invited suggestion, and which with him was characteristic. When I took leave of him, he accompanied me down the stairs, coming out to the steps of the portico at the White House; I asked him then, if there was anything further in the way of instruction that he wished to say to me. "No," he replied, "I have given you *carte blanche;* you must use your own judgment and do the best you can. I doubt if the States will ever come back."

It was nine o'clock of the hot morning of July 25 when Frémont was ferried across to St. Louis, and, without pausing for rest, he called a staff meeting at noon.[5] He immediately began the most strenuous activity of his life. He rose at five in the morning and labored almost without intermission till twelve at night. The problems before him were staggering. The curtain had risen on the drama called "the hundred days in Missouri" —the drama which tested Frémont's strength and weakness as never before, and which fixed in the popular mind a cruelly unjust impression of his character and capacities.

[4] MS. *Memoirs,* Bancroft Library.
[5] New York *Tribune,* August 9, 1861.

He had arrived at a critical moment, with disaster looming just ahead and prompt action imperative. Missouri, with a population of slightly more than a million, was attached to the South by blood, tradition, a common history, and similar institutions. When the Confederacy was formed, a militant minority took the view, at first partly concealed, that the state must join her southern sisters. This group included the governor, Claiborne F. Jackson, the lieutenant-governor, both United States Senators, and a majority of the legislature, and it had powerful newspaper support.[6] Another group, for a time larger and stronger, believed that secession might ultimately be necessary, but that it should not be attempted until every hope of a peaceable adjustment of the difficulties between the North and the South had been destroyed. This group included ex-Governor Robert M. Stewart, Alexander W. Doniphan, Sterling Price, and some influential editors. The trend of events slowly forced an alliance between many of its members and the uncompromising secessionists, but the tact of the Union leaders saved a large part of this faction for the Federal cause. Beneath the American banner rallied, not merely many of the Lincoln Republicans of Missouri, who had cast only one-ninth of the ballots at the last election, but many of the followers of Douglas, Breckinridge, and Bell, who were too much attached to the Union to countenance its disruption.

The struggle thus far in Missouri had been, in its main outlines, a contest between the astute secessionist governor, Claiborne Jackson, and the courageous Frank P. Blair, Jr., who was the brains and backbone of the Union element. Blair converted the Republican Wide-Awakes into Union Clubs. Decisive measures by him and Captain (later General) Nathaniel Lyon, a Connecticut veteran of the Mexican War, saved the St. Louis arsenal from the rebels when they were about to seize it. An equally decisive movement enabled Lyon to strike the rebel militia—for Governor Jackson, issuing a proclamation of war, had called fifty thousand militia into service for the

[6] Thomas Snead, *The Fight for Missouri in 1851*, p. 53*ff*.

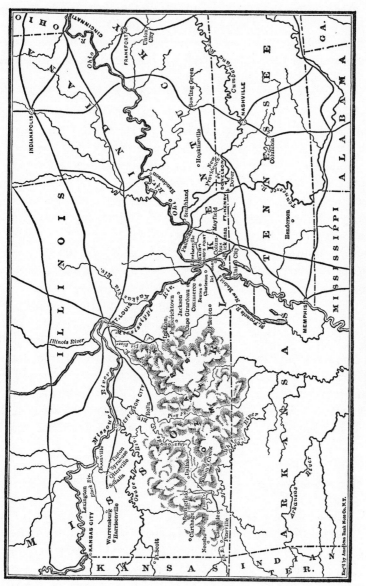

THE THEATER OF WAR IN THE WEST

Confederacy—at Booneville, a town on the Missouri River, and after a sharp engagement to put them to flight. The state capital at Jefferson City was meanwhile wrested from the Confederates. All this had occurred by June 17th, before Frémont had even landed in Boston.

The Unionists in the state had the advantage of superior numbers, for a heavy majority of the population were loyal; but after the initial steps by Blair and Lyon, the Confederates had the advantage of superior boldness, energy, and quickness. A genuine danger existed that the quickly rallying rebels would sweep all lower Missouri, take possession of Cairo and southernmost Illinois, where secessionist sentiment was strong, carry Kentucky into the Confederacy, and make even southern Indiana, where later the Knights of the Golden Circle flourished, doubtful territory. If they succeeded in this, the war might be virtually lost for the North. Rebel camps were formed throughout a great part of Missouri, commissions were issued in a skeleton rebel army, and adventurous young men of pro-slavery sympathies flocked to the Confederate standard, delighted at the prospect of army life. Governor Jackson and General Sterling Price united their forces, collected from these camps, in a formidable little army of about thirty thousand in the southwestern corner of the state. At Carthage they soon came into collision with the Federal forces under Franz Sigel, and in a comparatively bloodless battle, defeated him and drove him back upon Springfield. In southeastern Missouri the Confederates under Pillow were gathering another force of about twenty thousand, while Hardee with five thousand was said to be marching on Ironton.

When Frémont took command, sharp fighting was about to commence. Jackson and Price, flushed with their little victory, elated by the news of Bull Run, and pleased by reinforcements from Arkansas and a constant accession of volunteers, were moving northward. They would soon have full control of a rich lead-bearing region. To face them and the other armies, Frémont (according to Colonel Chester Harding's later evidence

before the Committee on the Conduct of the War) had only
15,943 men, scattered at nine points in Missouri, ill-equipped,
ill-trained, and ill-organized. As he had Jessie write to Montgomery Blair, he found the enemy already occupying in force
positions which he had intended holding against them; found
himself without money, arms, or moral support; found that
even St. Louis needed more men to keep its unruly elements
quiet. Jessie herself soon sent Francis P. Blair's daughter a
spirited picture of the situation: [7]

> You say all we need is "Generals." That is simply and literally
> the whole provision made for the Dept. An arsenal without arms or
> ammunition—troops on paper, and a thoroughly prepared and united
> enemy. Thick and unremitting as mosquitoes. The telegraph in the
> enemy's hands and the worse for us as not being avowed enemies.
> In Ohio and all the way we met Western troops on their way to the
> Potomac—the western waters left to defend themselves as best they
> might.... The President is a Western man and not grown in red
> tape. If he knew the true defenseless condition of the West it would
> not remain so. I have begged Mr. Frémont to let me go on and tell
> him how things are here. But he says I'm tired with the sea voyage
> —that I shan't expose my health any more and that he can't do with-
> out me.
>
> It's making bricks without straw out here and mere human power
> can't draw order out of chaos by force of will only.

The Union flag was upheld at Springfield in southwestern
Missouri by Lyon, who had reached there July 13th with a
combined force of Missouri and Kansas troops numbering between 7,000 and 8,000 men. But in spite of this strength,
Lyon's position was highly perilous. He had no adequate line
of communications at his rear. From St. Louis, three railways
then radiated—one toward the west, terminating at Sedalia,

[7] W. E. Smith, *The Francis Preston Blair Family in Politics*, II, p. 59.
Frémont in his own article on the situation later wrote that of 23,000 men
of all arms, only some 15,000 were available, the remainder being three months'
men. Most of his disposable force was being used by General John Pope in
North Missouri to check rebellion there. R. U. Johnson and C. C. Buel, eds.,
Battles and Leaders of the Civil War, I, p. 278 ff.

about three-fourths of the way across the state; one toward the southwest, ending at Rolla, scarcely halfway across the state; and the third toward the south, ending at Ironton, also hardly halfway across. Between Lyon's army and the nearest rail-head at Rolla, stretched 120 miles of broken country, with bad roads which any hard rain would make almost impassable. Provisions and supplies had failed to arrive as he had expected. Moreover, about half of his army consisted of the ninety-day men raised under President Lincoln's first proclamation, and their terms expired the middle of July. Many of these three-months volunteers would immediately reënlist for a longer term, and many would remain for the battle which seemed to be impending; but there was nevertheless much confusion, and the army was materially shrinking.[8]

If imminent danger threatened Lyon at Springfield, almost equally grave danger threatened the Federal forces at Cairo, the vital point at the junction of the Ohio and the Mississippi which must be used as a base for any advance into Kentucky. Major-General Leonidas Polk, commanding the Confederates at Memphis, made preparations early in July to lead his Tennessee contingent into Missouri for a campaign with a double objective. One column, under McCulloch, was to proceed against Lyon at Springfield; while the other was to march up the Mississippi under Generals Pillow and Hardee to cut off Lyon's retreat toward the East, was to take St. Louis if possible, and on its return was to enter Illinois and capture Cairo. This was too ambitious a program to be carried out. Nevertheless, about the time that Frémont arrived in St. Louis, Polk moved 6,000 troops up to New Madrid, where he reported that his force, with the German unionists of Missouri in front of them, were "full of enthusiasm and eager for the 'Dutch hunt.' "[9] It was rumored in Missouri and Illinois that a further advance by Polk's troops was imminent. The frightened Union

[8] See Nicolay and Hay, *Lincoln,* IV, Ch. 11, p. 23.
[9] *Official Records,* Series I, Vol. III, p. 617ff.; Nicolay and Hay, *Lincoln,* IV, p. 405.

commander at Cairo, General Prentiss, sent a series of urgent messages to Frémont, imploring him to send help to save this great strategic key to the Mississippi Valley. He wrote July 23rd: "Have but eight regiments here. Six of them are three-months men. Their time expires this week—are reorganizing now. I have neither tents nor wagons, and must hold Cairo and Bird's Point."

On the heels of this he informed Frémont that the rebels were about to capture Bird's Point, just across the Mississippi from Cairo, and that he had only two six-pounders ready to move. On July 29, 1861, he added another panicky appeal for aid:

> On yesterday, three thousand rebels west of Bird's Point forty miles; three hundred at Madrid and three regiments from Union City ordered there; also troops from Randolph and Corinth. The number of organized rebels within fifty miles of me will exceed twelve thousand—that is, including Randolph troops ordered and not including several companies opposite in Kentucky.

On August 1st came another telegram imploring immediate help. Prentiss stated that the previous day General Pillow had been at New Madrid with 11,000 well-armed and well-drilled troops, two regiments of splendidly equipped cavalry, and 100 pieces of artillery; that 9,000 more men were moving to reinforce him; and that he had promised to place 20,000 troops in that vital corner of Missouri at once. On September 4th, Polk's troops did occupy the strategic post of Columbus, Kentucky.

Frémont thus had to answer the demands of two widely separated commanders, each menaced by strong Confederate armies; he had to take steps to pacify Missouri, where a ghastly guerrilla struggle was beginning to break out; he had to organize the raw volunteers who were trickling into St. Louis, and to make frantic efforts to find them food, uniforms, and arms; and he had to keep the city, with its large popula-

tion of rebel sympathizers, under strict control. All this had
to be done by a man who had never commanded forces of
more than a few hundred, who had for years been engrossed in
civilian pursuits, and who was new to the city, the post, and
the problems about him. It had to be done with the most inadequate resources, under a War Department indifferent to
the West. The situation would have taxed the capacity of abler
men than Frémont.

His first decision was on the whole correct: to send word
to Lyon at Springfield that he had best fall back on his base
at Rolla, and to hurry reinforcements forward to Cairo. There
was no particular reason for holding Springfield. It was not
an important strategic point. There was, however, every
reason for safeguarding Cairo, which was vital for the command of the Ohio and Mississippi. If Pillow really had the
army credited to him, and if he could cross the Mississippi
above Cairo and cut off Prentiss's force, the result might be
a horrible disaster. Within a week after his arrival, Frémont,
though burdened with other business, had chartered a fleet of
eight steamboats, loaded them with soldiers and with artillery
and stores which he had ordered from the East, and set off
down the river.[10] He had labored like a slave to make this
expedition of nearly 4,000 men ready. The night before it set
out he retired at midnight, and was at his desk again at 4:30
A.M., where he remained till just before the departure of the
flotilla at three o'clock in the afternoon.[11]

The trip, however, gave him not only the first rest he had
enjoyed since he took up his command, but also the gratifica-
tion of a wildly enthusiastic reception by the nervous little
army under Prentiss. On five o'clock of an effulgent day, the
sun turning the Mississippi into a broad path of gold, his
flagship the *City of Alton* approached Cairo, and fired its
eight-pounders as a signal. At once the guns on shore replied.
For half an hour there was a perfect roar of artillery, the

[10] St. Louis *Republican,* quoted in New York *Tribune,* August 9, 1861.
[11] New York *Herald,* August 12, 1861.

echoes rolling away into the woods of Missouri and Kentucky. The banks of the two rivers were peppered with excited groups of soldiers. As the *City of Alton,* bedecked with evergreens and flags, churned in to the Cairo water-front, the wharves became black with uniformed men yelling "Frémont! Frémont!"; and when Prentiss led the General down the gang-plank and up to his headquarters at the St. Charles Hotel, the uproar was deafening. He had come in the nick of time. Prentiss's army was small, and much of it fast disintegrating; while in that swampy position, fever and dysentery were taking a heavy toll of it. Frémont had many of the sick transferred from the low ground to the breezy decks of his steamboats, and from that date made use of floating hospitals wherever he could.

Meanwhile, what of General Lyon? That commander was now in a mood which almost approached despair. He saw only retreat or ruin ahead of him. He must go back, he wrote Colonel Chester Harding at St. Louis, unless he received large reinforcements and supplies. "Our troops are badly clothed, poorly fed, and imperfectly supplied with tents. None of them have as yet been paid." [12] A little later he charged the Administration and General Scott with an inexcusable neglect of the West, and declared that they were allowing that section to become "the victim of imbecility or malice." Frémont had written to Montgomery Blair for "money and arms without delay and by the quickest conveyance," and Blair had replied from Washington on July 26th that "I find it impossible now to get any attention to Missouri or western matters from the authorities here. You will have to do the best you can and take all needful responsibility to defend and protect the people over whom you are specially set." [13] When Frémont opened his headquarters, three messengers were awaiting him from Lyon, all insisting that danger was imminent and that help must be sent him at once.

As it proved, there was a good fortnight in which help might

[12] Despatch of July 15, 1861, before Frémont's arrival.
[13] *Congressional Globe,* March 7, 1862; *37th Cong., 2d Sess.,* p. 1126.

have been despatched, and even a moderate force might have saved Lyon from defeat. But circumstances made it impossible for Frémont to furnish the required aid. It has been asserted that while he was taking 3,800 men to Cairo, he could also have sent several thousand by rail and wagon-road to Springfield, and so have saved the day. But, as a matter of fact, the troops were simply not available. Colonel Chester Harding later testified that while large numbers of volunteers were arriving in St. Louis in the first days of August, nearly all were unarmed, they were totally untrained and did not even know how to use a musket, and they were wholly without transport animals or wagons; and that regiment after regiment lay for days in the city without equipment, for the arsenals were empty. Having so few men, Frémont thought it unwise to divide his reinforcements. Above all, it can be urged in his defense that he expected Lyon to retreat, and issued orders with that definite end in view. As a matter of fact, he did on August 4th send two regiments marching toward Lyon's assistance, one from Booneville and the other from Leavenworth, Kansas—the only regiments available. He expected Lyon to retire to meet them. One of the messengers who reached him from Springfield, entreating him for "soldiers, soldiers, soldiers," told him that Lyon would fight at that town whether he got more troops or not; to which Frémont replied, "If he fights, it will be upon his own responsibility." [14]

By the beginning of August, the Confederate army under McCulloch numbered almost 13,000 men. It began its march toward Springfield, about fifty miles distant, on July 31st, and its approach filled Lyon with apprehension. He exaggerated its numbers, believing that almost 30,000 men opposed him, and even when he learned its true size, he realized that his plight was desperate. His own forces had by now shrunk to about 5,000 effective troops. If he remained stationary, he would be surrounded and captured; if he retreated from Springfield, he

[14] Snead, *Fight for Missouri*, p. 253; *Official Records,* Series I, Vol. III, p. 57ff.

would leave the southwestern section of Missouri, with its farm resources, lead-mines, and thousands of volunteers, to the enemy. He would have to traverse a rough country, and cross many difficult streams and ravines. To do this with some 5,400 disheartened men, his passage encumbered by four hundred army wagons, along roads blocked by crowds of refugees, would at best be a slow and painful operation. To do it with a powerful army hanging on his heels and a force of cavalry harrying his flanks might be dangerous.

Yet Lyon's duty was clear—it was to go back. A council of his officers three days before the battle showed that most of them believed a retreat proper and even imperative. The second in command was General John T. Schofield, who always declared that the fruitless sacrifice at Wilson's Creek was unnecessary and wholly unjustifiable. As he wrote long afterward, "our retreat to Rolla was open and perfectly safe, even if begun as late as the night of the ninth. A few days or a few weeks at most would have made us amply strong to defeat the enemy and drive him out of Missouri, without serious loss to ourselves." Schofield urged this opinion upon Lyon with vehemence. As for Frémont's orders, on August 6th he sent a letter to Lyon which reached the latter on the ninth; and although this letter has unfortunately been lost, we have two statements, corroborating one another, as to its contents. Both Schofield and Frémont tell us that it instructed Lyon that if he were not powerful enough to maintain his position at Springfield, he should fall back toward Rolla until he was met by reinforcements.[15] But Lyon was headstrong, he exaggerated the disaster to the loyal citizens of the region if he abandoned them to Confederate wrath, and he moved out to attack McCulloch's force of more than twice his numbers.

It was desperate, it was foolhardy, but it was sublime, and the news of that hopeless attack and its tragic result sent a thrill throughout the North. In the faint summer dawn of August 10th, Franz Sigel fell suddenly with 1,200 men upon the

[15] MS. *Memoirs;* John T. Schofield, *Forty-Six Years in the Army,* p. 40.

enemy's right flank, while simultaneously Lyon with 3,700 troops went into action against their left center. Sigel after some initial success was repulsed, but Lyon drove the enemy out of their camp, and then as the morning advanced threw back attack after attack by the Confederates, desperately trying to regain their positions. Within its limits, it was one of the fiercest encounters of the Civil War. The two main lines of battle, Federal and Confederate, were less than a thousand yards in length. Yet along this line almost every available company was brought into action. The Confederates would appear out of the billowing smoke in ranks three or four deep, one file lying down to fire, another kneeling, and one or two standing, and they sometimes pushed to within thirty or forty yards of the Union rifles and cannon before they were repulsed. Both Price and Lyon exhibited the greatest personal gallantry, Lyon receiving three wounds without going to the rear. At last a final heavy assault was made by the Confederates, and Lyon, leaping upon a horse and waving his hat in air, called to some fragments of reserves to close ranks and plunge into the mêlée. A part of the Second Kansas surged forward beside him, and as they met the Confederate line a ball pierced Lyon's breast. He fell from his horse and died almost instantly. A few minutes later, at half-past eleven in the morning, the chief surviving officers held a hasty council and gave the order to retreat.[16]

As graphic accounts of this battle of Wilson's Creek appeared in the northern press, and as Lyon's body with much pomp and public sorrow was taken from city to city to be buried at his New England home, the first loud criticism of Frémont arose. It was easy to say that he should have reinforced Lyon, and many said it. It was not so easy to say that Lyon should have retreated; nobody outside Missouri knew that Frémont had ordered him to do so unless he were certain of his safety, for Frémont never published his letter. Nobody knew how Cairo had been imploring Frémont for men, how in-

[16] *Official Records*, Series I, Vol. III, p. 62*ff*.

sistent President Lincoln had been that Cairo be safeguarded at all costs, and how limited were his forces in semi-hostile St. Louis. The consequence was that Frémont was attacked then and later for a catastrophe which it had been almost beyond his power to prevent. Later the Committee on the Conduct of the War reported that this first demand from Lyon had been pressed upon him so hastily, before he could measure his resources, "that even if he failed to do all that one under the circumstances might have done, still your committee can discover no cause of censure against him."

Once the criticism of Frémont was fairly loosed, it found much upon which to feed. No man on earth could have taken charge of the chaotic Department of the West, no general could have tried to bring well-prepared armies out of that confusion of unpreparedness, without committing blunders and making enemies. Frémont's blunders were peculiarly unhappy, and his enemies were soon a host.

His industry was unceasing, and within a few weeks he had to his credit an important list of achievements, to which his defenders were later able to point with warm praise. He policed the city, stopped the Confederate recruiting which had been openly conducted at the Berthold Mansion, and made life and property secure. He ordered General John Pope, another Mexican War veteran, to northern Missouri with instructions to organize local committees of safety and halt the guerrilla warfare being waged there by Confederate sympathizers. Since approximately ten thousand of the men under his command were three-months volunteers, and it was urgently necessary to keep them under arms while the raw recruits were being drilled, he personally guaranteed their pay if they would stay a fourth month. The morale of the officers showed immediate improvement following his arrival; tippling ceased, and the booksellers reported an unusual demand for Hardee's *Tactics* and Scott's *Tactics*.[17] He ordered a reorganization of the Reserve Corps in St. Louis, to be enlisted for the war, and to comprise infantry,

[17] New York *Herald*, August 12, 1861.

cavalry, and artillery units. In the first few days after assuming command he took possession of the Iron Mountain and the Pacific railroads, stationed small forces to protect them, garrisoned Ironton with a force under Colonel B. Gratz Brown, and took equal precautions for the safety of Cape Girardeau —these points being important for the defense of St. Louis.

Arms and money were still desperately needed; many of the soldiers had long been unpaid, and some volunteers as they arrived had to be set drilling with sticks, while even the trained men were armed with almost anything—some with smoothbores, some with rifled muskets, and some with nothing but sabers. As July closed, he appealed to the War Department agent in New York. The Adams Express Company, he wired, would bring by passenger train any arms directed to him; "send everything you have"; the arsenal was empty and "we must have arms—any arms, no matter what." At the same time he wrote directly to Lincoln, stating that he had found "nearly every county in an insurrectionary condition"; the enemy advancing in force from different points on the southern frontier; and besides the troops menacing Prentiss, 5,000 Tennesseans and Arkansas marching upon Ironton: [18]

I am sorely pressed for want of arms. I have arranged with Adams Express Company to bring me everything with speed, and will buy arms to-day in New York. Our troops have not been paid, and some regiments are in a state of mutiny, and the men whose term of service is expired generally refuse to enlist. I lost a fine regiment last night from inability to pay them a portion of the money due. This regiment had been intended to move on a critical post last night. The treasurer of the United States had here $300,000 entirely unappropriated. I applied to him yesterday for $100,000 for my paymaster-general, Andrews, but was refused. We have not an hour for delay. There are three courses open to us. One, to let the enemy possess himself of some of the strongest points in the state and threaten St. Louis, which is insurrectionary. Second, to force a loan

[18] *Official Records*, Series I, Vol. III, p. 416.

from secession banks here. Third, to use the money belonging to the government, which is in the treasury here. Of course I will neither lose the state nor permit the enemy a foot of advantage. I have infused energy and activity into the department, and there is a thorough good spirit in officers and men. This morning I will order the treasurer to deliver the money in his possession to Gen. Andrews, and will send a force to the treasury to take the money, and will direct such payments as the exigency requires. I will hazard everything for the defense of the department you have confided to me, and I trust to you for support.

Believing there was a shortage of both horses and arms in the United States, Frémont proposed to the Washington authorities that his former attorney F. P. Billings be allowed to buy the former in Canada, and that agents be hurried to France for the latter. The deficiency of arms was a terrible reality. But there were plenty of horses as near as Quincy, Illinois, at prices $30 a head lower than Frémont proposed to pay in Canada. The War Department forbade the Canadian purchases in a telegram which, because it was sent to a subordinate, aroused the General's anger.

Frémont's plan was to take the field with his army as soon as possible; and he reasoned that in order to hold St. Louis as his base he would either have to garrison it with a considerable force, or fortify it. As events turned out, St. Louis was soon perfectly safe. At the moment, however, his reasoning did not appear fallacious. He began digging a crescent-shaped line of intrenchments about the city, employing not the new recruits, who needed drilling and were in large part unfit for such heavy work in the August heat, but the laboring population of St. Louis. The city was full of turbulent men, their families in want, who presented a constant danger of riots; and government wages were an important factor in pacifying the community. In the same way, he planned to fortify Cape Girardeau, Ironton, Rolla, and Jefferson City, and thus enable small garrisons to hold the state tranquil.[19] Enlisting a confi-

[19] MS *Memoirs,* Bancroft Library.

dential agent or spy named Captain Charles D'Arnaud, the
General sent him within the Confederate lines to prepare a
correct map of the highways, bridges, and forts in Kentucky
and western Tennessee, and to ascertain the probable movements of the enemy. D'Arnaud shortly returned with much of
the desired information, and with useful maps showing the position of Fort Henry and Fort Donelson, then being constructed.

To expedite the transportation of troops, Frémont promptly
took two steps of great importance. The railroads entering St.
Louis had different terminals, some of them far from the
river. The General had a union station built and fortified on
the river bank, so that, upon a day's notice, 20,000 troops
could be moved through the city from a point on one railway
to a point on another. Troops arriving from Illinois could be
ferried directly to the station with all their supplies, without
need of wagons to haul them through the streets. It was a
common-sense step. At the same time, Frémont began to organize a river service. He asked Governor O. P. Morton of
Indiana, though ineffectually, for some regiments of men experienced in steamboating; and upon his own authority sent
for a veteran river captain in St. Louis, Thomas Maxwell, and
authorized him to organize a "marine corps" of pilots, engineers, mates, firemen, and sailors, three companies in all.[20]
On the very day he crossed the Mississippi to take command,
Frémont directed his chief of staff to find out what river boats
were available for refitting as gunboats. Asboth and Fiala, as it
happened, were familiar with the armed craft used by the
Austrians upon the lower Danube. On August 24th Frémont
ordered the construction of thirty-eight mortar-boats, and later
of eight steam-tugs to move them, and the adaptation of two
strongly built vessels as gunboats. The sides of all these craft
were lined with iron. Work was pushed on them by torch-light all
night long. Captain James B. Eads was frequently at headquarters, and the drawing of the plans was placed under his control.

[20] Sen. Exec. Doc. 412, 57th Cong., 1st Sess., p. 195ff.

Unfortunately, while Frémont was carrying through these constructive labors, he was making a series of errors, small in detail but large in the aggregate, which were destined to cost him dear. Reports reached the East that he was vain, capricious, and arrogant. It was complained that he had taken for headquarters an elegant private mansion at a rental of $6,000 a year; that the Hungarian and Garibaldian officers whom he had brought out as his personal staff wore gaudy uniforms and used fantastic titles; that he clattered through the streets with an ostentatious bodyguard; that he was so hedged about with sentinels that it was impossible to see him on business; that he issued commissions and gave out contracts in a shockingly irregular way; and that he and his assistants were preposterously extravagant. He was accused of surrounding himself with a knot of flatterers, and of ignoring able but plain-spoken men.[21]

In these charges there was a limited element of truth. Frémont's use of the splendid residence of Colonel J. B. Brant on Chouteau Avenue was entirely proper, for it enabled him to house under one roof the whole administrative activities of his Department. In a large second-floor room were desks for himself, his secretaries John R. Howard and William Dorsheimer, and Asboth and other staff officers. Large tables were placed in the room and covered with maps, diagrams, calculations of distances, and similar material prepared with care by Asboth. Downstairs were subordinate officers. The basement held a veritable arsenal, from which arms and ammunition were dealt out for emergency service. But Frémont guarded the approaches by so many sentries that men complained it was like capturing the Gorgon's head to fight their way in. General G. B. Farrar, who brought an important message from Springfield, declared that it took him three days to gain an audience with Frémont; that there were guards at the street corners, guards at the gate, guards at the outer door, guards at the

21 Nicolay and Hay, *Lincoln*, IV, p. 412.

office, and a whole regiment of troops in the adjacent barracks.[22]

The personnel and titles of Frémont's staff were certain to
grate upon rough and practical westerners. He had brought
with him not merely the Hungarians named, and Major Charles
Zagonyi, who organized a spirited cavalry battalion, but such
Italians as Captain Antonio Cattanco, Captain Ajace Saccippi,
and Lieutenant Dominica Occidone. Another officer was said
to be a natural son of Lord Byron. Frémont actually seemed
to prefer foreigners to Americans. On August 5th he wrote
Francis Lieber: "Are there any experienced artillerists, officers
or men, one or both, Germans, Prussian, or French, in New
York, who can be gotten immediately and sent to me here
without any loss of time? I am distressed for want of men to
man my guns and the enemy is at our door." He had twenty-
eight staff members, altogether too many. Some bore sonorous
and absurd foreign names—"adletus to the chief of staff,"
"commander of the bodyguard," "musical director," and "military registrator and expeditor." Among the fifteen aides-de-
camp were several politicians, who received no pay but served
in order to exert their influence upon affairs. They included
Owen Lovejoy, a portly, kindly, rhetorically eloquent gentleman, who sat in Congress for the Princeton district of Illinois,
and who, embittered by the death of his brother Elijah many
years before at the hands of an anti-Abolitionist mob, was
warmly opposed to slavery; John A. Gurley, well known as
an Abolitionist leader and a Representative from Ohio; and
Representative John P. C. Shanks of Indiana, also of radical
anti-slavery views. This trio was close to Frémont, as were
young Howard and Dorsheimer, his immediate secretaries.
Dorsheimer, a lawyer with a Harvard education, had ability,
and later rose to be lieutenant-governor of New York, but his
aristocratic elegance (he had a valet) amused many observers.

[22] Gustav Koerner, *Memoirs*, II, p. 170ff. The fact that Brant was a relative
of Mrs. Frémont made the $5,000 rental seem suspicious to some; actually it
was moderate.

FILLMORE AS A REPRESENTATIVE OF THE MODERATES

(From *American Caricatures Pertaining to the Civil War*, Brentano's, 1918)

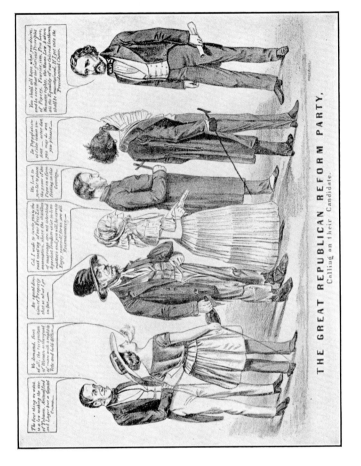

THE GREAT REPUBLICAN REFORM PARTY,
Calling on their Candidate.

THE LUNATIC FRINGE OF REPUBLICANISM

FRÉMONT IN 1861

BUILDING GENERAL FRÉMONT'S BRIDGE ACROSS THE OSAGE

(From *Harper's Weekly*)

BRILLIANT CHARGE OF GENERAL FRÉMONT'S BODYGUARD THROUGH THE TOWN OF SPRINGFIELD, MISSOURI, ON OCTOBER 24, 1861

(From *Harper's Weekly*)

GENERAL FRÉMONT'S ARMY ON THE MARCH THROUGH SOUTHWESTERN MISSOURI

THE F. P. BLAIR FAMILY IN POLITICS

F. P. BLAIR, JR.   F. P. BLAIR, SR.   MONTGOMERY BLAIR

(From W. E. Smith, *The Francis Preston Blair Family in Politics,*
by courtesy of The Macmillan Company)

BUST OF FRÉMONT FROM THE ORIGINAL BY AUSTIN JAMES

(Courtesy of Catherine Coffin Phillips)

Gustav Koerner, a brilliant young German-American, served on the staff as the representative of Governor Yates of Illinois.[23]

Unfortunate in some members of his personal staff, Frémont was unfortunate also in several officers of the regular army whom he found already stationed in St. Louis. The most important, bustling, and unpopular was Major Justus McKinstry, the quartermaster-general, who had become provost-marshal of St. Louis when the city was placed under martial law. He owed his command there to Blair himself. Before Frémont arrived the quartermaster-general in Washington had given McKinstry broad powers in making purchases, instructing him that while economy was important, promptness and efficiency were more so. A tall, dashing fellow, with dark complexion, resolute features, and "an eye like Mars to threaten and command," he looked, especially when galloping about the streets, the *beau idéal* of a soldier. But he had always been disliked in the army, and as censor of the activities of the St. Louisians he was hated by the people. His refusal to let any one enter or leave the city without passes, his rule that nobody should be on the streets after 9 P.M., and his restrictions on the press, aroused bitter complaint. He turned against Blair; and one of Frémont's worst blunders was to permit him to suppress the St. Louis *Republican,* a Unionist newspaper published by Blair's friends and close to Blair's heart. Blair came to consider this appointee of his own the most tyrannical and corrupt of the General's subordinates.

Frémont cannot be exonerated from blame for the chaos, friction, and extravagance which arose; a commander with more practical vigor would have cut through many of the difficulties directly. He would have mastered affairs, instead of

[23] Ida M. Tarbell, *Abraham Lincoln,* II, Ch. 24. As page in the Frémont headquarters there served a lad named Francis Grierson, who had been born in England and reared in Illinois, and who was destined to become a noted mystic and essayist. His impressions, recorded in a chapter of *The Valley of Shadows: Recollections of the Lincoln Country,* have slender historical value but great literary charm. He was impressed, as a boy would be, by the pomp and parade surrounding the headquarters and the strangeness of the foreign officers.

letting them master him. The General lacked high executive ability; still more, he lacked judgment of men. To be sure, much of the irregularity in letting contracts, the general confusion, and the tactless exclusion of important visitors, arose from the fact that he was crushed under a mountain of labor. He had to conduct an enormous correspondence with governors of the states and territories in his Department, with Washington officials, with his scattered commands, and with private citizens. It was more than Dorsheimer, Howard, and the devoted Jessie could manage. His troops were strewn all over the West—part in Missouri, part in Kansas, part in Chicago, part in southern Illinois, and soon part in Paducah, Kentucky. Once he kept his telegraphers busy thirty-six hours without intermission. With the lesson of Bull Run before him, he had resolved not to move forward till he had organized his force and collected adequate supplies; and Washington, intent on the eastern armies, hindered rather than aided him. But these excuses cover only part of his failure. Gustav Koerner correctly wrote Lyman Trumbull on November 12, 1861: [24]

There was a great amount of labor performed day and night but there appeared to be no proper system or method. Some of his most intimate friends were undoubtedly cheating and circumventing him, I thought. He is no judge of men at all, it seems to me, and he can readily be imposed upon by plausible knavery. I think he is honest and honorable himself, but too impulsive and too impressionable.

Necessarily, he had to depute much business to subordinates, who sometimes managed it badly. Breezy western citizens, who thought that everybody, whether President, Senator, or General, should stop and give them a half hour's chat, were turned back by sentries with a curt "What's your business?" or, if they gained entry, found Frémont preoccupied and hurried. They went out denouncing him as aristocratic and cold, when he was only protecting his time. Frémont's green staff helped him to make mistakes, for neither Howard nor Dor-

24 Trumbull Papers, Library of Congress.

sheimer knew the difference between a rascally contract hunter and a distinguished citizen of St. Louis, and sometimes admitted the former while debarring the latter. Their inexperience conspired with Frémont's own impatience of red tape to produce many irregularities. His unauthorized issuance of commissions became the despair of the War Department, while orders and requisitions were frequently signed without scrutiny. General Schofield tells us that he went repeatedly to Frémont for authority to have certain rifled guns in the St. Louis arsenal issued to his new artillery regiment; that he always received the authority, but before he got to the armory it was invariably countermanded by telegraph; and that finally he suggested to Frémont that he be sent East to procure fieldpieces and equipment. Frémont at once acquiesced, bade Schofield sit down and write the necessary order, and "signed it without reading." A well-known and able Missouri Congressman, John Phelps, came down the steps of the Brant House in high dudgeon, complaining that he could see nobody and get no business attended to. In many ways the Department of the West by mid-August, 1861, seemed in dire confusion.

Yet some were favorably impressed. John Hay, Lincoln's secretary, went to St. Louis late in August and for several days saw much of Frémont and Jessie. He thought the latter talked too much and too loudly. But Frémont "was quiet, earnest, industrious, imperious." Returning East, Hay wrote articles in two New York papers defending the General.

The increasing storm of criticism, made louder by prejudice and ignorance, and swelled by the clamor of selfish "patriots"— many of them Frank P. Blair's friends—who had been refused contracts for horses, beef, mules, or wagons, and who were highly disgruntled, dismayed Frémont. He winced under the attacks. A great deal of outright mendacity entered into them. An impartial Missouri observer, B. Rush Plumeley, later wrote Secretary Chase that he had taken the charges one by one and sifted them without regard to Frémont or Blair. "My dear friends, they are...lies." A friend of Blair, he added, had been the largest buyer of horses, and had supplied such miserable steeds that Frémont was compelled to issue an order that no more Missouri stock should be bought. The records of the War Department bear this out. They contain a number of Blair's brief notes to McKinstry. "Dear Major: If you buy any more horses, I wish you to give Jim Neal a fair chance. He is a personal friend of mine and a sound Union man." Again, "Dear Major: I shall be obliged to you if you can give Mr. Alec Peterson a contract for buying horses. He is a good friend of mine..." And to still another officer, "General Meigs: If you want horses in Missouri, I most cordially recommend Mr. Farrar to purchase them for you." It was Farrar who supplied the most defective animals. Frémont was fiercely criticized for a purchase of Hall's carbines to arm his half-defenseless troops, and since this purchase involved no less a person than young J. Pierpont Morgan, the accusations have been repeated and embroidered in numerous books. But a careful investigation has shown that the much-denounced transaction was really prudent and commendable.[25]

While the storm of attacks increased, the military situation in these first weeks after Lyon's defeat and the retreat of his shattered army to Rolla seemed full of the gravest peril. Union leaders believed that there were now 60,000 or 70,000 armed rebels in the state, of whom perhaps 40,000 were Missourians. Troops had suddenly appeared in great force from Arkansas, Tennessee, and other states, and with the benefit of comprehensive military plans matured by Leonidas Polk and others, had overrun half the state. Living on the country, they were seizing horses, grain, meat, clothing, and other supplies from Union citizens. Meanwhile, in central and northern Missouri the rebel guerrillas, recruited from the countrysides, were en-

[25] Koerner, *Memoirs*, II, p. 168; on Frank Blair's desire for contracts, W. E. Smith offers a fair treatment in *The Francis Preston Blair Family in Politics*, II, p. 67. McKinstry published a pamphlet defense of himself which contains a mass of material on contracts and corruption, and which is more severe upon Frank Blair than Frémont; *Vindication of Quartermaster-General McKinstry*. For this whole subject of wartime corruption see Appendix II.

gaging in appalling outrages. They were burning bridges, wrecking railway trains, cutting telegraphs, raiding farms, and falling in sudden force upon exposed Union units, only to scatter again in a hundred directions. Their warfare was driving the loyal population by thousands to take refuge, penniless, in Illinois, Iowa, and Kansas. There seemed danger that parts of the state would become a stark wilderness.[26] And nobody knew where Pillow and McCulloch would strike next.

Under these circumstances Frémont, believing some decisive stroke to be necessary, resolved suddenly upon a proclamation of military emancipation. In this step he was unquestionably urged forward by his immediate associates. Two parties had arisen among the loyal citizens of Missouri, the radical Union men or "charcoals," and the conservatives, or "claybanks." The former, who included most of the Germans, believed in aggressive, uncompromising action, while the latter advocated patience, conciliation, and caution. The latter were led by Frank Blair and provisional Governor Hamilton R. Gamble; it was the former who surrounded Frémont, and who, with the radical Lovejoy, Gurley, and Shanks among their spokesmen, had obtained a marked ascendancy over him. They held a decided conviction that the slaves of rebels ought to be forfeit. Secession, they reasoned, had destroyed all constitutional protections and safeguards which formerly shielded southern citizens; it was now perfectly legal to confiscate the property of men in arms, and slaves were of course property. Every report of outrage and destruction in peaceful Union counties, of depredations by bushwhackers and guerrilla gangs, was an argument for stern measures. Men were being killed and their homes wiped out. Should the Federal Government hesitate to free the slaves of miscreants responsible for such acts? To this view Mrs. Frémont was completely won over, and she added her arguments to those of Lovejoy and Gurley.

How long Frémont debated the question with himself and

[26] Compare *Official Records*, Series I, Vol. III, p. 417.

others, we do not know; but his wife tells us that at the end he moved with his accustomed impetuosity: [27]

The State outside of the fortified points was becoming more and more unsettled. The farmers would, when notified, join the camps of the rebel commanders in great numbers, suddenly augmenting their forces, and then, if the projected raid or attack was deferred, would return again to their homes, reducing the force correspondingly.

In this manner, however, it was impossible to foresee which point would be threatened next, and failing sufficient troops to control the State through force of arms, it became necessary to devise some means to prevent this guerrilla warfare. The credit of the government was about used up, and it had so lost prestige through the non-payment of its debts to the soldiers, and those who furnished the supplies, that it was regarded with contempt by the Secessionists, and many Unionists came to doubt its power to compel. For many days and nights the situation had been a most anxious one for Gen. Frémont; with unfilled requisitions in Washington, commanders of troops demanding reinforcements where there were none to give, troops clamoring for pay when there was no money....He determined to force the rebel sympathizers, who did not join the rebel armies as soldiers, to remain at home, and to make them feel that there was a penalty for rebellion, and for aiding those who were in rebellion.

On the morning of the 30th of August, shortly after daybreak, Mrs. Frémont found Gen. Frémont at his desk. He had sent for Mr. Edward Davis, of Philadelphia, who arrived as she came. It was sufficiently light to see plainly, and the General said, "I want you two, but no others." Then in the dawn of the new day, he read the Emancipation Order, that first gave freedom to the slaves of rebels, and which he had thought out and written, in the hours taken from his brief resting time.

The proclamation with which Frémont thus astonished the nation declared that he found it necessary to thrust aside the provisional governor and assume the administrative powers of the disordered state; that all Missouri would thenceforth be

[27] MS *Memoirs,* Bancroft Library.

under martial law; that the lines of the Union Army should for the present extend from Leavenworth by way of Jefferson City, Rolla, and Ironton to Cape Girardeau on the Mississippi; that all persons found with arms in their hands north of these lines should be tried by court-martial, and if guilty, should be shot; and that "the property, real and personal, of all persons in the state of Missouri directly proven to have taken an active part with their enemies in the field is declared to be confiscated to the public use, and their slaves, if any they have, are hereby declared freemen." His intention was to penalize the disloyal slave-owners of northern and central Missouri who were organizing or supporting the guerrilla warfare of those regions. But his action had a far wider significance. The conflict had thus far been a war to preserve the Union, and no members of the Administration and no general had suggested any other object; Frémont's proclamation, if its principles were sustained and applied to other fields, would convert it into a war to liberate the slaves.

Already many radical-minded Northerners, including, of course, the Abolitionists, had demanded just this. Gerrit Smith, in an open letter of July 12th to Frémont's staff assistant, Owen Lovejoy, had said that the government did right to call for millions in money and hundreds of thousands of soldiers if they were really needed to put down the rebellion. "But why take a costly and weary way to put it down," he asked, "when a cheap and short one is at hand? Why choose crushing burdens of debt and immense human slaughter when both can be avoided? The liberation of slaves has obviously become one of the necessities and therefore one of the rights of the country. Let the President, in his capacity as commander of the army, proclaim such liberation and the war would end in thirty days." Moncure D. Conway was putting through the press a book, received enthusiastically by the newspapers and by radicals like Sumner, entitled *The Great Method of Peace*, which declared emancipation the master-key of victory. Announce it, he wrote, and "every Southerner would have to hurry

home to be his own home-guard and his own home-provisioner."
Even those who held no such illusions thought, as the *Tribune*
said, that it was "time to be in earnest; that handling traitors
with kid gloves is not the way to subdue them." [28]

Frémont's proclamation of August 30th, therefore, coming
at a moment of growing antagonism between radical and conservative Northerners, and his action immediately afterward
in setting up a commission to take evidence and in issuing deeds
of manumission to slaves, fell upon the country like a thunder-
bolt.

[28] New York *Tribune,* July 28, 1861 (for Gerrit Smith's letter); September
1, 1861.

XXX

Frémont *vs.* Blair and Lincoln

B EYOND question Frémont issued his proclamation simply as a war measure in Missouri, and with little if any thought of its effect outside that state. He has been accused by Nicolay and Hay of drafting it as an appeal to the support of the northern radicals, and as a last desperate attempt to regain the popularity which he had lost through Lyon's defeat. No foundation exists for this view, which is unjust in attributing to the impetuous General a measure of shrewd, scheming calculation which he never possessed. He planned the proclamation merely as a weapon against the guerrillas who were laying northern Missouri waste; he designed it, as he said, "to place in the hands of the military authorities the power to give instantaneous effect to existing laws, and to supply such deficiencies as the conditions of war demand." It was characteristic of him that he did not wait to consult the Administration on so momentous a step; had he paused to think of its effect outside turbulent Missouri, he would have done so. But he did not know how fiercely the radicals and Lincoln were already at odds over emancipation.

He was warned, as he read it to his wife and friend in that gray August dawn, that Washington would be hostile. "General," said Edward Davis, "Mr. Seward will never allow this. He intends to wear down the South by steady pressure, not by blows, and then make himself the arbitrator." "It is for the North to say what it will or will not allow," replied Frémont, "and whether it will arbitrate, or whether it will fight. The time has come for decisive action; this is a war measure, and as such I make it. I have been given full power to crush rebellion in this department, and I will bring the penalties of rebellion home to every man found striving against the Union." [1]

The reception met by the proclamation has been described by many historians, and it is sufficient to say that it aroused the enthusiasm of radical anti-slavery elements in the North as nothing had done since the firing on Fort Sumter. New England was jubilant. From all parts of the Middle West came reports that men were saying, "Now the Administration is in earnest," or "That looks like work!" In Lincoln's own state of Illinois the outburst of applause was such as to give the President genuine pain. The German-Americans rose *en masse* to this new and higher object which Frémont seemed to have given the war; recruiting increased by a sudden leap. The press of the North was almost a unit in commendation. In Chicago, the *Tribune;* in Washington the *National Intelligencer;* in Boston, the *Post;* and in New York, Raymond's *Times,* Horace Greeley's *Tribune,* and Bryant's *Evening Post* all praised the proclamation in high terms. Even James Gordon Bennett's *Herald,* lately on the side of the South, and the Chicago *Times,* which was at one time briefly suppressed as a copperhead organ, joined the chorus of approbation.[2] George Julian, an Indiana member of Congress, later wrote that "it stirred and united the people of the loyal States during the ten days of life allotted it by the Government far more than any other event of the war." Perhaps the most extraordinary fact was that Simon Cameron, the Secretary of War, who was at his home ill, thought it an admirable stroke, and telegraphing his congratulations to Frémont, returned to his desk ready to give it hearty endorsement. He was surprised to find that Lincoln was hostile.[3] Sumner was enthusiastic. From that moment, Frémont became more than a general—to millions, especially in New England and among the German and Yankee elements

---

[1] MS *Memoirs,* Bancroft Library.

[2] The Chase MSS, Library of Congress, contains a mass of approbatory letters; see Frank Moore, *Rebellion Record,* III, 33*ff.* for press comment.

[3] Cameron advocated arming Negro soldiers; *Diary of Edward Bates,* p. 203.

of the West, he became a symbol. His name represented the crusade for the extinction of slavery.

How Lincoln, with his usual calm sagacity, took a broader and wiser view; how with the necessity of conciliating the hesitant Kentuckians in mind, he patiently and kindly asked Frémont to modify his proclamation—this, too, is an old story. His letter of September 2nd to the General is worth quoting in full: [4]

MY DEAR SIR: Two points in your proclamation of August 30th give me some anxiety:

First: Should you shoot a man, according to the proclamation, the Confederates would very certainly shoot our best men in their hands in retaliation; and so, man for man, indefinitely. It is, therefore, my order that you allow no man to be shot under the proclamation without first having my approbation or consent.

Second. I think there is great danger that the closing paragraph, in relation to the confiscation of property and the liberating slaves of traitorous owners, will alarm our Southern Union friends and turn them against us; perhaps ruin our rather fair prospect for Kentucky. Allow me, therefore, to ask that you will, as of your own motion, modify that paragraph so as to conform to the first and fourth sections of the act of Congress entitled, 'An act of Congress entitled, "An act to confiscate property used for insurrectionary purposes," approved August 6, 1861, and a copy of which act I herewith send you.

This letter is written in a spirit of caution, and not of censure. I send it by special messenger, in order that it may certainly and speedily reach you.

This request for a modification Frémont foolishly refused. His eyes were bent wholly upon Missouri, without thought of the other border states, and he tells us in his unpublished *Memoirs* that the effect there was striking. "The Union people rejoiced openly. The class of sympathizers with the South became quiet and careful, finding that they must respect the laws

[4] Nicolay and Hay, *Lincoln,* IV, Ch. 24, give it and the circumstances.

of the land they lived in. To the rebels everywhere it was a
blow. It affected not only their principles but their property."
He wrote to Lincoln a stubborn explanation: [5]

Trusting to have your confidence, I have been leaving it to events
themselves to show you whether or not I was shaping affairs here
according to your ideas. The shortest communication between Washington and St. Louis generally involves two days, and the employment of two days in time of war goes largely toward success or
disaster. I therefore went along according to my own judgment,
leaving the result of my movements to justify me with you. And
so in regard to my proclamation of the 30th. Between the rebel
armies, the Provisional Government, and home traitors, I felt the
position bad and saw danger. In the night I decided upon the
proclamation and the form of it. I wrote it the next morning and
printed it the same day. I did it without consultation or advice
with any one, acting solely with my best judgment to serve the
country and yourself, and perfectly willing to receive the amount
of censure which should be thought due if I had made a false movement. This is as much a movement in the war as a battle, and in
going into these I shall have to act according to my judgment of
the ground before me, as I did on this occasion. If, upon reflection,
your better judgment still decides that I am wrong in the article
respecting the liberation of slaves, I have to ask that you will openly
direct me to make the correction. The implied censure will be received as a soldier always should the reprimand of his chief. If I
were to retract of my own accord, it would imply that I myself
thought it wrong, and that I had acted without the reflection
which the gravity of the point demanded. But I did not. I acted
with full deliberation, and upon the certain conviction that it was a
measure right and necessary, and I think so still. In regard to the
other point of the proclamation to which you refer, I desire to
say that I do not think the enemy can either misconstrue or urge
anything against it, or undertake to make unusual retaliation. The
shooting of men who will rise in arms against an army in the military occupation of a country is merely a necessary measure of
defence, and entirely according to the usages of civilized warfare.
The article does not at all refer to prisoners of war, and certainly

[5] *Official Records*, Series I, Vol. III, p. 477.

our enemies have no ground for requiring that we should waive in their benefit any of the ordinary advantages which the usages of war allow to us.

Already Frémont had been asked by the Confederate commander to explain his article upon the shooting of prisoners. On receipt of Frémont's despatch, Lincoln in a courteous letter made a public order:

Your answer, just received, expresses the preference on your part that I should make an open order for the modification, which I very cheerfully do. It is therefore ordered that the said clause of said proclamation be so modified, held, and construed as to conform to, and not to transcend, the provisions on the same subject contained in the act of Congress entitled, "An act to confiscate property used for insurrectionary purposes," approved August 6, 1861, and that said act be published at length, with this order.

The news was received by many in the North with gnashing of teeth. Judge George Hoadly of Cincinnati wrote that the prevalent sentiment in his city could be described only by the word "fury." [6] "How many times," asked James Russell Lowell, "are we to save Kentucky and lose our self-respect?"

This rebuke by the President in the sight of the nation was but the first of a series of disasters which befell Frémont. The next and the most catastrophic was an open estrangement between him and the powerful Blair family. The Blairs, as Lincoln later told some friends in a confidential chat, were a proud clan, with the spirit of a close corporation, and with a tendency to go in a headlong rush for any object. Related to the Bentons through the Preston family of Virginia, they and the Frémonts had long been close friends. The two sons, Montgomery and Frank, had gone to Missouri to have the benefit of Senator Benton's influence in practising law; while Jessie had spent much time with the "old gentleman," Francis P. Blair, on his attractive estate at Silver Spring, just across

6 Chase MSS, Library of Congress.

the Maryland line, whither he had retired with his slaves, dogs, and books. To this place, with its groves and grottoes, she had brought her second baby daughter in 1853 to die. Lincoln later testified that he had appointed Frémont as western commander at the earnest solicitation of the Blairs, and that he was their "pet and protégé." There seemed every reason for complete harmony. Yet a swift and angry breach ensued—a breach which disrupted the Unionists of Missouri, and shook the whole Northwest.[7]

The reasons for this duel between Frémont and the Blairs, with political results that tormented the Lincoln Administration till the last year of the War, were complex. Temperamentally, the men were certain to clash. Frank Blair, who had taken the helm in Missouri, had gained thereby a national reputation. He was shrewd, direct, practical, and aggressive, and the erratic, impetuous, visionary traits of Frémont grated upon him. Both were hot-tempered and tenacious. Frank Blair expected to continue to be the directing force in Missouri affairs, while Frémont had no intention of letting anybody dominate them but himself. Already the Blair clan had shown what it would do with any commander who crossed its path in that state. A few months earlier, it had taken General William S. Harney in hand because he seemed slow and conservative, and had broken him with cruel despatch. Frank had pulled all the wires he could in Missouri; his brother the Postmaster-General, "the Pisistratus of his race," had exerted pressure at the capital; and Harney had been ignominiously removed. Now Frank desired to have his wishes treated as something like commands, and was chagrined when Frémont, with Jessie at his back, followed his own course. Missouri had shown promise of becoming a political enclave of the Blairs; it dismayed them to see Frémont taking steps which rallied the Germans at his back and looked like the erection of a possible machine of his own. Finally, Frank had many Missouri friends who, having helped

---

[7] For a vigorous sketch of Frank Blair, see G. W. Nichols, *Story of the Great March*, p. 97*ff*.

him "save" the state, thought they were entitled to the contracts which were being lavishly distributed; while Frémont had contract-hungry friends of his own—men whom Blair called "California vultures." [8]

For a time after Frémont's arrival, matters had gone with fair smoothness. Montgomery Blair supported him loyally in Washington. He encouraged the General in his expenditures, and criticized the Secretary of the Treasury for his parsimonious ways—"Chase," he wrote, "has more horror of seeing Treasury notes below par than of seeing soldiers killed." He talked with Lincoln about Frémont's needs, and criticized Lincoln, too— "he is of the Whig school, and that brings him naturally not only to incline to the feeble policy of the Whigs, but to give his confidence to such advisers." [9] Frank Blair was much at Frémont's headquarters, and asked and received not a few favors. Quite naturally, he requested consideration in contracts for his friends among the important merchants and manufacturers of St. Louis; and this consideration was cheerfully granted. But the time came when Frémont denied some of Blair's requests. In particular, he and McKinstry declined to grant two friends of Blair a contract to supply clothing and other equipment for forty thousand men—Frémont not believing he needed so much.[10] Frank believed in this and other contracts; he did not believe in others which Frémont was letting—some of them shown later to be full of fraud—to men whom he characterized as "obscene birds of prey." There was fault on both sides. When Frank wrote east, his father showed that he also had some grasping ideas. The old gentleman sent Frémont a decidedly irritated letter, in which he suggested "a copartnership in the West," and said that he and his sons would do everything in their power to aid the commander, if on his part he would

---

[8] W. E. Smith, *The Francis Preston Blair Family in Politics*, II, p. 67*ff*., reaches my own conclusion that the principal basis of the Frémont-Blair quarrel lay in rival ambition for power and prestige. Missouri was not big enough for both men.

[9] Report, *Committee on Conduct of the War*, Part III, p. 115*ff*.

[10] Report, *Committee on Conduct of the War*, Part III, p. 178*ff*.; p. 202*ff*.

be obliging to them. Frank, he added, wanted a new military post.[11]

I shall expect you to exert your utmost influence to carry my points, and now to begin, I want to have Frank made a militia major-general for the State of Missouri. This, I presume, Gov. Gamble can do, and as Major-General Frost nipped his military honors in the bud, by turning traitor and absconding with Jackson, it would seem but a completion of what was gained in substituting Gamble for the abdicating governor, to make Frank, as the military man of the State, take the position deserted by Gen. Frost. Frank might have accepted a generalship, offered him by Lincoln, but he felt that he might be useful in Congress·and hence declined a commission from that quarter which would have vacated his seat in the House. He has no commission now and acts only as colonel by the election of the regiment and courtesy of the army.

Frémont felt unable to grant this unblushing demand and said so. He tried to soften the refusal by writing the Blairs that Frank's regiment would amount to a brigade, but the rebuff stung them. Actually, he hoped that Frank Blair would accept a command in the East and so cease to complicate the Missouri situation. But the elder Blair continued to insist, by letters and telegrams, that Frémont yield to and coöperate with his son. He believed that Frank was on the high road to the Presidency, and was determined that nothing should check his son's promising career. Montgomery also thought that Frank was, as Gideon Welles records, "the greatest man in the country." All the ambitions and the wishes of the family were concentrated upon the young man. As Lincoln shrewdly put it, "Frank is their hope and pride." [12]

In so far as they were motivated by political ambitions and

[11] Frémont MSS, Bancroft Library.

[12] But Frémont did write Provisional-Governor Hamilton R. Gamble on August 18th requesting that as a special favor he "immediately commission with the rank of Brigadier-General the Honorable Frank P. Blair, now colonel of the 1st Missouri Volunteers." Gamble lacked power to do so. Gamble Papers; courtesy of Miss Marguerite Potter. For Welles on Frank Blair, see his Diary, III, p. 408.

a desire for personal favors, the Blairs appear to poor advantage in their attack on Frémont; but there was a better side. Frank Blair came honestly to believe that Frémont lacked the high military talents his position required. He thought that St. Louis was overwhelmingly loyal, and objected to the measures which Frémont and McKinstry took to police it under martial law. Later, he declared that Frémont's acts were "the offspring of timidity, seeking to prevent imaginary dangers by inspiring the terrors with which he himself was haunted." There was room for a sincere divergence of opinion upon this policing, and it is not easy to say which man was right. Most merchants were sympathetic with secession, and even after Frémont's work was done, the secessionist candidates for officers of the Chamber of Commerce and the Mercantile Library Association, two powerful organizations, were elected by heavy majorities.[13] Frémont's force of effective troops was much smaller than it appeared to be, and he knew that he might have to denude the city of men to answer some urgent call from the East or the West. On the whole, his precautions appear to have been justified.

Again, Blair condemned the fortification of St. Louis as another evidence of the same wasteful timidity, and as a step both useless and in its execution needlessly extravagant. These defensive works included ten forts, and the labor on them was prosecuted until the middle of October, when the War Department ordered them dropped. It is impossible to say that they were useless. There seemed genuine need in July and August, 1861, for protective measures of this character, and the precaution was probably wise. Washington was heavily fortified; General Ormsby Mitchel took great care in the summer of 1861 to fortify Cincinnati. But Blair was right as to the extrav-

---

[13] *Congressional Globe,* March 7, 1862. Frémont thought the Board of Police Commissioners for St. Louis, which had been appointed by ex-Governor Jackson, disloyal. He wrote Provisional-Governor Gamble on August 18th urging that they be dismissed, and suggesting men to take their place. Action should be taken without delay, he declared. But Gamble found himself without power to remove them except on formal complaint (Gamble Papers).

agance. Frémont, who should have assigned the work to army engineers, gave it instead to a Californian named Beard, who did it incompetently and made extortionate profits. A leading army engineer later testified that if the War Department had not interfered, the government would have lost $240,000 on forts useless for defense.

The defeat and death of Lyon, a close friend, was a severe shock to Frank Blair, and in itself raised a doubt in his mind of Frémont's capacity. Lincoln tells us that at first he had spoken of Frémont with high admiration and warm hopes for the future. "But at last," said Lincoln, "the tone of Frank's letter changed. It was a change from confidence to doubt and uncertainty. They were pervaded with a tone of sincere sorrow and of fear that Frémont would fail." General John M. Schofield states that the change in Frank's attitude was manifest just after Lyon's defeat. Late in August, Schofield and Blair called together upon Frémont at the Brant mansion: [14]

The general received me cordially, but, to my great surprise, no questions were asked, nor any mention made, of the bloody field from which I had just come, where Lyon had been killed. . . . I was led at once to a large table on which maps were spread out, from which the general proceeded to explain at length the plans of the great campaign for which he was then preparing. Col. Blair had, I believe, already been initiated, but I listened attentively for a long time, certainly more than an hour, to the elucidation of the project. In general outline the plan proposed a march of the main army of the West through southwestern Missouri and northwestern Arkansas to the valley of the Arkansas River, and thence down that river to the Mississippi. . . . As soon as the explanation was ended, Col. Blair and I took our leave, making our exit through the same basement door through which we had entered. We walked down the street for some time in silence. Then Blair turned to me and said: "Well, what do you think of him?" I replied, in words rather too strong to repeat in print, to the effect that my opinion as to his wisdom was the same as it always had been. Blair said: "I have been suspecting that for some time."

[14] J. M. Schofield, *Forty-six Years in the Army*, p. 48*ff*.

It was a family maxim that: "When the Blairs go in for a fight, they go in for a funeral." [15] So it was this time. The quarrel was heated enough when Frémont issued his emancipation proclamation. That made it worse, for the Blair family took the President's view that it was necessary to conciliate the people of the border states, and to refrain from direct attacks upon slavery. Frank Blair when aroused had all the dour fury of his Scotch Covenanter blood. His letters shortly stirred up a hornet's nest in Washington. On the other side, Mrs. Frémont came to her husband's aid with all the invincible tenacity and vigor she had inherited from her father. It was a duel to the death. When the smoke of battle cleared away, Frémont was a ruined man, and the political future of the Blairs was almost hopelessly compromised.

The public gained its first clear intimation of this quarrel early in September, when Lincoln despatched Postmaster-Blair and his brother-in-law, Quartermaster-General Meigs, to St. Louis to make a thorough inquiry and a report, and also to give Frémont friendly advice and admonition. They bore a letter from Lincoln to General David Hunter in Chicago. "General Frémont," wrote the President, "needs assistance which it is difficult to give him. He is losing the confidence of men near him, whose support any man in his position must have to be successful. His cardinal mistake is that he isolates himself, and allows nobody to see him; and by which he does not know what is going on in the very matter he is dealing with. He needs to have by his side a man of large experience. Will you not, for me, take that place?" [16] Montgomery Blair and Meigs arrived at St. Louis on September 12th. Their friends gave it out that their purpose was to look after the overland mails, but this deceived nobody. Popular gossip at once decided, said the St. Louis correspondent of the New York *Herald*, that the gov-

[15] Compare E. C. Kirkland, *The Peacemakers of 1864*, p. 145; A. G. Riddle, *Life of Benjamin Wade*, p. 287. It must be remembered, in interpreting Montgomery Blair's attitude toward such enemies of Frémont as General John Pope, that he himself had received a West Point training.
[16] Nicolay and Hay, *Lincoln*, IV, p. 413.

ernment was discontented "with the way General Frémont has expended money and made proclamations, while at the same time he does nothing in the way of getting the state into Federal possession." Frémont himself saw the handwriting on the wall, for he later wrote: [17]

Early in September, I began to feel the withdrawal of the confidence and support of the Administration. The visits of high officials charged with inquiry into the affairs of my department, and the simultaneous and sustained attacks of leading journals accumulated obstructions and disturbed my movements. In fact, my command virtually endured little over one month. But the measures which I had initiated had already taken enduring shape.

It was inevitable that Montgomery Blair, after talking with the embittered Frank and with others who were thoroughly prejudiced against Frémont, should come back with an unfavorable report. Deciding to his own satisfaction that the public welfare required Frémont's removal, on his return he recommended steps to this end.[18] Writing to Sumner, he declared that his brother was thoroughly aroused. Frank, he asserted, "cannot tolerate trifling in a great cause, and when he discovered that Frémont was a mere trifler, he was not to be reconciled to seeing the State overrun by pro-slavery myrmidons, by an empty proclamation threatening to deprive them of their negroes." Nothing could have been more unfair than to call Frémont "a mere trifler," and yet this was the impression the Blairs were vigorously attempting to diffuse both east and west.

At the same time the provisional governor of Missouri, Hamilton R. Gamble, who had been appointed by a state convention, was seeing Frémont on behalf of the President, and meeting none too cordial a reception. Lincoln had heard that Frémont as a radical Unionist and Gamble as a very conservative Unionist were not getting on well, and he sent Gamble a letter to show to the General. Their meeting took place at headquarters

[17] Frémont MSS, Bancroft Library; New York *Herald*, September 18, 1861.
[18] See *Report, Committee on the Conduct of the War*, Part III, p. 170.

on the fourteenth. According to Gamble's account, Frémont was very odd in manner, sitting silent and apparently distracted much of the time. But he made it clear that he did not believe that Gamble had coöperated properly with him, complaining that the governor had not made militia appointments which he desired, and had not dismissed various officers upon request. Gamble pointed out that he was bound by constitutional limitations. Next day Frémont sent the governor a note requesting another interview. Thereupon Gamble stayed in the city for two days before returning to the capital at Jefferson City; but on the first day Frémont failed to make an appointment, and on the second he failed to keep one that he himself had made! Gamble, according to his own story, waited half an hour in an anteroom, and then not being admitted, went away in disgust. Of all this he sent Lincoln a circumstantial though indirect report, which left it plain that he thought little of Frémont's capacity.[19]

Meanwhile, Mrs. Frémont, angry and overwrought, had embarked upon a course which made matters ten times worse for her husband. Aware of the fast-growing distrust in Washington, she resolved to strike at once and strike hard. She would go to Washington with a confidential letter from Frémont to Lincoln explaining the Western situation. She would seek a special interview with the President, defend her husband roundly, and denounce his accusers as they deserved. This was much the same hot-headed course which Benton had followed with Polk when a court-martial threatened Frémont. Doubtless the General knew that it would be better to keep the fiery Jessie at home, but she would suffer no restraint. On September 8th she set out, taking her English maid. After sitting for two nights and two days in the hot, overcrowded trains, at the close of the 10th she reached Washington, and drove to Willard's Hotel to meet some friends from New York.

---

[19] Gamble Papers; these were kindly searched for me by Miss Marguerite Potter. Gamble asked for arms for his state troops; Frémont promised them, but Gamble nevertheless wrote immediately afterward that he had no expectation of getting them.

Of her ensuing interview with Lincoln we have two accounts by the two participants. The President, in an informal conversation with some associates more than two years later, recorded by one of his secretaries, remarked:

> She sought an audience with me at midnight, and tasked me so violently with so many things, that I had to exercise all the awkward tact I have to avoid quarreling with her. She surprised me by asking why their enemy, Montgomery Blair, had been sent to Missouri. She more than once intimated that if General Frémont should decide to try conclusions with me, he could set up for himself.[20]

It is difficult to believe this last. Mrs. Frémont's story differs from Lincoln's in essential particulars. Her narrative is probably more accurate than Lincoln's casual conversation, some two years after the event, casually jotted down later by John Hay, for the interview must have been burned deep into her retentive memory. She writes: [21]

> I went for Gen. Frémont to Washington to give his letter into President Lincoln's hands—both of us doubted its reaching him in the usual way.
>
> I got in at the end of the day, tired, for I had travelled night and day from St. Louis in an ordinary car, and at once sent my card (from Willard's Hotel) with a written request to know when I might deliver the letter to the President.
>
> The messenger brought back a card on which was written, "Now, at once, A. Lincoln."
>
> It was nearly 9 P.M., the date September 10 [1861].
>
> As I had not been able to undress or lie down since leaving St. Louis I had intended taking a bath and going to bed at once. But I walked over immediately, just as I had been for two days and nights, in my dusty black mourning dress.
>
> Judge Edward Coles of New York city was with me.
>
> We were asked into the usual receiving room, the red room, next the large dining room. After some little waiting the President came in from that dining room by the farther door, leaving the door partly

[20] Nicolay and Hay, *Lincoln*, IV, p. 415.
[21] No date; Jessie Benton Frémont MSS, Bancroft Library.

open. As he crossed the room that door was still more widely set open.

I introduced Judge Coles, who then stepped into the deep doorway leading to the blue room—we were just by it—and there he remained walking to and fro, keeping in sight and hearing, just within the range of the doorway. For he was struck at once, as I was, by the President's manner, which was hard—and the first tones of his voice were repelling. Nor did he offer me a seat. He talked standing. and both voice and manner made the impression that I was to be got rid of briefly.

I often told over this interview to friends. It was clear to Judge Coles as to myself that the President's mind was made up against General Frémont—and decidedly against me. It would be too long to give you fuller detail. Briefly, in answer to his "Well?" I explained that the general wished so much to have his attention to the letter sent, that I had brought it to make sure it would reach him. He answered, not to that, but to the subject his own mind was upon, that *"It was a war for a great national idea, the Union, and that General Frémont should not have dragged the Negro into it— that he never would if he had consulted with Frank Blair. I sent Frank there to advise him."* The words italicized are exactly those of the President.

He first mentioned the Blairs, in this astonishing connection.

It was a *parti pris,* and as we walked back Judge Coles, who heard everything, said to me, "This ends Frémont's part in the war. Seward and Montgomery Blair will see to that, and Lincoln does not seem to see the injustice, the wrong of receiving secret reports against him made by a man authorized to do so, and as everyone knows, with his mind often clouded by drink and always governed by personal motives."

The President said he would send me his answer the next day.

The next day passed and nothing came from him. But Mr. Blair, Sr., came and told me many things. I had known him always and liked him, though Mr. Frémont did not. He was very angry with me for not letting Montgomery "manage things." He talked angrily and freely, as was natural to one who had grown up to defer to him, and in his excitement uncovered the intentions of the Administration regarding the protection of slavery.

That caused me to write note number two to the President. The originals of these must have been in possession oɪ the secretaries. I have the copies which I kept for Gen. Frémont. I confined my request to asking for the promised letter, and for copies of the charges against Mr. Frémont.

In the President's answer he says "not hearing from me," he had sent the answer by mail and declined to give letters without consent of owners. Yet he acted on them injuriously to the reputation of Gen. Frémont.

I did not risk a direct telegram to Gen. Frémont, but through my English maid I sent a cipher telegram in her name to an operator at headquarters, a man we could trust, and in that way the general was warned against being trapped into any steps aimed at by a show of "friendship" from Postmaster-General Blair. I returned immediately to St. Louis and found him working to "modify" and reshape the General's course—but he had been listened to only, and my arrival ended all attempts at concealing their real conduct. I did not speak to him then, or ever again.

In a later document, the unpublished part of the biographical *Memoir* of the explorer written by his wife and son, Mrs. Frémont adds some significant details to this brief narrative. She states that when she handed the President the General's letter, "he smiled with an expression that was not agreeable," and stood under the chandelier to read it. Meanwhile, trembling with fatigue, she sat down uninvited. When he had finished, the President told her that he had already written the General, and that he knew what the Administration wished done. To this she replied that Frémont thought it would be well if Mr. Lincoln explained personally his ideas and desires, for "the General feels he is at the great disadvantage of being perhaps opposed by people in whom you have every confidence." Lincoln was a little startled. "What do you mean? Persons of different views?" he inquired. Thereupon Mrs. Frémont began to talk about the difficulty of conquering by arms alone, and the necessity of appealing to the sentiment of England and other nations by a blow against slavery; expressing ideas that had certainly not been in Frémont's head when he issued his proclamation as an effort to intimidate the farmer-guerrillas of northern Missouri. Apparently nettled, the President remarked, "You are quite a female politician." He at once went on to speak vehemently of Frémont's mistake in converting a war for the Union into a war against slavery.

Mrs. Frémont also writes that when Francis P. Blair came to see her early the next day, he grew heated. "Well," he said, "who would have expected you to do such a thing as this, to come here and find fault with the President? Look what you have done for Frémont; you have made the President his enemy!" The old editor, saying that Montgomery would talk with Frémont "and bring him to his senses," gave her to understand that five days earlier Lincoln had received from Frank Blair a letter containing various charges against Frémont; and that it was because of this letter that the Postmaster-General had been sent to St. Louis to make an examination. As she has related, she asked Lincoln in "note number two" for a copy of these charges. The President's reply was brief:

It is not exactly correct, as you say you were told by the elder Mr. Blair, to say that I sent Postmaster-General Blair to St. Louis to examine into that department and report. Postmaster-General Blair did go, with my approbation, to see and converse with Gen. Frémont as a friend. I do not feel authorized to furnish you with copies of letters in my possession, without the consent of the writers. No impression has been made on my mind against the honor or integrity of General Frémont, and I now enter my protest against being understood as acting in any hostility towards him.

Taken together, Mrs. Frémont's display of temper in Washington and Montgomery Blair's highly prejudiced report concerning affairs in St. Louis unquestionably deepened the President's feeling that Frémont had been an unfortunate choice for the Western Department. Jessie, having done irreparable harm, turned back to St. Louis. Lincoln still showed patience with the General. But Mrs. Frémont had no patience with any one. Her burning resentment against the Blairs, her belief that they

had devised a conspiracy against her husband, made her anything but a calm and prudent assistant at headquarters. She
was no sooner back at the Brant Mansion than she inspired
another of Frémont's indiscreet steps.

This was nothing less than the arrest of Frank Blair, September 18th, on a charge of insubordination. Frémont telegraphed Cameron that "information of such positive character
has come to my knowledge, implicating Col. F. P. Blair, Jr.,
1st Missouri Volunteers, in insidious and dishonorable efforts
to bring my authority into contempt with the government, and
to undermine my influence as an officer, that I have ordered
him in arrest, and shall submit charges to you for his trial." [22]

The hatred between the two men was now so intense that
neither would listen to reason regarding the other. Blair sin-
cerely believed that Frémont was a confused, incompetent
trifler whose continued control would soon lose the whole state
to the Confederates. Frémont sincerely believed that Blair was
an ambitious scoundrel, frequently drunk, and always eager
to advance his own fortunes by any means whatever. He and
Mrs. Frémont make much in their manuscript *Memoirs* of the
clothing contract and similar matters; they believed Blair willing to wreck the Union cause to satisfy his private plans and
grudges. Mrs. Frémont, as Montgomery wrote a friend, was
mainly responsible for the arrest—it was "General Jessie's
doing." The Postmaster-General sent Frémont a sensible telegram, asking his brother's release, and concluding: "This is no
time for strife except with the enemies of the country." [23] But
for a time Blair refused to be released, demanding a trial at
which his charges could be sifted. Meanwhile, St. Louis was in
a furor of excitement over the affair, and the Unionist party
suffered.

For both Frémont and the Federal cause, the episode could
hardly have occurred at a more unhappy time; for once again
a heavy military blow was about to fall.

[22] MS *Memoirs*, Bancroft Library.
[23] W. E. Smith, *The Blair Family*, II, p. 77.

The military situation in the West had developed rapidly in early September, and had now reached a point where in one quarter it offered the brightest hopes, while in another it threatened a second heavy disaster. The hopeful quarter was the Mississippi River area near and below Cairo and Paducah. Two or three days before Mrs. Frémont set off for Washington, a new brigadier-general named Ulysses S. Grant marched into Paducah, at the mouth of the Tennessee River a short distance below Cairo, and took possession of this portal to a great water-way. He had acted in the nick of time, without orders from Frémont, for Leonidas Polk was about to seize the town. Frémont deserves credit, however, for having on August 28th placed Grant in command of southeastern Missouri and southern Illinois with headquarters at Cairo; the region where the great campaign to open up the Mississippi was certain to develop. He gave Grant written instructions to take possession of points threatened by the Confederates on the Missouri and Kentucky shores. In his manuscript *Memoirs* the explorer states that he chose Grant for this position, when men near him would have sent General John Pope, because he had discerned his unusual qualities:

I believed him to be a man of great activity and of promptness in obeying orders without question or hesitation. For that reason I gave General Grant this important command at this critical period. I did not then consider him a great general, for the qualities which led him to success had not had the opportunity for their development. I selected him for qualities I could not find combined in any other man, for General Grant was of unassuming character, not given to self-elation, of dogged persistence and of iron will.[24]

Grant had the able John A. Rawlins with him.

A great part of Frémont's troops were now disposed in this quarter, and he looked forward to a rapid advance down the river. The letter he sent to Lincoln by Mrs. Frémont was pri-

[24] MS *Memoirs*, Bancroft Library.

marily an outline of this plan, and shows a genuine comprehension of the strategic situation: [25]

I...ask your attention to the position of affairs in Kentucky. As the rebel troops driven out from Missouri had invaded Kentucky in considerable force, and by occupying Union City, Hickman, and Columbus were preparing to seize Paducah and attack Cairo, I judged it impossible, without losing important advantages, to defer any longer a forward movement. For this purpose I have drawn from the Missouri side a part of the force which had been stationed at Bird's Point, Cairo, and Cape Girardeau, to Fort Holt and Paducah, of which places we have taken possession. As the rebel forces outnumber ours, and the counties of Kentucky, between the Mississippi and Tennessee Rivers, as well as those along the latter and the Cumberland, are strongly secessionist, it becomes imperatively necessary to have the cooperation of the loyal Union forces under Generals Anderson and Nelson, as well as of those already encamped opposite Louisville, under General Rousseau.

I have reinforced, yesterday, Paducah with two regiments, and will continue to strengthen the position with men and artillery. As soon as Gen. Smith, who commands there, is reinforced sufficiently to enable him to spread his forces, he will have to take and hold Mayfield and Lovelaceville, controlling in this way the mouths of both the Tennessee and the Cumberland Rivers.

Meanwhile, General Grant would take possession of the entire Cairo and Fulton Railroad, Piketown, New Madrid, and the shore of the Mississippi opposite Hickman and Columbus. The foregoing disposition having been affected, a combined attack will be made upon Columbus, and if successful in that, upon Hickman, while Rousseau and Nelson will move in concert by railroad to Nashville, Tenn., occupying the State capital, and, with an adequate force, New Providence.

The conclusion of this movement would be a combined advance toward Memphis, on the Mississippi, as well as the Memphis & Ohio Railroad, and I trust the result would be a glorious one to the country.

[25] *Official Records*, Series I, Vol. III, p. 478.

In its main outlines this was a sensible plan, which did credit to Frémont. But while the prospects in this quarter looked bright, in northwest Missouri another defeat was imminent. Here Colonel James A. Mulligan, with the Chicago Irish Brigade and some Illinois and Missouri troops, had just taken up a position at Lexington, some 160 miles up the Missouri River. Reaching it on September 9th, he had hastily thrown up entrenchments. A Confederate army under Sterling Price immediately advanced upon him from southwestern Missouri, where the battle of Wilson's Creek had brought a large influx of Confederate volunteers. Mulligan appealed for reinforcements, and labored frenziedly in gathering munitions and forage. After preliminary skirmishing, on September 18th Price began his attack in force. His army far outnumbered the Federals, and the result was never in doubt. Though the Irish soldiers made a gallant defense, their water supply was finally cut off, and on September 21st they were compelled to surrender. It was an even more stinging reverse than the defeat of Lyon. With a loss of only twenty-five men killed, Price exultantly reported the capture of 3,500 men (including home guards), 7 guns, large quantities of munitions, and $100,000 worth of commissary stores. When men realized that a small army had been lost in the center of a supposedly Union State, a tremendous cry of indignation went up. For a week the fate of Lexington had been in the balance, and the press had reported every scene in the drama to an anxious nation.

The Missouri River, though low at that season, was open. It seemed feasible to send Federal troops up it by steamboat. Union detachments were stationed at various points in northern Missouri, some within short marching distance. Why, men demanded, did not Frémont hurry reinforcements to Lexington in time? Frank Blair's organ, the *Evening News,* carried an angry editorial on September 23rd. Mulligan, it declared, had been confident "that with forty thousand friendly Federal troops within a few days' march of him," he would be rescued. "But the heroic officer calculated too largely on the coöperation of the authorities at St. Louis." They, with their 40,000 men, their vast stores of munitions, their command of all the railroads and steamboats, had let a ragged, ill-armed, unpaid Confederate army march all the way from Springfield and bag an important town, an army, and invaluable supplies.

Certainly Frémont should never have sent Mulligan to his exposed position in Lexington without guarding against movements which might cut him off. Nevertheless, he was in part the victim of circumstances. His Department, far from having 40,000 men available, was desperately poor in properly trained troops. Schuyler Colfax, arriving in St. Louis on September 14th, when the whole city was excited by news that Price was advancing upon Lexington, hurried to Frémont and asked if he could not send rescuing troops. The General replied: "Mr. Colfax, I will tell you confidentially how many men we have in St. Louis, though I would not have it published on the streets for my life. The opinion in the city is that we have 20,000 men here, and this gives us strength. If it were known here what was the actual number, our enemies would be promptly informed." He rang for the muster-rolls. They showed that the city had but 6,800 men, home guards and all; and of this force there were only two full regiments, the remainder being fragmentary, undisciplined detachments of 200 to 600 men. Said Colfax: "This is not really enough for the proper defense of St. Louis; but even so, couldn't you spare some for the emergency?" He tells us that tears stood in Frémont's eyes as the General handed him two telegrams.

One from Secretary Cameron, dated September 14th, stated that the President had determined to call upon him for "five thousand well-armed infantry, to be sent here without a moment's delay." The other was from Winfield Scott of the same date. "Detach five thousand infantry from your department, to come here without delay," it ordered, "and report the number of troops that will be left with you. The President dictates." Colfax asked Frémont if he could not expostulate with the government. "No," said he, "that would be insubordination, with which I have already been unjustly charged. The capital must be again in danger, and must be saved, even if Missouri fall and I sacrifice myself." [26]

Frémont hurriedly telegraphed Governors Morton of Indiana and Dennison of Ohio for aid, but both replied that they were under orders to send all available troops to the East. He sent orders on September 13th and 14th to Generals Pope at Palmyra, Sturgis at Mexico, and Jefferson C. Davis at Jefferson City, to march troops at once to the relief of Lexington; this a full week before the capitulation.[27] Pope promised that by the 18th he would have two full regiments of infantry, a detachment of cavalry, and 4 pieces of artillery in the threatened town, and that by the 19th he would have 4,000 soldiers there. Yet none of them arrived. Jefferson C. Davis set out, but let his troops fire into each other in the darkness, and failed to reach his objective. Sturgis came within a few miles of the river opposite Lexington, and then hearing of Price's heavy forces (which rumor exaggerated to 35,000 men), and learning that he had seized the ferries, timidly retired, though if he had hurried on he might have saved the day. In a word, three commanders showed insufficient energy, and Frémont was left to shoulder the blame for their failures.

It was now a perfect storm of abuse that he faced, and only the fervent belief of great masses of northern haters of slavery in his ability and earnestness enabled him to continue his work. After the *Evening News* published its bitter editorial on the fall of Lexington, he suppressed it for a day and arrested Blair's friend Charles G. Ramsay, its proprietor—an indiscreet step, for which friendly Eastern newspapers properly criticized him. A malignant letter appeared in the *National Intelligencer*, asking why with his 60,000 splendidly equipped soldiers, "the very élite of the West," he did not drive the half-naked, ill-armed rebels out of the state.[28] So he now had 60,000 men!

[26] Colfax tells this in *Congressional Globe*, March 7, 1862, p. 1128.
[27] Frémont Order Book, Bancroft Library.
[28] See New York *Herald*, September 21, 1861.

This letter was reprinted all over the North. Signed "A Missourian," it bore sufficient resemblance to the *Evening News* editorial to indicate that Frank Blair inspired or wrote it. Despatches from Washington declared that the President and his Cabinet were "amazed" that Frémont had failed to relieve Mulligan.[29] Meanwhile, exaggerated stories of the extravagance in his Department passed from tongue to tongue. His enemies sneered at one of his orders for 500 tons of ice, and talked of the sherry cobblers which his officers expected to enjoy; the fact being that the ice was supplied on a requisition from the surgical staff for use in Western hospitals. He was accused of surrounding himself with a set of sharpers from California, and winking at their thievery. Worst of all, Frank Blair and others gave currency to the report that he was thinking of erecting a western military republic, similar to that which Sam Houston had set up in Texas. It was a ridiculous charge, but it found believers even in Washington. Lincoln's secretary Nicolay left a sealed envelope in his manuscripts endorsed "A private paper, Conversation with the President, October 2, 1861." The first sentence ran: "Frémont ready to rebel." It is safe to say that Frémont never entertained a disloyal thought in his life.[30]

On September 26th Frank Blair, who had now been released from arrest, filed formal charges against Frémont, which through Adjutant-General Lorenzo Thomas were laid before Lincoln. They included neglect of duty, disobedience of orders, conduct unbecoming an officer, extravagance and waste, and despotic and tyrannical conduct. Among the specific charges were Frémont's alleged failure to repair to St. Louis promptly; his neglect to reinforce Lyon and Mulligan; his suffering Brigadier-General Hurlburt, "a common drunkard," to continue in command; his refusal to see people who sought him

[29] New York *Herald, Tribune,* September 23, 24, 1861.

[30] Helen N. Nicolay, *Personal Traits of Abraham Lincoln.* See Ida M. Tarbell, *Lincoln,* II, Ch. 24, for Dr. Emil Preetorius's angry statement on this charge. A shrewd St. Louis observer, he pronounces Frémont "a patriot and a most unselfish man."

on urgent public business; his violation of Presidential orders in the emancipation proclamation; and his persistence in keeping disreputable.persons in his employ. It was a blanket indictment. Every one who knew the situation in Missouri was aware that it grossly misrepresented Frémont's conduct there; every one who knew Frank Blair was aware that all his statements demanded a liberal discounting. His fits of temper were always leading him into extravagant utterances and rash acts. The Blair papers reveal that on October 7th Frank Blair was writing his brother Montgomery in the following terms:[31]

I think God has made up his mind to ruin this nation, and that the only way to save it is to kick that pack of old women who compose the Cabinet into the sea. I never since I was born imagined that such a lot of poltroons and apes could be gathered together from the four quarters of the globe as Old Abe has succeeded in bringing together in his Cabinet, and I believe that the first duty of every patriot is to stop fighting Jeff Davis and turn in on our own Government and make something out of it with which to carry on the war against the traitors. Jeff Davis and his whole crew have not done us half the harm that has been inflicted upon the country by the cowardice, ignorance, and stupidity of Lincoln's Administration.

At a later date the nation learned more about Frank Blair's infirmities of temper; in 1868 his wild utterances cost the Democratic ticket of Seymour and Blair all its slender chances of victory. But at this time his name was still potent and his charges impressed the country. The New York *Times* under Henry J. Raymond took them up and called for Frémont's dismissal. The harried commander in St. Louis could now see how much his failure to conciliate the powerful Blair clan was costing him. Whether Frémont was right or Frank Blair was right on specific matters of fact was a minor question. The major consideration was that their quarrel was dividing the Unionists of Missouri into two glowering factions, and was going far

[31] Smith, *The Blair Family*, II, pp. 83, 84.

toward paralyzing all their activities in the war. Such a division could not long be tolerated. And no matter how much of the right was on Frémont's side, Lincoln could not forget that Montgomery Blair was in his Cabinet; he, who thought constantly of the wavering border, could never forget that the Blairs were the most powerful personal force in the Border States. He was still keenly resentful of the radical demand that he make the extinction of slavery a direct object of the war, and he knew Frémont was a radical hero.

XXXI

The End of the "Hundred Days"

THE first summer of the War was passing into autumn; McClellan was still drilling his Army of the Potomac, still sneering at the Administration in letters to his wife, still exaggerating the forces of the enemy; Secretary Cameron was rapidly losing the confidence of intelligent observers; and northerners looked back upon a series of defeats—Bull Run, Ball's Bluff, Wilson's Creek, Lexington—with scarcely a victory to counterbalance them. The uneasy nation was beginning to demand that the Administration give it commanders who would move forward and win victories. To this demand, McClellan was deaf; while Frémont, with a weaker and much more poorly equipped force, was necessarily keenly aware of it. Working night and day under a sword of Damocles, he knew that within a few weeks the thread which sustained it would probably break. He had but one hope. Before those weeks expired, he must win a victory which would restore his prestige and cause the Administration to stay its hand.

Frémont had realized this fact at once when Lexington fell. Reporting the disaster to Winfield Scot, he added, in an effort to forestall criticism: "I am taking the field myself, and hope to destroy the enemy, either before or after the junction of the forces under McCulloch. Please notify the President immediately." Scott replied that the President was glad to see him hastening to the scene of action; "his words are, 'he expects you to repair the disaster at Lexington without loss of time.'"

Sterling Price, with his booty and prisoners, was retreating from Lexington to join McCulloch's army in southwestern Missouri. Frémont at once reorganized his available troops in five divisions, and ordered the commanders, Pope, McKinstry, Hunter, Sigel, and Asboth, to concentrate at Springfield, still held by the enemy. It was easy to give the order, but for the commanders to obey was a different matter; for the divisions were without adequate transportation, rations, uniforms, or munitions for a campaign. Congresman Gurley was frenziedly writing Lincoln on October 1st that the lack of supplies was scandalous, and that if Frémont were not given men, money, and arms, even St. Louis might fall.

Although Lincoln had now virtually made up his mind to re-move Frémont, with his usual patience he determined first to send Secretary Cameron, who had inclined to Frémont's side, to make a personal inquiry.[1] He gave Cameron authority to displace the General at once if he thought it expedient, but asked for careful action. The Secretary stopped in St. Louis, where he talked with the Blair-Gamble group, and received a vivid impression of the schism in the Union ranks. Near the middle of October he reached Frémont's new field headquarters at Tipton, Missouri. He found the camp in confusion, with the troops badly in need of arms, ammunition, and clothing. Evi-dently Cameron had made up his mind in St. Louis to remove Frémont, but he now—seeing the general's energy—changed it:

I had an interview with General Frémont [he wrote Lincoln on October 14th], and in conversation with him showed him an order for his removal. He is very much mortified, pained, and, I thought, humiliated. He made an earnest appeal to me, saying that he had come to Missouri, at the request of the government, to assume a very responsible command, and that when he reached this state he found himself without troops and without any preparations for an army; that he had exerted himself, as he believed, with great

[1] Attorney-General Edward Bates wrote his brother-in-law, Governor Gamble, on September 27th: "I thought (I wrote so to several of my friends at St. Louis) that Frémont would certainly be relieved, but this day I find that that result is not probable, therefore I am in deep trouble on account of our poor betrayed and sacrificed state.... General Frémont is not to be removed— at least until he has had a full opportunity to retrieve his fortunes, or to ruin our state utterly and endanger our cause."

energy, and now had around him a fine army, with everything to make success certain; that he was now in pursuit of his enemy, whom he believed were now within his reach; and that to recall him at this moment would not only destroy him, but render his whole expedition useless. In reply to this appeal, I told him that I would withhold the order until my return to Washington, giving him the interim to prove the reality of his hopes as to reaching and capturing the enemy, giving him to understand that, should he fail, he must give place to some other officer. He assured me that, should he fail, he would resign at once.[2]

Both Pope and Hunter gave Cameron a highly unfavorable opinion of Frémont's military capacity and acts, and both regarded the apparent plan of campaign with mystified astonishment. Nevertheless, Frémont was actively taking the field while McClellan, with every advantage of supplies and official support, was still drilling his army in Virginia. Cameron did well to refrain from dismissing a commander really eager to fight.

But from the moment he left St. Louis Frémont felt that he was between two enemies, the Confederates in front, his personal assailants in the rear. Frank Blair was continuing his attacks with increasing bitterness. Released from arrest at Montomery's request on September 24th, he had been stung to rage by rebukes from Frémont, who accused him of using his family position to lay deliberately false statements before the President. In submitting his formal charges against Frémont, Blair published a letter to Adjutant-General Lorenzo Thomas which answered this accusation in withering terms.[3] For this and his continued efforts to undermine the General, Frémont had him rearrested; and though this episode was soon terminated, it left him (as his biographer says) a raging lion. With Blair against him, with provisional-Governor Gamble against him, with several of his own generals against him, Frémont was in an agonizing position. Just before leaving St.

---

[2] Nicolay and Hay, *Lincoln*, IV, p. 430.
[3] Published in New York *Herald*, October 9, 1861.

Louis for the field he poured out his bitter emotions in a letter
to a New York friend:[4]

I...send you this hurried note in the midst of the last arrangements before leaving.

We have to contend with an enemy having no posts to garrison
and no lines of transportation to defend or guard, whose whole
force can be turned at will to any one point, while we have from
Leavenworth and from Fort Scott to Paducah to keep protected.

I wish to say to you that, though the position is difficult, I am
competent to it, and also to meet the enemy in the field. I am not
able at the same time to attend to the enemy at home. It is a shame
to the country that an officer going to the field, his life in his hands,
solely actuated by the desire to serve his country and win for himself its good opinions, with no other objects, should be destroyed
by a system of concentrated attacks utterly without foundation.
Charges are spoken of when there are none to be made. What is the
object of the repetition of these falsehoods, except to familiarize the
public mind to the idea that something is wrong? Already our
credit, which was good, is shaken in consequence of the newspaper
intimations of my being removed. Money is demanded by those
furnishing supplies. To defend myself would require the time that
is necessary to and belongs to my duty against the enemy. If permitted by the country, this state of things will not fail to bring on
disorder....My private character comes in only incidentally. I defend it because, naturally, his reputation is dear to any man; but
only incidentally. This is the foundation of many of my acts, and
will be if I stay here. Everything that hurts, impedes, or embarrasses
the work entrusted to me I strike at without hesitation. I take the
consequences. The worst that can happen to me is relief from great
labor.

The advance toward southwestern Missouri in pursuit of
Price's retreating army lurched forward as rapidly as unfavorable circumstances would allow. When Frémont and his staff

4 Published in St. Louis *Democrat*, September 28, 1861. This journal, like the
Republic, was as friendly to Frémont as the *Evening News* was hostile. But
Frank Blair believed that Frémont had obtained their friendship by a mixture
of threats and material inducements.

reached Jefferson City on September 27, 1861, they found a
multitude of difficulties awaiting them at Camp Lilly, as the
place had been named in honor of his daughter. A thousand
wagons sent him from the East had proved to be made of rotten
wood, and were breaking down everywhere on the roads and
in the streets.[5] By October 7th, all the troops which Frémont
had been able to collect were on the road for Tipton, one hundred sixty miles from St. Louis, where they again paused.
Rations were scanty, and sometimes the men were on half their
proper allowance of food. Large herds of cattle had to be collected by foraging parties and tons of corn brought in to be
ground at Frémont's portable mills. The dearth of horses and
vehicles continued, and the march, as one young aide said, was
a continual "wait for the wagon."

Yet the obstacles were slowly overcome, and Frémont's hopes
rose higher and higher. Writing to Jessie in St. Louis, he declared that his men would emulate the fine marches of the
California Battalion. "The army is in the best of spirits, and
before we get through I will show you a little California prac-
tise, that is, if we are not interrupted." Dreams of a spectacular
achievement floated before his eyes. He would scatter Price's
army and push rapidly on south. "My plan is New Orleans
straight," he wrote, "Foote to join on the river below. I think
it can be done gloriously, especially if secrecy can be kept. . . .
It would precipitate the war forward and end it soon and vic-
toriously." [6]

Mid-October found his steadily growing army under way for
Warsaw on the Osage River, where the fleeing Price had burned
the bridge behind him. Here a trained engineer, using men
from the ranks, succeeded in stretching a pontoon bridge, eight
hundred feet long, across the stream within thirty-six hours.
Some of the lumber came from the demolition of old houses,
but most of it was cut green in the neighboring woods. It was
no sooner finished than the army was streaming forward again

[5] John R. Howard, *Remembrance of Things Past*, Ch. 19.
[6] Jessie Benton Frémont, *The Story of the Guard*, pp. 72ff., 85.

upon Springfield, the key to that section of the state and the city near which Lyon had met defeat two months earlier. The General had communicated his dream of a march down the Mississippi to his men, and the watchword went about: "New Orleans and home again by summer!" [7]

Frémont paid little heed to obstacles in this march, and where horses and wagons were lacking, sent off into the country about for them. He had established supply depots with about a million rations at Tipton and two million at Jefferson City; but he was enough of a frontiersman to know how to subsist in large part on the country and to meet problems as they arose. Food taken from loyal citizens was paid for in government orders; that taken from secessionists was simply confiscated.[8] Most of his division commanders showed the same spirit and coöperated zealously in the advance. The glaring exception was John Pope, whose unexpected failure to reinforce Mulligan at Lexington, after promising to do so, still rankled in Frémont's mind. "Pope," said Frank Blair later, out of intimate knowledge,[9] "is a braggart and a liar, with some courage, perhaps, but not much capacity." Rising in time to high command, he made an utter botch of his brief campaign against Lee. He had done well in stamping out the guerrilla warfare in northern Missouri, but he now showed nothing less than a spirit of insubordination.

When Frémont ordered him to join in the forward movement, Pope wrote Hunter that he was stupefied by the way in which the General ignored actual conditions. "There is not transportation enough," he declared, "to move this army one hundred yards." He complained that the troops had not been properly organized into brigades and divisions, and that he had no supply trains or cavalry. These statements were partly inaccurate, and showed a disposition to magnify every possible difficulty. The ragged, ill-armed, ill-supplied Confederates,

[7] *Ibid.*, pp. 45, 46.
[8] MS *Memoirs*, Bancroft Library.
[9] Welles, *Diary*, I, pp. 104, 119.

living on the country, found no difficulty in moving where they liked. Pope had caught the spirit of contempt for Frémont in certain St. Louis and Washington circles, and knew that powerful men would only too gladly support his recalcitrance. To Hunter, he wrote a few days later in a tone of sheer impudent scorn of his commander: [10]

I received your note yesterday morning and I am really sorry I could not come down to see you before I left Syracuse. I am anxious to know the result of the Secretary's visit and its object. Upon his action on the subject, in my judgment, rests the safety of this command from great suffering. If we attempt to go south of the Osage without supplies for at least a month, and without much better preparation for everything that exists now, I do not believe that one half of these troops will ever return alive. The winter is coming on us. The men of this division are without overcoats, their clothes in rags, and only one blanket apiece; no provision trains or depots organized, and, so far as I can see, no object in view.

I shall, however, move from here and occupy the point designated, with five regiments, being all I can get anything like transportation for. I can, perhaps, carry eight or ten days' rations for the five regiments by making very short marches....

Each division commander is left to himself. I don't know where to look for provisions short of St. Louis, or where for quartermaster or any other stores, short of the same place, neither do I know to whom I can apply for anything this side of St. Louis. I have written and telegraphed for 300,000 rations, as I intend to establish at Otterville a depot of provisions and of such stores as I can get for my own command. Altogether, this is the most remarkable campaign I ever saw, heard of, or read of.

Frémont was led by his scouts to believe that at a point a little beyond Springfield the Confederates would face about and give battle. We now know that this was actually their intention. Price wrote his superiors: [11]

[10] Copy in Frémont MSS, dated October 18, 1861; Compare *Official Records,* Series I, Vol. III, p. 527.

[11] *Official Records,* Series I, Vol. III, pp. 731, 732.

I am now falling back on Pineville, where General McCulloch and myself have concluded to make a stand. Should the Federal forces advance from Springfield for the purpose of attacking us, we will act on the defensive, depending on the rugged nature of the country to compensate for any inequality in numbers. Our position will be so chosen that we will be able to make our artillery effective. . . .

McCulloch also wrote that he had agreed with Price to fight a battle in Missouri, although the combined Confederate armies amounted only to about seventeen thousand men, and he feared the outcome. Pineville is a county seat in the extreme southwestern corner of Missouri. But Pope, Hunter, and the Washington authorities, lacking Frémont's special information, felt almost certain that the Confederates would not pause until they were safe in the wilds of Arkansas, and that Frémont was conducting a wildgoose chase. To Pope, it seemed a criminal enterprise, and he wrote Hunter:[12]

When our forces have succeeded in reaching Neosho, or Arkansas itself, what is to be accomplished, or rather what does any sane man suppose will be the result? The prospect before us is appalling, and we seem to be led by madmen. Of course, Gen. Frémont and the men around him, whose official existence depends upon his not being superseded, are desperate. But should they be permitted to drag to destruction, or at least to great and unnecessary suffering, the 30,000 men of this army, for no other purpose than to save, if possible, their own official lives?

While Major Zagonyi and his so-called Frémont Bodyguard of picked cavalrymen, 150 strong, were delivering a victorious and memorable charge against the Confederate garrison at Springfield,[13] and while Frémont's army was pushing beyond that town, the sands of the President's patience were running out. He feared the loss of invaluable troops in the hills of

[12] Copy in Frémont MSS; Pope to Hunter, October 26, 1861.
[13] For accounts of this spirited affair see Moore, *Rebellion Record,* III, pp. 235-239. Zagonyi had three companies, while the garrison numbered 2,000 men. Zagonyi wrote that he had never seen such bravery as his cavalry showed: "Their war cry, 'Frémont and the Union,' broke forth like thunder."

Arkansas. Adjutant-General Lorenzo Thomas had gone to St. Louis with Cameron and made an inspection of his own; and upon his return he published a report caustically arraigning Frémont for incompetence, extravagance, and irregularity.[14] Thomas had moved exclusively in the Blair circle in Missouri and formed his conclusions there. He declared, naturally enough, that in the opinion of many observers Frémont "is more fond of the pomp than of the realities of the war—that his mind is incapable of fixed attention or strong concentration—that by his mismanagement of affairs since his arrival in Missouri, the State has almost been lost—and that if he is continued in command the worst results may be anticipated." This conclusion he supported by a series of hearsay allegations. Obviously, none but a prejudiced witness would talk about the state being lost when order was wholly restored and the last important Confederate force was scurrying for Arkansas. It was widely known that Thomas disliked Frémont, that he had opposed Frémont's appointment, and that from the beginning he had spoken abusively of Frémont.[15] It was also obvious that his allegations, when analyzed, contained little specific evidence. He reported that there had been irregularities in the pay department, and that the chief paymaster complained of improper orders; that the quartermaster in St. Louis instanced confused and irregular requisitions; and that many people were suspicious of the contracts Frémont had let. While all this was true, irregularities and fraudulent contracts marked every stage of the initial war effort East and West, from Cameron's office down; the country could better condone them than excessive caution and inactivity. Of such evidence as a court of law would admit Thomas offered little. Nevertheless, as a general impression his report was damaging.

And, unfortunately for Frémont, Thomas by no means stood alone. General Hunter had categorically told Cameron that he

---

[14] *Official Records,* Series I, Vol. III, p. 540ff.; New York *Tribune,* October 30, 1861.

[15] Jessie Benton Frémont, *Story of the Guard,* pp. 86, 87.

did not think Frémont fit for the command. Lincoln had hoped that Frémont would make Hunter his adviser and guide; but the two had not got on—Hunter underrated Frémont, and Frémont, thinking that Hunter wished to harass him, detached him for a comparatively unimportant field command. Brigadier-General S. R. Curtis of St. Louis expressed the same conclusion. "In my judgment," he wrote the President, "General Frémont lacks the intelligence, the experience, and the sagacity necessary to his command." [16]

At the same time Elihu B. Washburne, who visited St. Louis at the head of a Congressional subcommittee upon government contracts, wrote members of the Administration that "such robbery, fraud, extravagance, peculation as have developed in Frémont's department can hardly be conceived of." He spoke of a "horde of pirates" ruining the credit of the government.[17] His phraseology was exaggerated; he had accepted without independent investigation the stories of the Blair circle and of some disappointed contractors; moreover, he was an economical Yankee (later known in Congress as a Treasury Watchdog) who had not yet grasped the fact that it is impossible to wage war without a lavish expenditure. All Frémont's contracts for fortification, supplies, foodstuffs, arms, steamboats, and so on, totaled only about twelve million dollars. At the moment, however, Washburne's voice carried great weight. Moreover, even men cordially disposed toward Frémont joined the chorus of criticism. Gustav Koerner wrote his wife that the confusion was preposterous and that he might resign at any time. The evidence for the essential features of the indictment against the General seemed overwhelming.

It was a bizarre situation. It was bizarre in that the commander of the West, while thus denounced as incompetent by

[16] Nicolay and Hay, *Lincoln,* IV, Ch. 24. A friend of Governor Gamble's in Washington, Charles Gibson, also preferred charges against Frémont to the President; Gibson to Gamble, September 27, 1861 (Gamble Papers).

[17] See his letter to Chase, October 31, 1861 (Chase MSS). Gideon Welles states that Washburne had the reputation of being the meanest man in the House; *Diary,* I, p. 234.

a vigorous group in Missouri and by the Administration's best observers, was regarded with admiring devotion by his army, applauded by most Unionists of the state, and looked upon as a hero by nearly all the radicals of the North. It was bizarre in that Frémont, exalted one hour by his expectation of crushing Price's army and turning triumphantly against the Confederates on the Mississippi, was depressed the next by Pope's and Hunter's insubordination and the fear of a sudden removal. His letters to Jessie show a feverish alternation of hope and despair. Just as he had the West well in hand, he felt that he was being stabbed in the back. "I assure you I am getting pretty well tired of being badgered in this way," he wrote, with an express threat of resignation.[18] To drop his load would be a relief, he added; but he could not think calmly of the scoundrels who were throwing away brave lives and imperiling the war to gratify their base ambitions.

To Lincoln it appeared that a change was imperative. Yet even at the last he acted with characteristic forbearance. Attorney-General Bates's diary shows that as late as October 22nd the Cabinet hesitated, with Seward, Chase, and Cameron all for delay, and the President in "painful and mortifying doubt." On October 24th, Lincoln wrote an order relieving Frémont from his command, which was to be given to General Hunter; and he despatched it by a personal friend to General Curtis in St. Louis:

Dear Sir [he wrote Curtis], On receipt of this, with the accompanying enclosures, you will take safe, certain, and suitable measures to have the enclosure addressed to Major-General Frémont delivered to him with all reasonable dispatch, subject to these conditions only, that if, when General Frémont shall be reached by the messenger—yourself or anyone sent by you—he shall then have, in personal command, fought and won a battle, or shall then be in the immediate presence of the enemy in expectation of a battle, it is not to be delivered, but held for further orders. After, and not

[18] Jessie Benton Frémont, *The Story of the Guard,* p. 174ff.

till after, the delivery to General Frémont, let the inclosure addressed to General Hunter be delivered to him.

Under these circumstances, the final scene of the "hundred days" was played out. Frémont's army on November 2nd was encamped just beyond Springfield, with all dispositions made for an immediate advance and battle; for on information furnished him by Generals Sigel and Asboth, division commanders, he learned that the advance guard of the enemy was on Wilson's Creek, nine miles distant. The spirit of the troops was high. With nearly all of them the commander was enormously popular, and they were convinced that a victory was at hand. He was serenaded and cheered at every opportunity. The official messenger with the order of dismissal entered the camp by stratagem, and after much difficulty in gaining an audience was taken at nightfall before Frémont.

The general [he tells us], was sitting at the end of quite a long table facing the door by which I entered. I never can forget the appearance of the man as he sat there, with his piercing eye and his hair parted in the middle. I ripped from my coat lining the document, which had been sewed in there, and handed the same to him, which he nervously took and opened. He glanced at the superscription, and then at the signature at the bottom, not looking at the contents. A frown came over his brow, and he slammed the papers down on the table and said, "Sir, how did you get admission into my lines?" [19]

Frémont had lost his command—lost it under circumstances of the most humiliating character. Many of his officers were dismissed with him, without pay, on the ground that their commissions had been irregularly issued. But the sting of the blow was largely taken away by the outburst of feeling which it produced in his army and all over the North.

The intelligence, spreading like a prairie fire through the camps at Springfield, aroused indescribable indignation and

[19] Tarbell, *Lincoln*, II, Ch. 24. Frémont writes: "The order had been hurried forward by General Hunter, who superseded me." *Battles and Leaders*, I, p. 287.

excitement.[20] Officers by the dozen declared they would resign at once. Many companies threw down their arms, saying they would fight under nobody but Frémont. Impromptu mass-meetings were held in every tented street. The General had to spend much of the evening expostulating with officers and men and urging them to stick by their posts. The German soldiers talked loudly of resisting General Hunter when he came to assume command, and Frémont felt impelled to issue strict orders that there should be no insubordination and no demonstration when he left. Finally the troops quieted down, but their spirit was gone. "It would be impossible to exaggerate the gloom which pervaded our camps," wrote the New York *Herald's* correspondent of the scene the next morning, "and nothing but General Frémont's urgent endeavors prevented it from ripening into general mutiny." Hunter was delayed in arriving to assume the command. Every one believed still that the enemy was close in front, and that but for this change of command a decisive success might have been achieved. Finally, toward evening of November 3rd, Frémont promised the officers who thronged his quarters that if Hunter did not arrive, he would lead the army to the attack next morning.

There ensued one of the strangest scenes of the war. "I never saw anything at all approaching the excitement this announcement created," wrote an observer.[21] Officers ran from the headquarters shouting the news. Men threw their hats in air. Wave after wave of cheering arose, spreading from camp to camp and growing more remote as distant regiments heard the news. Band after band began to play, and soon twelve of them were massed in front of the General's tent, serenading him simultaneously. The universal depression changed to exultant joy, and everybody prepared to start for the battle-field at daylight. A battle might soon have taken place, for McCulloch really did await the attack. He later reported to the Confederate gov-

20 New York *Herald*, Springfield correspondence, November 3, 4, 1861.
21 *Ibid.*, November 8, 1861.

ernment that he intended to turn and fight, the ground to be selected by Price and himself.

But unfortunately for the soldiers' hopes, at ten that night Hunter arrived. Frémont handed over the command, and prepared to leave the next day. The generals spent two hours in conference, and Frémont outlined his plan of battle. But Hunter had received strict orders from Lincoln that he was not to continue a risky pursuit of the elusive Confederates. "You are not likely to overtake Price," wrote Lincoln, "and are in danger of making too long a line from your own base of supplies and reinforcements." The President clearly implied his condemnation of what he supposed to be Frémont's general strategy: "While, as stated in the beginning of the letter, a large discretion must be and is left with yourself, I feel sure that an indefinite pursuit of Price, or an attempt by this long and circuitous route to reach Memphis, will be exhaustive beyond endurance, and will end in the loss of the whole force engaged in it."

In St. Louis, the news of Frémont's arrival produced the same shock of excitement and anger, followed by the same general gloom. Citizens put their flags at half mast or draped them with black. Soldiers dashed their arms to the cobblestones in the streets, declaring that they were through with the war. The local authorities were fearful, as on an earlier occasion when a false rumor of Frémont's dismissal had been published, that a mob would lynch Frank Blair and his associates, and the angriest threats were heard against Blair's life. When Frémont arrived in the city on November 8th he was met by a tumultuous assemblage, which welcomed him with bands of music, and cheering vociferously, surrounded his headquarters. A committee of German-Americans read a complimentary address, and handed him a set of resolutions, declaring that "we recognize in John C. Frémont the embodiment of our patriotic feeling and political faith," that "he has performed his arduous and responsible tasks with all possible energy and honesty," and that they believed that "a wise Providence may have reserved him for a still wider sphere of action in future times." [22] Jessie, who had denounced the treatment of her husband, left to organize and lead his army without money or the moral aid of the government, as "treason," was with him to lend her comfort and voice a resentment which he never publicly expressed.

Unquestionably, Lincoln did wisely in removing Frémont. The antagonisms he had aroused would alone have made his continuance in command impossible. Nevertheless, a great body of observers in Missouri believed then and always that he had acted, not merely with high patriotism, but with sagacity and efficiency. Many members of his command defended both his integrity and devotion. One of his soldiers, George E. Waring, Jr., later eminent as a civic leader in New York, records in his autobiography: "He was the life and the soul of his army, and it was cruelly wronged in his removal." The views of his adherents are well expressed in a letter which W. G. Eliot, later president of Washington University, a close and shrewd observer of Missouri events, had written Secretary Chase late in October:[23]

I can easily understand that to unfriendly eyes Gen. Frémont may have laid himself open to censure in many particulars. There has been at times a degree of military demonstration, a seeming tendency to extravagant parade, a boldness in taking responsibility even at the risk of exceeding his authority, that has surprised and alarmed the semi-loyal. Even some hearty Unionists have doubted his wisdom and desired a greater degree of conciliation and caution. But we must consider the extreme difficulty of his position. Many things which would be wrong in time of peace, are right and wise in time of war, and promptness of action is sometimes better than

[22] *Appleton's Annual Cyclopaedia,* 1861, p. 494.

[23] Frémont MSS. Eliot (of the same family as the president of Harvard) was a bold opponent of slavery, an active assistant of Lyon and Blair in the opening days of the war, and one of the leaders in the Western Sanitary Commission—the appointment of which by Frémont was an important and valuable act. It has been said of him (*Appleton's Cyclopaedia of Biography,* II, 325) that "he was engaged in all sorts of public and philanthropic enterprises, and has probably done more for the advancement of St. Louis and all the Southwest than any other man that has ever lived in that section." His judgment demands respect.

caution and refusal to take responsibility. It should be remembered that Frémont assumed command at a time of the greatest difficulty, just after the Manassas disaster, when the Union cause was at the lowest ebb. He found St. Louis terribly demoralized. The Secessionists were in ecstasies, and had little doubt of speedy success. One of them openly said to me that "there was a bullet moulded for every Yankee Abolitionist in St. Louis." Many of our wealthiest men openly declared themselves for the South. At one of the most conspicuous corners of the city, Fifth and Pine Streets, in the well-known Berthold mansion, the Confederate headquarters were established, with the Confederate flag conspicuously flying, and recruits were openly enlisted for the Confederate cause. The city authorities did not dare to interfere. There was not a United States flag to be seen anywhere, and Union men spoke with bated breath. The city was not secure from insurrection or the State from secession.

Now without going into details, at the end of two or three weeks after Frémont's arrival, everything was changed. The Union flag went up and the Confederate flag came down. The secession headquarters were closed, and troops of Union soldiers from Iowa and Illinois and Missouri poured into the city attracted by the prestige of Frémont's name. The bold demonstration of strength created strength. The prompt declaration of martial law throughout the State, by many denounced as an extreme measure, held in check the disloyal tendencies, and in a short time gave a totally new aspect to affairs. By erection of earthworks around the city, employment at high wages was given to two or three thousand discontented laborers, all of whom were required to take the oath of allegiance, thus controlling effectually the most unruly part of the population.

The general result is that the city is now safe from attack or insurrection. The defences around it are equal to an army of 20,000 men for resisting an attacking force, and for the control of the city itself. I do not know that they were strictly necessary from a military point of view, but the moral effect has been great, and if any unexpected reverses should occur, they will be of great use. So long as the city is held, the pacification of the State is only a question of time. St. Louis may be now regarded as a thoroughly loyal city. The thought of secession is getting to be absurd. Such is now the public sentiment of the better classes and the final settlement seems sure.

I do not claim that the whole credit of this great change belongs to Frémont, but he has been the responsible leader, and as the blame of every disaster is laid upon him, he should have a measurable share of the praise for what is good. A commander-in-chief is properly judged by the general effect of his administration, rather than by the special incidents of progress. He is sorely blamed for not sending reinforcements to General Lyon, but I doubt if he could have done so consistently with his more imperative duties in the occupation of Cairo and Bird's Point, which were sharply threatened by the Confederate forces. The official documents will show.

I have almost no personal acquaintance with Gen. Frémont, and have nothing to lose or gain through him, except as a loyal citizen of Missouri. I am pleading not for him, but for the cause he represents. He is now at the head of an enthusiastic army, almost in the presence of the enemy. It would not only be unjust and unfair but unwise, to supersede him until a battle is fought.

But outside Missouri a great number of Frémont's adherents cared little about defending the details of his military administration. He had become a symbol. To a multitude in the North and the West his name stood for the radical demand that the abolition of slavery be made an object of the war. If the modification of his proclamation had caused a storm, his removal now aroused a perfect hurricane of wrath. The very threat of it had checked recruiting in Ohio and other states. Many felt implicit confidence in him, and no attack by Frank Blair or Lorenzo Thomas could shake it. In Cincinnati a great county mass meeting had cheered his proclamation "with the wildest outburst of continued applause that was ever witnessed" there, "screaming, yelling, stamping, whooping, throwing hats, and embracing each other." [24] In New England men had agreed with Garrison's *Liberator,* which greeted it with a *"Laus Deo,"* as "the beginning of the end." Ben Wade had written Frémont in the middle of October that "all your enemies have yet been able

[24] Chase MSS, September 15th, to October 1st, contain many letters defending Frémont and picturing the popular anger over his treatment.

to do has not in the least shaken the unbounded confidence which the people have ever had in you, and we all hope you will persevere in the course you have thus far pursued. No greater misfortune could befall the country than that you should retire at this period." [25] Now that the blow had fallen thousands were embittered and angry. Whittier wrote:

> Thy error, Frémont, simply was to act
> A brave man's part, without the statesman's tact,
> And, taking counsel but of common sense,
> To strike at cause as well as consequence.
> O, never yet since Roland wound his horn
> At Roncesvalles, has a blast been blown
> Far-heard, wide-echoing, startling as thine own,
> Heard from the van of Freedom's hope forlorn!

Secretary Chase's confidential agent in St. Louis had informed him at the first ill-founded report of Frémont's removal that "if the President had emptied the arsenals of the government into the camps of the rebels, he could not have so effectively strengthened them." His agent in Pittsburgh wrote him that some capitalists there were so enraged that they would not put a cent into government securities:

Is it known to the Administration [demanded the editor of the Cincinnati *Gazette* in a letter to Chase], that the West is threatened with a revolution? Could you have been among the people yesterday, and witnessed the excitement; could you have seen sober citizens pulling from their walls and trampling under foot the portrait of the President; and could you hear today the expressions of all classes of men, of all political parties, you would, I think, feel as I feel, and as every sincere friend of the government must feel, alarmed.

Professor C. E. Stowe of Andover, Massachusetts, wrote in the same terms: "I wish you could hear the voices of surprise, indignation, disgust and contempt which now everywhere find

[25] Frémont MSS, Bancroft Library.

utterance at the removal of Frémont. The feeling is frightfully earnest." Few believed that the reports of Meigs, Cameron, and Thomas were fair. "The thing," declared Simeon Nash of Gallipolis, Ohio, "has been done in a way to destroy public confidence in its honesty." Another correspondent wrote Chase that he had just returned from a tour as far west as Iowa, and that "I never have seen such excitement, such deep indignant feeling everywhere I have travelled." [26]

"Where are you," demanded Thaddeus Stevens of his fellow-radicals in Congress, "that you let the hounds run down your friend Frémont?" Stevens was a formidable political figure, and he did not stand alone. A mass meeting at Cooper Institute on November 27, 1861, listened to an oration by Charles Sumner warmly laudatory of Frémont, and—with Schuyler Colfax, David Dudley Field, Charles King, William M. Evarts, and other distinguished men on the platform—adopted resolutions indorsing his doctrine upon the emancipation of the slaves of rebels. Henry Ward Beecher asked the General to come to Plymouth Church one Sunday morning, and in his sermon harshly condemned Daniel Webster as a statesman who had timidly compromised with slavery. "He died, and is dead," said Beecher. "But," turning to Frémont, "your name will live and be remembered by a nation of freemen."

If from the voice of his contemporaries Frémont could derive much comfort, he could feel a little later that he had been publicly vindicated. The Committee on the Conduct of the War, after an elaborate investigation, reported in the spring of 1863 that he was not to blame for the failure to reinforce Lyon or Mulligan; that he had acted with energy and promptness; that various of his measures, such as the building of gunboats, had been of the highest value; and that his administration of the Western Department "was eminently characterized by earnestness, ability, and the most unquestionable loyalty." Its members, Ben Wade, Zachariah Chandler, John Covode, and George W. Julian, were politically sympathetic toward Frémont, yet

[26] Chase MSS, especially November 4, 5, 6, 1861.

their verdict carried weight. In Congress, his record was enthusiastically defended by Schuyler Colfax, Roscoe Conkling, and others, though Colfax regarded himself as a family friend of the Blairs.

The consensus of historical opinion has been less kind. James Ford Rhodes, John Fiske, and Nicolay and Hay have all agreed that Frémont's record shows that he was poorly fitted for the command which he took. In this judgment they are unquestionably right. He was deficient in ability to organize the complex and multifarious activities of his Department, his estimate of men was highly faulty, he showed a signal lack of tact, and his characteristic impulsiveness led him into a cardinal and fatal error—the emancipation proclamation, which he should never have issued without consulting the President. A man with genuine military genius would have managed to save Mulligan, and possibly Lyon as well; Frémont showed no spark of that rare quality. A leader with more address and adaptability would never have estranged Blair and his supporters so completely and quickly as Frémont did. He admitted to the Committee on the Conduct of the War that he had done much war business "a little loosely"; that a great deal in the Department "was not consistent with strict military propriety, a great deal." He never learned to coördinate his forces properly, and in his military plans, as in all else, he remained something of a dreamer— prone, as General Curtis said, to "dash at a shadow."

But this is not all the story, and most historians have done less than justice to Frémont. His earnestness, zeal, and patriotism were above question. He labored with almost superhuman energy, and gave his best talents to the cause. The difficulties of his position, tossed as he suddenly was into a Department without organization, money, arms, or stores, without anything but raw recruits, asked not merely to raise and use armies but to equip them, left to shift largely for himself by an Administration intent upon the eastern front, and compelled to deal with sedition at home as well as organized enemies in the field, can hardly be exaggerated. They would have tried the capacities of the ablest men. Grant himself might have failed. With all his shortcomings, Frémont in three months did bring an army into being, did virtually clear Missouri of the enemy, did order gunboats, tugs, and motor-boats, and take other practical measures important for the future, and did help to place in Kentucky a force and a commander, the then unknown Grant, who were destined to win the first real victories of the War.[27]

[27] For a generous estimate of Frémont's constructive services in Missouri, see William Wood, *Captains of the Civil War* (Yale Chronicles of America), p. 119. See also T. Harry Williams, "Frémont and the Politicians," *Journal of the American Military History Foundation*, II, No. 4. Ben Wade wrote Charles A. Dana, a few days after Frémont concluded his testimony before the Committee on the Conduct of the War, a remarkable letter, in which he bitterly asserted that the general was the innocent victim of a wicked plot, and that "no public man since Admiral Byng...has suffered so unjustly as General Frémont." Dana Papers, Library of Congress, February 3, 1862.

XXXII

The Mountain Department

WHEN Frémont left the army at Springfield and with the Zagonyi Guard and his personal staff as escort set out for the railhead at Rolla, his associates were struck by his gaiety; as he cantered along, he laughed and chatted like a schoolboy set free for a holiday. These high spirits remained with him in St. Louis. He busied himself for a fortnight collecting documentary evidence upon the transactions of the Western Department, to be used in his defense. He continued to suffer various humiliations. Not merely was the Zagonyi Guard mustered out without pay, quarters, or rations, on the ground that at Springfield they had expressed disloyal sentiments, but all his contracts had been suspended, and officers were now sent from Washington to determine whether the bills he had incurred should be paid. Yet his aides tell us that the Brant mansion resounded with vivacity and humor. The General, wrote one in his diary, was "absolutely on the rampage with fun and fire. Our table is about the jolliest, most sociable, most enjoyable spot of its kind that I have experienced." [1]

Underneath this buoyancy, however, lay a smoldering sense of injustice; and from this moment Frémont was a confirmed opponent of the Administration. He shared the belief of many Republicans that its military, political, and diplomatic policies were inept and inefficient. His papers show that, feeling he had been grossly wronged, he was convinced that part of the Administration—especially the Blair element—had acted under the influence of selfish and malignant motives. Why had it failed

[1] John R. Howard, MS Diary, November 16, 1861.

to supply him with funds and munitions? Why, at the moment when Mulligan was reported in danger and every man was needed at Paducah, had it stripped his command of 5,000 well-armed troops, not revoking the order till the harm was done? Why had Secretary Cameron and General Thomas left him in command when they thought he was stuck fast in the mud at Tipton, but removed him when he had extricated himself and was about to defeat Price or drive him from the state?

Jessie's wrath exceeded his own. Her indignation was so intense that for a time it led her to believe that Frémont was the victim of a traitorous conspiracy on the part of the Blairs. Throughout the hundred days, her anxieties and labors had matched those of her husband. In a curious scrap of autobiography, she tells us that when Frémont was in pursuit of Price a well-known St. Louis merchant, Thornton Grimsley, had come and told her that confidential information of the Union movements was being treacherously smuggled to Price's headquarters, and that the enemy was thus aware that neither Hunter's nor Pope's divisions would join Frémont's army. Mrs. Frémont, in a frenzy of anxiety, hurried a trusted Negro off with the news to her husband. She was oppressed all day by fears of some frightful disaster. That night at dinner her cousin, Mrs. Brant, remarked: "We have had such a rain to-day that I can't understand why your hair is all dusty." Nobody thought more of the subject; but the next morning her English maid began combing the hair, and stopped suddenly with tears in her eyes. "It had been a chestnut brown," writes Mrs. Frémont, "but now every hair was marked with an alternating white patch about an inch apart, giving an odd look of mottled gray to the whole." [2] At this time she was only thirty-six.

If this indicates the emotional stress under which she had labored, another autobiographical fragment indicates how sternly she nursed her wrath. Returning to New York, the Frémonts stayed for a time at the Astor House, where they

[2] Jessie Benton Frémont MSS, Bancroft Library.

received much attention from radical Senators and Congress-
men; they then took apartments on Fourth Avenue, and shortly
went to Washington, so that Frémont might aid the investigation into the Western Department. Early in 1862 they were
invited to the famous party of February 5th at the White
House, the last really brilliant social occasion till the war
ended. Many members of Washington society refused; a friend
told Jessie that Mrs. Lincoln had shown her eighty declina-
tions, among them one by Senator Wade, who wrote upon the
card: "Are the President and Mrs. Lincoln aware that there
is a civil war? If they are not, Mr. and Mrs. Wade are, and
for that reason decline to participate in feasting and dancing."
But the President sent a messenger to say that he especially
desired Frémont to be present, and they joined the five hundred
guests. The morning before the ball Dorothea Dix told Jessie
that she had just left the White House, where Lincoln was
deeply perturbed by the illness of his son Willie:[3]

The President spoke of the ball, and wanted to stop it, but it
came off. The only alteration made was that there was no dancing.
It was announced officially that on account of the illness in the
house there would be no dancing; but the Marine Band at the foot
of the steps filled the house with music while the boy lay dying
above. A sadder face than that of the President I have rarely seen.
He was receiving at the large door of the East Room, speaking
to the people as they came, but feeling so deeply that he spoke of
what he felt and thought, instead of welcoming the guests. To Gen.
Frémont he at once said that his son was very ill and that he feared
for the result. On seeing his sad face and grieved appearance, the
feeling with which we had gone gave way to pity, and after expressing our hopes for the lad's recovery we passed on to make
our respects to the President's wife. The ball was becoming a ghastly
failure....
The political feeling of the country was represented there that
night by strangers, members of Congress, and persons brought down

[3] *Ibid.* Willie, who had taken a cold which turned into fever, died February
20th. The doctor had said before the party that there was as yet no reason for
alarm, and Jessie's account is characteristically overdrawn.

to Washington by the business of the war. Uniforms and ladies' evening dress gave their brightness, but almost angry feeling for and against emancipation, and for a quick sharp conduct of the war, found its expression there that night. The President was so sad, so bowed down by the thought of the coming loss of his son, that it seemed to depress the company, and they shifted around until the larger portion had congregated on the other side of the East Room, where Gen. Frémont was standing. The whole talk was on the necessary peremptory pursuit of the war to make the South realize that it could not maintain slavery under the protection of the North.

So many criticized the conduct of the war and...there was so much feeling of sorrow that Gen. Frémont's policy of emancipation was not to be carried out, that it became embarrassing, and we left. I had hardly got my wraps on before we were recalled by Mr. Sumner, who came with a message from the President saying that he wanted us to return, that he specially wanted Gen. Frémont. It seemed the President had found that Gen. McClellan and Gen. Frémont had never met....

As we crossed the long East Room, the President came forward to meet the General; took him by the arm leading him to Gen. McClellan who was at the upper end of the room, and introduced them to each other, then introducing Mrs. McClellan and myself. We bowed, but as each seemed to wait for the other, neither of us spoke a single word. One look showed me she was dressed in the Secession colors. A band of scarlet velvet crossed her white dress from shoulder to waist, and in her hair were three feathers of scarlet and white. If this was intentional, it was unpardonable in the wife of the commander-in-chief of the Union armies, and yet it seemed impossible to have been quite an accident. After a few minutes' talk between the President, Gen. McClellan, and Gen. Frémont, we left.

At this moment the pressure for Frémont's reappointment to a military command was becoming irresistible. Many radicals and many even of the moderate German-Americans were implacable in their anger over his treatment. When early in 1862 Frémont had appeared before the Committee on the Conduct of the War, reports had reached the public that it was "staggered" by the ease with which he disproved every accusation. In March he gave the press the full text of his defense, including numerous documents. The *Tribune*, publishing it complete in an extra sheet, seized the occasion for a long and belligerent editorial defending his record and declaring that no other commander had been pursued with such unjust malevolence. A great part of the press both East and West took his side. There ensued an immediate explosion in Congress. Frank Blair, on March 7th, made a vitriolic speech attacking Frémont's Missouri record, and the Congressional radicals rushed to the fray. The leading address in Frémont's behalf, delivered by Schuyler Colfax, was a masterly presentation of his case. Lincoln saw that it was best to yield to the storm, and give Frémont another opportunity in the field.

The general was immediately assigned to head the newly created Mountain Department, which comprised western Virginia (where Rosecrans had commanded), eastern Kentucky, and a part of Tennessee. Proceeding with his wife and two children to Wheeling, Frémont there relieved Rosecrans on March 29, 1862. He took his own staff, many of them young Germans, Hungarians, and Frenchmen, whose foreign tongues—as in St. Louis—created a prejudice against him. His first headquarters were at the McLure Hotel in Wheeling, where Jessie placed herself in an anteroom and did her utmost to protect his time. Assuring important callers that he was so busy with his plan of campaign that his moments were gold, she turned them over to staff members and yet made no enemies. The general devoted himself entirely to military affairs, leaving all orders touching civil policy and the relations of Unionists and Confederate sympathizers to his Judge-Advocate, Corwine, and to Governor Francis H. Pierpont of West Virginia.[4] He knew that much was expected of him in the field. Though his force was small, amounting to about twenty-five thousand men on paper, and actually to much less, and though it was badly equipped, his Department represented a pet idea of the President's.

[4] C. H. Ambler, *Francis H. Pierpont*, pp. 144-147.

Lincoln believed it feasible to march from western Virginia over the mountains into East Tennessee and seize the railroad at Knoxville, rescuing the Unionists of that region. This would have been impossible even for a much larger force. As Jacob D. Cox has written in *Battles and Leaders*, extensive operations across the Alleghenies from east or west were impracticable, because a wilderness a hundred miles wide, traversed by few and wretched roads, rendered it impossible to supply troops from depots on either side. The country was so wild that it did not afford even forage for mules. Yet Frémont was put in a position where he had to promise to attempt the feat.

A month after he took command, he departed for the military frontier; his plan being to march into the Shenandoah Valley, and then (as he had arranged with Lincoln) move to break the Virginia & Tennessee Railroad. Unfortunately, Lincoln's whole disposition of forces in this region was at fault, and in the next few months Stonewall Jackson made a spectacular demonstration of the fact at the expense of the three generals opposing him. These were N. P. Banks, who had a small army at Strasburg in the Shenandoah—9,000 men at the time of Jackson's raid; Frémont, with about 15,000 troops at different points in the Shenandoah; and McDowell, who was at Fredericksburg charged especially with the defense of Washington, but who at the critical moment despatched 20,000 men up the valley to help bag Jackson. These three forces should have been under the command of a single general. Instead, the only central command was that which Lincoln and Stanton themselves, acting on telegraphic advices to Washington, undertook to furnish.

The story of Jackson's brilliant and spectacular Valley campaign against the three generals has often been told, and needs no rehearsal in detail.[5] He had some 17,000 effective men, and the armies brought against him outnumbered his troops by at least two to one. Yet by daring rapidity of movement, by the

[5] J. G. Ropes, *Story of the Civil War*, II, p. 115ff.; James Ford Rhodes, *History of the United States*, IV, p. 13ff.

ability to appear at unexpected points and to dodge pursuit, Jackson managed to strike blow after blow, to defeat or evade each opposing commander, and, after throwing Washington into a panic, to return to a safe position with rich spoils and thousands of prisoners. Meanwhile, he had prevented Mc-Dowell's 40,000 men from joining the Union army before Richmond. He whipped Schenck at the village called Mc-Dowell, overwhelmed Banks at Winchester and drove him across the Potomac in wild disorder, eluded Frémont, who was checked at Cross Keys by Ewell, crushed two brigades under Tyler at Port Republic, and got safely away; all this between May 19 and June 10, 1862. James Ford Rhodes places the blame for this chiefly on Lincoln. Issuing orders by telegraph, he devised a plan that "was too complicated to succeed," and that Lee himself would never have risked.

Frémont in this campaign has been accused of showing a lack of energy. If he and McDowell had met at Strasburg on May 30th they could possibly have cut off Jackson's retreat, but Frémont did not get there even by the thirty-first, when he could do no more than strike at Jackson's rear. Moreover, he was ordered by Lincoln at an earlier stage of the campaign to march to Harrisonburg, and instead turned up at Moorfield. For all this, he is censured, at least by implication, by the historian Rhodes.[6] But the censure is hardly deserved. When Lincoln early in June sent Carl Schurz to the scene to make a confidential report, Schurz exonerated the commander upon both heads. "It is a fact which admits of no doubt," he wrote the President, "that when you ordered Gen. Frémont to march from Franklin to Harrisonburg, it was absolutely impossible to carry out the order. The army was in a starving condition, and literally unable to fight. ... Thus it seems to have been necessary to move back to Moorfield, in order to meet the supply trains." He added that the troops had proceeded by forced

<hr/>

[6] Rhodes, *op. cit.*, IV, p. 15*ff*. Frémont himself wrote later that Cross Keys "was not indecisive. I was engaged with General Jackson for eight days with constant sharp skirmishing driving his force before me, I with an inferior force, he burning bridges and culverts to delay us." Frémont MSS, Bancroft Library.

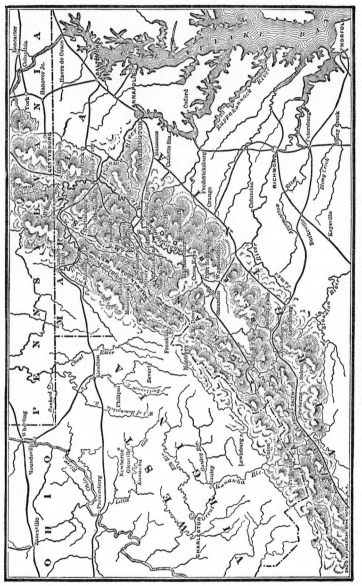

THE THEATER OF WAR IN THE EAST

marches to Strasburg, leaving most of the baggage and knap-
sacks behind. "The march was difficult, and owing to the lack
of provisions, very hard on the men. The army failed to arrest
Jackson at Strasburg, and although it seems that Jackson's
rear guard might have been attacked with more promptness
and vigor, yet it is undoubtedly a very fortunate circumstance
that Gen. Frémont did not succeed in placing himself across
Jackson's line of retreat." Frémont had at most 10,000 men,
"in a wretched condition," and Jackson's larger army would
almost certainly have defeated the ill-conditioned force.

As Schurz wrote later, a highly resolute, self-reliant commander would have taken the risk of this defeat and strained
every nerve to be at Strasburg on time; yet Frémont believed
that he had done all that was humanly possible. He declared
that nothing could have excelled the devotion with which his
tired, ill-clad, ill-fed troops pursued Jackson's rear-guard after
the action at Strasburg:

The road was strewn with arms, blankets, and clothing, thrown
away in their [the rebels'] haste, or abandoned by their pickets where
they had been surprised, and the woods and roads were lined by
their stragglers, unable to keep up with the rapid retreat. For nine
days we kept in sight of the enemy—the pursuit interrupted only
by the streams where the enemy succeeded in destroying the bridges
for which our advance was in continual contest with his rear.[7]

After Cross Keys, Lincoln telegraphed him, "Many thanks to
yourself, officers, and men for the gallant battle of last Sunday"; and he later added, in another message: "You fought
Jackson alone and worsted him"—which was not precisely true.

Schurz had heard much of Frémont, and studied the General with curiosity. He found him a man of "elegant build,
muscular, and elastic, dark hair and beard slightly streaked
with gray, a broad forehead, a keen eye, fine regular features."

[7] For Frémont's letter see New York *Tribune*, February 12, 1863; compare
Col. G. R. F. Henderson, *Stonewall Jackson and the American Civil War*, I,
Ch. 11.

He praised his air of refinement, his easy and unaffected manners, and his low, gentle tone of voice, which carried a suggestion of reticence. "The whole personality," he concluded, "appeared rather attractive—and yet, one did not feel quite sure." In his report to Lincoln, Schurz included a sage word of political warning: [8]

This morning I found General Frémont in a somewhat irritated frame of mind, and I must confess I understand it. The government has plenty of provisions, and our soldiers die of hunger; plenty of shoes, and they go barefooted; plenty of horses, and we are hardly able to move. I would entreat you let it not be said that this army is more neglected than any other. It would appear that it is willfully so, and you know how this will be interpreted. The task this army has before it is an important one, and it ought to have the means to fulfill it.

But Lincoln had been too thoroughly imbued by the Blairs' prejudices to trust Frémont, and under any circumstances the General's services would have been brief. In the middle of June, Frémont asked the President to increase his force, promising that if it were augmented to 35,000 men, the strength originally promised him, he would capture Staunton, seize the Richmond-Newbern Railroad, and prevent the enemy from using western Virginia as a rich granary. The correspondence which ensued reveals Lincoln's deep-seated distrust for his commander. Frémont had been courteous in reminding the President of his promise of a larger army. "I now ask from the President the fulfillment of this understanding," he wrote, "and ask it only because, under the conditions of war, I should be able to render good and immediate service." But the President telegraphed a reply next day which showed not a little asperity:

Your dispatch of yesterday, reminding me of a supposed understanding that I would furnish you a corps of 35,000 men, and

[8] Compare Carl Schurz, *Reminiscences*, II, 343-346.

reminding me of the "fulfillment of this understanding," is received I am ready to come to a fair settlement of accounts with you on the fulfillment of understandings.

Early in March last, when I assigned you to the command of the Mountain Department, I did tell you I would give you all the force I could, and that I hoped to make it reach 35,000. You at the same time told me that within a reasonable time you would seize the railroad at or east of Knoxville, Tenn., if you could. There was then in the department a force supposed to be 25,000, the exact number as well known to you as to me. After looking about two or three days, you called and distinctly told me, that if I would add the Blenker Division to the force already in the department, you would undertake the job. The Blenker Division contained 10,000, and at the expense of great dissatisfaction to Gen. McClellan I took it from his army and gave it to you. My promise was literally fulfilled. I have given you all I could, and I have given you very nearly, if not quite, 35,000.

Now for yours: On the 23d of May, largely over two months afterward, you were at Franklin, Va., not within three hundred miles of Knoxville, nor within eighty miles of any part of the railroad east of it, and not moving forward but telegraphing here that you could not move for lack of everything. Now, do not misunderstand me. I do not say you have not done all you could. I presume you met unexpected difficulties; and I beg you to believe that as surely as you have done your best, so have I. I have not the power now to fill up your corps to 35,000. I am only asking of you to stand cautiously on the defensive; get your force in order, and give such protection as you can to the valley of the Shenandoah and to Western Virginia.

Have you received the orders and will you act upon them?

Lincoln's despatch showed all too clearly that he was unconvinced of Frémont's military capacity and ready to find fault with his acts. As a matter of fact, its criticism was hardly fair. Military critics have agreed that Lincoln's plan for the capture of Knoxville was romantic and highly impracticable. Blenker's division, which was to raise Frémont's army to 35,000, was not ordered to him until the beginning of April

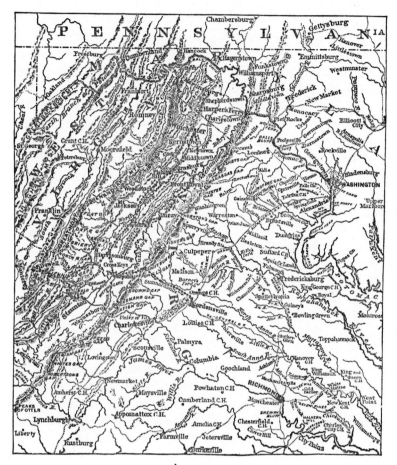

SCENE OF JACKSON'S SHENANDOAH CAMPAIGN

and did not reach his Department until May 5th, then coming in ragged, shoeless, tentless, without sufficient provisions, and tired. Frémont could not argue with the President. He sent a brief and submissive reply, saying simply that the orders had been received, and that he would of course act upon them, as he was already acting. But he read between the lines of the message its full significance, and it played its part in his almost immediate decision to withdraw.

For this decision the President furnished before the end of June what Frémont regarded as sufficient reason. Lincoln, wisely but belatedly, consolidated the forces of Frémont, Banks, and McDowell into one army, to be called the Army of Virginia, and placed it under the command of John Pope, the troops of the Mountain Department being constituted the First Corps under Frémont's command. Since his removal in Missouri, Frémont detested Pope only less than he detested Frank Blair. They were avowed enemies. He believed that Pope had been disloyal and insubordinate, and had tried to encompass his defeat. He could not bring himself to hold any intercourse with the man. It would perhaps have been wiser— it would certainly have been more patriotic—had he sunk his personal resentment and stuck doggedly to his work until, as was inevitable, Pope demonstrated his utter incapacity. But such a course did not square with his or Jessie's pride, with their sensitive conception of personal honor; and he requested that the President relieve him of his command. Lincoln promptly did so, turning the corps over to Sigel. Before the summer ended, Pope had sustained one of the worst defeats of the war at the second battle of Bull Run.

All these events naturally increased the antagonism between Frémont and the Administration. Lincoln was more convinced than ever that Frémont was intractable and unsafe. He regarded the explorer as a troublesome man providentially shelved. Frémont, chafing for action, but unwilling to surrender his dignity, was convinced that he had been the victim of a new indignity, and that he could never expect justice from

Lincoln or the Blairs. He returned to New York, taking his personal staff with him, in an embittered frame of mind. For a time he kept his peace. He was still one of the high officers of the Army, and he had hopes that some conjunction of circumstances might recall him to the field. His radical friends and the radical press were vociferous in urging his claims; Mrs. Frémont pulled whatever wires she could reach. Among others, she approached Hannibal Hamlin. "What can I do?" the Vice-President wrote her. "The slow and unsatisfactory movements of the Government do not meet my approbation, and that is known, and of course I am not consulted at all, nor do I think there is much disposition in any quarter to regard any counsel I may give much if at all." Still, he tried. Others tried, with equal lack of success. At one time they seemed likely to succeed. In the first weeks of 1863 a highly important command was arranged expressly for Frémont by Stanton. Both the command and his designation to it received the approbation of the President; but the post was finally given to another officer. Frémont continued to draw pay, but used it, as he publicly announced, to relieve wartime distress. Watching Lincoln's policies with increasing disapproval, he looked forward to the time when he might cross swords with his enemies—and that time was soon to come.

XXXIII

The Defeat of the Blairs

THE year 1864 opened with storm-clouds billowing thickly about the Lincoln Administration, and Frémont watching the omens of trouble with keen interest. Discontent was rife in every quarter—in the Cabinet, in Congress, in the country at large; and everywhere it was breeding political machinations against the President. In these plots, Frémont had no mind to play an active rôle. He had turned at once to his private business pursuits and was willing to lose himself completely in them. But he fully realized that to hundreds of thousands of voters his name still possessed a magical ring.

A new Congress had convened the previous December, and had promptly shown that it was under the domination of radicals who were thoroughly unfriendly to the Administration. Lincoln's candidate for the speakership had been decisively defeated—defeated by the brilliant Indianian, Frémont's warm defender, Schuyler Colfax. The important committees had been filled by men who opposed Lincoln's conservative policy. In the Senate, Charles Sumner, icy, solemn, and pontifical, felt a personal cordiality for Lincoln, but sternly deplored his official course. Zachariah Chandler, a rough backwoods type of politician, blunt and ruthless, took the same attitude. He, like Lyman Trumbull, the irrepressible Illinoisan, John P. Hale, a supercritical, nagging New Englander, and that domineering egotist, Benjamin F. Wade, was a member of the Committee on the Conduct of the War. Wade as chairman had made this body a thorn in Lincoln's side. Its final report on April 3, 1864, was a resounding blast in favor of a more vigorous prosecution of the conflict. Then a new joint committee of the same name was organized, and with much the same personnel resumed the attack on the President.

In the House, the foremost place among Lincoln's opponents was taken by the bitter, narrow, patriotic Thaddeus Stevens, now aged and bowed by disease, but unrelenting as ever. Beside him stood the dashing and comparatively youthful Henry Winter Davis of Maryland, who disputed control over that state with the Blair dynasty. Another who shared their views was George W. Julian of Indiana, who had been disgusted by Lincoln's slowness in proclaiming emancipation. He would never have proclaimed it, Julian believed, if he had not feared that Congress would refuse to vote supplies unless the war were placed upon a definite anti-slavery basis.[1] Lincoln in his December message had proposed to Congress a moderate and tolerant plan for reconstructing the lost states, and the radicals had lost no time in preparing to knife it. Thaddeus Stevens had exploded a little earlier that he was "tired of hearing damned Republican cowards talk about the Constitution," and that the North should give the rebels "reconstruction on such terms as would end treason forever." Now Henry Winter Davis brought forward a bill which was intended to destroy Lincoln's reconstruction scheme and furnish a harsher system in its stead. The hostility of all these men toward Lincoln's renomination was open and bitter. Young James A. Garfield, who had fought at Shiloh and had just entered Congress from the Ashtabula district of Ohio, wrote that "we hope we may not be compelled to push Lincoln four years more."

If Congress seemed alive with discontent and opposition, the Cabinet was even more savagely divided. Stanton, a man compounded of disagreeable qualities, jealousy, arbitrariness, ambition, and ill temper, and yet laborious, enormously energetic, a vast organizing force, a thorough patriot, seemed at times to hold Lincoln in utter contempt. He had called him

[1] Julian, *Political Recollections*, p. 227.

a gorilla and talked of his "painful imbecility." [2] At other times, his loyalty and admiration appeared perfect. Salmon P. Chase was at work day and night laying mines, stringing wires, and planning to make himself President in the stead of the Illinois lawyer whose powers he distrusted and whose aims he thought inadequate. After some initial coyness, his candidacy was perfectly open, and Lincoln had to tolerate it. Wade and Winter Davis gave him their support, while various Congressional radicals and prominent citizens formed a committee— the Republican National Executive Committee—under Senator Samuel C. Pomeroy of Kansas to push his candidacy. From this body shortly came a vigorous pronunciamento, declaring that if the anti-slavery principle was to triumph, if the war was to be vigorously prosecuted and the country made safe, the voters should rally to elect Chase instead of Lincoln.[3] Chase clubs began to spring up over the North. Meanwhile, other members of the Cabinet were hopelessly antagonistic to each other.

The principal cause of the Cabinet antagonisms was evident to every observer—the Blairs. The Postmaster-General, Montgomery Blair, had early become a storm center. Like his father and brother, he basked in Lincoln's favor, which the whole family repaid with warm-hearted devotion to the President; but other leaders regarded the tall, angular Missourian with dislike. His talk of solving the slavery question by measures of colonization and compensation enraged the radicals. When emancipation was proposed, the emancipation for which Sumner and Greeley, Wade and Beecher were calling, he had stubbornly opposed it to the last. He declared it inexpedient and would have postponed it even when Lincoln decided to issue his proclamation. Upon the reconstruction issue, the radicals thought him equally perverse. The whole Blair family was for treating the South mildly and kindly, and restoring its rights promptly. Montgomery Blair loosed a tremendous broadside

[2] Morgan Dix, *John A. Dix*, II, p. 19.
[3] *Annual Cyclopaedia* (1864), p. 783; Nicolay and Hay, *Lincoln*, VIII, p. 319.

against the men who stood for "amalgamation, equality, and fra-
ternity" with the Negro race.[4] To the old Abolitionists and to
all who, like Zachariah Chandler and Thaddeus Stevens, thought
that the Negroes should be treated as friends and the rebels
as enemies, the Blairs had become anathema.

Commanding the President's support, Montgomery Blair
might have seemed in a position to hold his Cabinet portfolio
without making enemies in the President's official family. Instead, he quickly surrounded himself with feuds and antagonisms, which by 1864 had become dangerous in their intensity.
He and Seward felt nothing but dislike for each other. The
elder Blair had by some strange process of reasoning associated
Seward and Frémont as allies, and regarded them as twin
agents of the Abolitionist cause, an opinion which he took no
pains to conceal. Montgomery Blair believed that Seward had
tried deliberately to provoke the clash between the North and
the South, and made reckless and unfounded charges to that
effect.[5] As for Attorney-General Edward Bates, the Blairs had
systematically undermined and opposed him in Missouri politics, and he well knew it. The peppery Stanton and the in-
triguing Montgomery Blair did not get on at all. Montgomery,
recalling Stanton's record as a member of Buchanan's Cabinet,
doubted his loyalty and zeal in the Union cause, while the two
were utterly incompatible in temperament. Stanton was never
a man to repress his private hatreds, and he struck out at the
Blairs by having some of their Maryland relatives arrested
on the charge that they had smuggled supplies of medicine
over to the Confederates.[6] When it came to Chase, of course,
Blair's enmity was still more open.

Outside official circles, there seemed—to the superficial observer—many evidences of popular chilliness toward Lincoln.
The correspondence of Chase and Lyman Trumbull is filled
with letters from bitter-enders who resented the President's

[4] Kirkland, *The Peacemakers of 1864,* p. 185.
[5] T. K. Lothrop, *William Henry Seward,* p. 123.
[6] Kirkland, *op. cit.,* p. 187.

seemingly tepid policy. The northern pulpit was largely un-friendly. The strongest church magazine, Henry Ward Beecher's *Independent,* declared that: "Great statesmen are few in any country, but few as they are we must make diligent search to find one for the next presidency." Of course, the Democratic newspapers were shrill in abuse; James Gordon Bennett's *Herald,* which the President himself read for its unrivaled war news, lashed the Administration unmercifully. But part of the Republican press was not much less hostile. Greeley's *Tribune* declared that Lincoln's nomination would at once awaken "the fear that the disasters, the burdens, the debts, and the hopes deferred will be revived." Utterances of similar purport could be found in William Cullen Bryant's dignified *Evening Post.* Both Bryant and Greeley believed that the nomination of a Republican candidate for the Presidency should be deferred until the close of the summer of 1864, in order that the people might know whether the overthrow of the Rebellion was in sight, or its speedy termination was out of the question. If the battles of July and August showed that it was impossible to crush the Rebellion at once, then another and better leader than Lincoln could be called to the helm. But some editors were for rejecting Lincoln out of hand. The youthful Whitelaw Reid of the Cincinnati *Gazette* declared that the President was ready to "surrender the cause of human freedom to the masters of slave plantations." [7]

It was inevitable that much of the opposition to Lincoln should crystallize about the name of Frémont. He was sin-cerely indifferent to any movement of the sort. Giving up all hope of military employment, he had plunged with his usual enthusiasm into a new business field—railroad building. The newspapers had suggested that if he was not to be allowed a command, he might be appointed military governor of North Carolina or one of the other reconquered states. The great task in these states, said the *Tribune,* was to organize the eman-

[7] New York *Tribune,* June 6, 1864, and subsequent issues; for Reid see Wil-liam E. Dodd, *Century Magazine,* Vol. 114, p. 48.

cipated slaves: "The first condition for the success of such an effort is to win their confidence. We cannot do it by sending them a general whom they do not know. But Frémont's name has been a watchword in every cabin since 1856, and will be heard at once as a war-cry by the slaves waiting to rally under the Union flag." Lincoln, however, refused to heed such suggestions. When George Julian called at the White House to urge a post for the explorer, the President replied that he was willing, but that he did not know where to place him. The situation, he said, reminded him of the old man who advised his son to take a wife, to which the son replied, "Whose wife shall I take?" There were important positions in sight, but they could be reached only by removals which he did not care to make.

A somewhat different answer was given to a deputation which, including Senator Henry Wilson, Wendell Phillips, Moncure D. Conway, and Oakes Ames, came to the President to discuss the governorship of North Carolina. Some one suggested Frémont, and Lincoln tolerantly indicated why he thought the proposal bad. "I have great respect for Gen. Frémont and his abilities," said the President slowly, "but the fact is that the pioneer in any movement is not generally the best man to carry that movement to a successful issue. It was so in old times, wasn't it?" he continued with a smile. "Moses began the emancipation of the Jews, but didn't take Israel to the Promised Land after all." The truth was that Lincoln could not have appointed Frémont without offending his conservative supporters, and he did not think it necessary to act.

While Chase was coming brazenly into the open in his pursuit of the nomination, while Thaddeus Stevens was expressing the sagacious view that Ben Butler would make a much better President than Lincoln, and while Greeley was declaring in the *Tribune* that Chase, Frémont, Butler, and Grant ought all to be considered, the explorer had immersed himself in railway operations. His enthusiasm for the development of the great trans-Mississippi region was as fresh as ever. The action of

Congress in richly endowing a Pacific railroad stirred his imagination. Commanding large funds on the credit of Mariposa, having a name valuable to any enterprise, and personally familiar with western topography, he felt that this offered an ideal field for his energies. In June, 1863, the New York press announced with applause that he had put his hand to the helm. Capitalists had been reluctant, with the war raging, to undertake new lines across the plains. But now Frémont had come forward with Samuel Hallett, widely known, as the *Tribune* said editorially, "in moneyed circles as a man of large financial experience, combined with an energy and indomitable will to which all obstacles are made to succumb." [8] They intended to build a line through the state of Kansas—what was later known as the Kansas Pacific—connecting on the east with the Missouri River terminals; and for this purpose, took over a paper railway called the Leavenworth, Pawnee, & Western. A new directorate was chosen, and Frémont elected president. In a few weeks he was advertising from his Beaver Street offices for bids to deliver 4,000 tons of iron rails at Leavenworth or Kansas City.

But if he would willingly have kept aloof from politics, an increasing number of radicals were insistent that he be drafted for service in 1864. Many German-Americans and Abolitionists preferred him above all other candidates; while, as the weeks passed, supporters began to drift in from other camps. Butler's name aroused more derision than enthusiasm. The Chase candidacy, blazing brilliantly in the political heavens in February, came down like a rocket-stick in March. Pomeroy's circular in behalf of the Secretary of the Treasury aroused wide comment. But on February 22nd, the Republican National Committee, sitting in Washington, virtually came out for the renomination of Lincoln, and called the Republican Convention to sit for that purpose at Baltimore in June. More decisively, on March 5th, the Republican caucus of the Ohio Legislature refused to endorse Chase as a "favorite son," which meant

[8] New York *Tribune,* June 4, 1863.

that Ohio was for Lincoln. Chase reluctantly and ungracefully withdrew, though his desire to see Lincoln supplanted was as strong as ever; and many of his adherents turned toward Frémont.

The first token of the way the wind was veering appeared on March 19th, when radical and old-school Abolitionists of New York came together at Cooper Union in an earnest "Frémont meeting," of which Frémont knew nothing in advance. The men in charge were for the most part obscure. Under the blazing gas jets in Room 20 the erudite Friedrich Kapp declaimed, with a marked accent, upon the need for a change of government. A Mr. Whipple gained the floor, and launched into personal abuse of Lincoln. He had himself seen, he said, the bad effects of liquor and the evil influence of slavery. A platform calling for "vigorous, consistent, concentrated prosecution of the war" was read amid cheers. Then there was a stir at the door, a sudden clapping of hands, and everybody arose as the loose, ill-clad figure of Greeley shuffled in. The editor's remarks, as reported by his own journal, were confused, but he squeakily made three facts clear. First, that he thought it would have been well to postpone all nominations and campaigning until people could see what Grant would do in the summer campaigns; second, that he advocated a single term for Presidents; and third, that while he expected to support the regular nominee of the Republican Convention, he believed that "the people of New York were in favor of putting down the rebellion and its cause, and sustaining Freedom, and he believed that John C. Frémont would carry out such views." [9]

As luck would have it, at this moment Frank Blair executed a stroke which aroused the radicals to a new pitch of anger. The current seemed to be setting against the President. Pennsylvania, Massachusetts, and New York were apparently hostile to him. All Frank Blair's innate recklessness and pugnacity came to the surface. As major-general he had no right to hold civil office, but he had made an arrangement by which

[9] New York *Tribune,* March 20, 1864.

he had surrendered his commission temporarily and Lincoln placed it in a secret drawer, to be restored upon demand. By this adroit if illegal maneuver, Frank was able to return to Congress. In January, he had begun to make war upon Secretary Chase by calling for an investigation of certain Treasury regulations. Now, on April 23, he suddenly arose in his place and made the most sensational and ferocious speech which Congress had heard in years. He accused Chase of public and private corruption; he declared that he had squandered public funds, wrung from a hard-pressed people, to advance his candidacy; and he charged that he had used hundreds of Treasury agents to build up his machine. To support this tirade, he read a letter from a New York financier, which spoke of reports afloat that Chase had given his son-in-law, Governor Sprague, a permit to buy cotton at the South by which the latter would probably make two million dollars.[10]

This vicious and ill-considered attack created an uproar among the radical leaders and editors, and increased the resentment with which they viewed the Administration. The New York *Tribune* declared that it had left a more painful impression than any other utterance in the House in years. Chase denounced the speech as an "outrageous calumny." The special car in which he left Washington that day for Baltimore fairly "trembled with his rage." [11] There seems no question that Lincoln was much annoyed by Blair's indiscretion. The man had kicked over another beehive, he said; and for a time he hesitated to restore Blair to his military command, though he had already given the needed instructions. But the radicals naturally believed that Lincoln had done something to instigate Blair's onslaught, and that he had taken satisfaction in it. After this event, Chase and Montgomery Blair glared daggers at each other whenever they met in the Cabinet room.

But Chase was out of the running for the presidency, and it was now evident to everybody that Lincoln would be nom-

---

[10] *Congressional Globe,* 38th Cong., 1st Sess., Part II, p. 1831*ff.*
[11] A. G. Riddle, *Recollections of War Times,* pp. 267, 268.

inated at Baltimore at the beginning of June. It was by no means so clear that he would be successful in November. James A. Garfield wrote despondingly: "Lincoln will be nominated and a copperhead will be elected. Not a dozen men in Congress think otherwise." Chase grumbled to the governor of Ohio: "The Convention will not be regarded as a Union Convention, but simply as a Blair-Lincoln Convention, by a great body of citizens whose support is essential to success." But even to have the President again placed at the head of the Republican party was a bitter dose to many of the extremists, and they turned to the idea of a third ticket. It might be used to obtain the withdrawal of Lincoln from the race; it could certainly be used to increase the chances of his ultimate defeat. On May 4, 1864, a group of radical Republicans who were known to favor the choice of Frémont sent out an invitation to a mass convention in Cleveland, to meet May 31st for the purpose of forestalling the action of the regular Republicans. The signers did not constitute an impressive group. Representing only eleven states, they included no names more distinguished than those of B. Gratz Brown, Friedrich Kapp, Emil Preetorius, and James Redpath. However, their call was shortly reinforced by one emanating from a number of minor state officials in New York, and one sent out by a considerable number of Abolitionists.[12]

Frémont's papers do not indicate that he was excited by the prospect for another nomination for the presidency, or that he had any illusions as to the chances for his election; indeed, it appears that he was by no means certain of consenting. His papers do show that he was urged to take a receptive position by such men as Governors Andrew and Curtin, and David Dudley Field. The coming convention was derided by William Lloyd Garrison. "General Frémont, as yet," he wrote, "has not shown a single state, a single county, a single town or hamlet in his support. Who represents him from Massachusetts, on the call for the Cleveland Convention? Two men,

[12] *Annual Cyclopaedia*, 1865, p. 783*ff*.

both non-voters, I believe, and neither of them has a particle of political influence." [13] But men like Wendell Phillips and Schuyler Colfax, women like Elizabeth Cady Stanton, were for Frémont, and when the Convention actually met, it had a good press. Even the Democratic journals, for selfish reasons, spoke well of it.

It opened formally on May 31, 1864, in Cosmopolitan Hall in Cleveland, with ex-Governor William F. Johnston of Pennsylvania calling the motley body of about four hundred Radicals, Germans, and War Democrats to order. Many of the delegates had no credentials, though they represented various political organizations. Sixteen states had sent members. For the most part everything went like clockwork. Frémont was nominated by acclamation, General John Cochrane of New York was named for Vice-President, though many had supposed that the honor would go to B. Gratz Brown, and a platform was adopted which expressed radical ideas from beginning to end. It called for uncompromising prosecution of the war, the constitutional prohibition of slavery, free speech and a free press, and a one-term presidency; for leaving reconstruction exclusively to Congress, and for the confiscation of rebel lands to be divided among active soldiers and sailors. Frémont promptly accepted the honor, declaring that "today we have in this country the abuses of a military dictation without its unity of action and vigor of execution"; but he dissented from the plank upon the confiscation of rebel property.

For the moment, his nomination was regarded in Administration circles with comparative indifference. Lincoln, upon hearing of the proceedings, opened his Bible at the twenty-second chapter of I Samuel and read aloud: "And everyone that was in distress, and everyone that was in debt, and everyone that was discontented gathered themselves unto him; and he became a captain over them: and there were with him about four hundred men." As June began, in fact, everything seemed going well for the President. Sherman was pressing forward

[13] New York *Evening Post*, June 3, 1864.

upon Atlanta; Grant was facing Lee on the Chickahominy, and the nation's trust in Grant was enormous. It had been made emphatically clear that the Republican rank and file wanted Lincoln. As Bryant put it: "In the first place, he is popular with the plain people, who believe him honest, with the rich people, who believe him safe, with the soldiers, who believe him their friend, and with religious people, who believe him to have been specially raised up for this crisis; and in the second place, because many of the thieving and corrupt scoundrels of the political mews, who know the fact of his popularity, have eagerly attached themselves to the car of his success."[14] Lincoln had the votes, and nobody else had. The Baltimore Convention witnessed a spontaneous outburst of enthusiasm for the President. The delegates, trying again and again to burst through parliamentary forms, nominated him amid deafening cheers and cries of "God bless him!"

But the week of Lincoln's triumph was a week of humiliation for the Blairs. They had made enemies on every hand who were now gathering to crush them. The first blow fell upon the head of the much-hated Frank Blair. His diatribe against Chase had prompted Thaddeus Stevens to introduce in the House a resolution asking the President to explain just how Frank had been able to be a major-general and a member of Congress at the same time. The House responded by passing a resolution which declared that Blair had never possessed a legal right to his seat as Representative, and another asserting that any officer of the United States Army who had severed his connection with it by written resignation or by service in Congress must have a second appointment, in the manner required by the Constitution, before he could resume his sword.[15] This was a stinging rebuke, but worse was to come. For three years denunciation and dislike of the Blairs in Missouri, their special political barony, had been growing. Men there looked back upon Frank Blair's acts in 1861 and decided that he had

14 New York *Evening Post,* June 3, 1864.
15 *Congressional Globe,* 38th Cong., 1st Sess., Pt. II, p. 1854*ff.;* Pt. IV, p. 3389*ff.*

been a marplot and a curse. In the spring of 1864, this opposition had come to a head, and the radicals, meeting in State
Convention, had sent an implacably anti-Blair delegation to
Baltimore. Another gathering sent a set of delegates friendly
to Blair.

Which delegation should be admitted? On June 8th, this
question came before the Baltimore Convention, and Preston
King of the committee on credentials read a report excluding
the Blairites. The Convention rocked with joy, and all proceedings were suspended while the tide of applause rose and
ebbed. Then the report was put to a vote. State after state cast
votes for its approval, until Maryland and Delaware were
reached, and they voted "aye" too! Once more the Convention
broke into thunderous applause, which still echoed around the
hall when it was announced that the anti-Blair delegates had
been seated by a vote of 440 to 4.[16] In effect, the Republican
Party served notice upon Lincoln that it had no use for the
"Blair malcontents." This notice was underlined when, at the
instance of the Missouri delegates, a resolution was passed declaring for the reorganization of the Cabinet—which meant
that Montgomery Blair should go.

If in early June the skies had seemed bright for Lincoln, in
July and August they grew overcast again. The losses at Cold
Harbor and the Wilderness, when the people at last realized
them, had a stunning effect. Heavy fighting by Grant in front
of Petersburg ended in a checkmate. The hospitals were
choked with wounded, and the Army of the Potomac was exhausted. The spectacular raid of General Early at the beginning
of July brought Washington within an inch of capture—so close
that the Navy Department hastily prepared a vessel to carry
the President down the Potomac. The Treasury was empty, and
greenbacks fell during part of the summer to forty cents on
the dollar. Gloom was general throughout the North, and it
found an inevitable outlet in dissatisfaction with Lincoln. The
elder Blair, in something like a panic, employed the closing

[16] New York *Tribune;* New York *Evening Post,* June 9, 1864.

days of July in visiting various leaders in New York City—
Bryant, Greeley, James Gordon Bennett, and McClellan, now
about to be made the Democratic candidate—and pleading
with them to support Lincoln, or at least to refrain from opposing him. He and Montgomery even hoped that they could
influence McClellan to decline the Democratic nomination, but
in this they utterly failed. On August 5th the Administration
sustained a new blow—for that day appeared the bitter manifesto of Ben Wade and Henry Winter Davis against Lincoln's
reconstruction policy. Greeley wrote Lincoln on August 9th
that if the election were held next day, the Democrats would
sweep New York and Pennsylvania by one hundred thousand
majority; while near the middle of that month Thurlow Weed,
one of the most sagacious of practical politicians, told the
President that his reëlection was an impossibility.[17]

This sudden and steady drop of the Republican barometer
produced an equally sudden change in the Administration's
attitude toward Frémont. It was seen that his candidacy might
be disastrous. His followers were intensely in earnest, and a
great part of the German press had rallied to his side. He
would poll a large vote, and would poll it in states likely to
be close. The ticket was considered strong, for Cochrane was
a War Democrat of radical views—a former congressman, a
brigadier-general till his health failed, and an early advocate
of the policy of calling the emancipated slaves to arms. It was
recalled by political wiseacres that a third party in 1844, the
Abolitionists under Birney, had beaten Clay for the Presidency,
and that another third party in 1848, the Free Soilers under
Van Buren, had beaten Cass. Some Bostonians of prominence
were so alarmed by the outlook that they published a letter
proposing that both Frémont and Lincoln withdraw in favor
of a compromise candidate, and to this Frémont returned a

---

[17] New York *Sun* in late June and early July, 1889, published a series of letters in reply to Nicolay and Hay's *Lincoln,* showing that the Frémont movement was a very serious matter, and placed the Lincoln ticket in actual jeopardy.
By mid-June, twenty-six German-language papers had come out for Frémont,
New York *Herald,* June 15, 1864.

somewhat inconclusive but generally favorable reply. A movement was begun to use the Frémont party as a nucleus for the nomination of Grant, with the object of forcing Lincoln out of the field.

With affairs in this posture, Frémont soon learned that a number of practical politicians were holding consultations with Lincoln upon the best means of strengthening his presidential prospects. The participants included Elihu Washburne, Senator Harlan of Iowa, James M. Edmunds of the Union League, and most active of all, Zachariah Chandler. Much alarmed by the Wade-Davis manifesto, Chandler first bent his efforts to conciliate these redoubtable leaders. He, Cameron, and Wade in the stormy days before the war had made a triple alliance to take up each other's quarrels if insulted by any Southern Senator; and as a result of this early friendship, Chandler could appeal to Wade—like himself a quick-tempered, rough-spoken, aggressive man—with some confidence. Their interview at Wade's home near Ashtabula is described by David H. Jerome of Detroit, who was present, as "rather titanic." Wade finally demanded as his ultimatum the withdrawal from the Cabinet of Montgomery Blair, whom he thought at heart a Democrat. Chandler then went directly to the President, and—according to two different authorities, both good—obtained Lincoln's pledge that if the negotiations he had undertaken proved successful, Blair would be retired. Then visiting Henry Winter Davis in Baltimore, Chandler easily persuaded him to promise party loyalty on the same condition made by Wade. His next problem was to obtain the withdrawal of the Frémont-Cochrane ticket. In a letter written long afterward, he said that he deemed this of vital importance, and procured the consent of Lincoln and the chairmen of both the National and Congressional Committees for his negotiations.[18]

[18] On this subject I have drawn my material from the Frémont MSS; Chase MSS; Charles Moore's letter in the *Century Magazine*, July, 1895, based on conversations with David H. Jerome and others; the diaries of Edward Bates, Gideon Welles, and Orville H. Browning; Donnal V. Smith, *Chase and Civil War Politics*; W. E. Smith, *The Blair Family*; and Charles R. Wilson, "New Light on the Lincoln-Blair-Frémont 'Bargain' of 1864," *American Historical Review*,

Going to New York, Chandler established headquarters at
the Astor House. Assisted by George Wilkes, a capable war
correspondent, he approached Frémont, who divided his time
between Nahant and New York, and several interviews followed in the office of Frémont's attorney and political adviser,
David Dudley Field. Field prepared the way by telling the
general that while the war had plainly not been conducted
with sufficient energy and ability, the assurances of a change
in Administration policy were so full that he thought it best
for him to do what he could for party unity. Chandler then
made his appeal. Lincoln would not withdraw, he said, and
yet he would certainly be defeated by McClellan if Frémont remained in the field. He was empowered, he went on, to say
that if Frémont would step out, he would immediately be given
active service in a high command, while those who had perse-
cuted him (meaning the Blairs) would be placed where they
could do him no further harm. Frémont wrote to friends for
advice. Wendell Phillips urged him to stay in the field; Whittier paid him a special visit at Nahant to ask him to withdraw. One reply he had from Nathaniel P. Sawyer of Pittsburgh, dated September 13th, throws light on the negotiations: [19]

Your esteemed favor of the 7th reached me yesterday....In reply, if you have assurance of Mr. Blair's immediate removal and
also Mr. Stanton's and the assurance that Mr. Seward will not be
reappointed, my advice is that you withdraw as soon as practicable
in favor of Lincoln and Johnson.

Something tells me that Lincoln will never fill a second term. If
I am right, Johnson will be the President, a man who I have loved
since Sixty-one. I have no doubt he will do you and your friends
justice. There is no man living I would sooner see President.

It will be time enough after the election to consider the propriety
of accepting a position. For the present I would advise you to

XXIX, p. 71ff. The subject is intricate, but the evidence that Frémont was offered a bargain and rejected it is to my mind conclusive.

[19] This extraordinary letter, whose author seems to have anticipated Lincoln's assassination, is in the Andrew Johnson Papers, Library of Congress,
Vol. 48.

entertain no proposition. I have perfect confidence in Horace Greeley and have no doubt he will be able to carry out any promises he may or has made.

If you withdraw, Gov. Johnston and myself will support Lincoln and Johnson....

It is evident from this that Chandler was trying to strike a bargain with Frémont. The promise that Blair would be retired was but a minor part of this bargain—that promise had already been made to Wade and Davis, and the retirement would occur no matter what Frémont did; but the promise of an active position was important. Some evidence exists that Frémont had temporarily considered withdrawing in favor of McClellan, a purpose which would heighten the eagerness of Lincoln's friends to buy his friendship. But the general, after due consideration, indignantly declined the proffered inducements. For this we have two pieces of evidence. One is a statement he left in his manuscripts. Offered "patronage to my friends and disfavor to my enemies," he writes, "I refused both. My only consideration was the welfare of the Republican party." The other evidence is a telegram which Col. R. B. Marcy sent from St. Louis to McClellan at this very time. He had learned from Frémont's friend Justus McKinstry, he telegraphed, that Chase and Henry Wilson had approached the explorer with the promise of a Cabinet position and of the dismissal of both Blairs "if he would withdraw and advocate" Lincoln. Frémont had replied that this was "an insult." [20]

The tone of Frémont's letter of withdrawal, published September 22nd, is further evidence that he had rejected a bargain as dishonorable. Had he made a dicker, he would have treated Lincoln gently. Instead, his language was harsh. "In respect to Mr. Lincoln," he declared, "...I consider that his Administration has been politically, militarily, and financially a failure, and that its necessary continuance is a cause of regret for the country." He withdrew not because he approved of Lin-

[20] McClellan MSS, September 22, 1864; compare William Starr Myers, *General George Brinton McClellan*, p. 448.

coln's policies, he wrote, but because McClellan had declared
in effect for the restoration of the Union with slavery, and the
Democrats must therefore at all costs be defeated. While between the two parties no man of liberal convictions could hesitate, he believed that Lincoln's reëlection was simply the lesser
of two evils.

But if Frémont was above a bargain, Wade and Davis were
equal to it. Now that Frank Blair had been humiliated, it was
the turn of the Postmaster-General. He had lately increased the
number of his bitter enemies. When Early's troops made their
raid north of Washington, they burned Montgomery Blair's
beautiful home, Falkland, at Silver Spring. A friend expressed
sympathy, and Blair burst out with the bitter remark: "Nothing better could be expected while politicians and cowards
have the conduct of military affairs." Halleck heard of this
and wrote a letter about it to Stanton, which Stanton angrily
laid before the President. In consequence, Stanton and Blair
ceased to speak. But Montgomery was now disliked in every
quarter. He had been barred from the Union League; a radical
committee including George S. Boutwell and John Covode had
lately demanded his dismissal; Henry Wilson wrote Lincoln
that his retention would cost tens of thousands of votes. Men
spoke of the Blairs as "a nest of Maryland serpents." On
September 22nd, Chandler, accompanied by David H. Jerome,
later governor of Michigan, had a private interview with Lincoln. He announced the complete success of his labors; he
had gotten Frémont out of the race, though not by the means
he had expected. That afternoon the Washington papers contained Frémont's card of withdrawal, and next day Lincoln
asked for and received the resignation of Montgomery Blair,
to take effect at once.

It was an unexpected stroke. Montgomery, joining his associates Bates and Welles as they emerged from a Cabinet meeting at the White House, took their breath away by coolly remarking: "I suppose you are both aware that my head is
decapitated—that I am no longer a member of the Cabinet."

As Welles gasped, Blair took Lincoln's letter from his pocket and read it aloud. Couched in cordial terms, it reminded him that he had frequently stated that he was willing to leave the Cabinet when the President thought it best, and informed him that the time had arrived. Both Welles and Blair agreed that Frémont was not the moving cause. Welles muttered something about Chase; but, "Oh," said Blair, "there is no doubt Seward was accessory to this, instigated and stimulated by Weed." Such was the fraternal spirit in the Cabinet! None of the three thought of Zach Chandler as the principal agent.

Jessie tells us that she had thoroughly approved of Frémont's refusal of a field-command or Cabinet office as part of the proposed bargain; "with a feeling of joy akin to ecstasy I heard his decision to remain in private life." Though his withdrawal might have been phrased more generously, it effected its purpose. With a united party behind him, Lincoln received a majority of nearly a half million votes at the polls. Long afterward, in 1889, Jessie wrote the poet Whittier to thank him again for helping Frémont to reach the right decision: [21]

Among the words I remember from you are: "There is a time to do and a time to stand aside." I never forget your saying this to me at our Nahant cottage in 1864 when you had come to say them to Mr. Frémont. Wendell Phillips, who saw the *do* more clearly than the *stand aside*, insisted I had dreamed your visit. "Whittier goes nowhere. He never visits. His health does not let him," and laughing arguments against your wise and necessary view of what the time demanded of Mr. Frémont—to renounce self for the good of the greater number. Do you not remember it too? It was a **deciding** word, coming from you.

[21] Catherine Coffin Phillips, *Jessie Benton Frémont,* pp. 271, 272.

XXXIV

A Financial Debacle

THE virtual ending of Frémont's public career left him free to turn his attention to private affairs, and opened one of the strangest chapters of his career. It is a chapter marked by dramatic incident and tragic climax. When the war began, Frémont was a multimillionaire; a dozen years later, he was so nearly penniless that but for a few loyal friends he and Mrs. Frémont would hardly have known where they could lay their heads or obtain their next meal.

On the morning of December 13, 1864, a large and curious crowd surged into the Manhattan courtroom in which Judge Mason was presiding over Part Three of the State Supreme Court. The famous trial of ex-Mayor George Opdyke against Thurlow Weed for an alleged libel was about to begin. Every newspaper had sent its reporters to write columns of matter. The ablest lawyers of the city were enlisted, William M. Evarts and Edwards Pierrepont appearing for Weed, and David Dudley Field and former Judge Emott for Opdyke. In later years, men looked back upon the trial as heralding the disclosures of graft in national and city affairs which have made the Reconstruction period seem so shameful in our history. The principal charges published by Weed were that Opdyke had defrauded the city in claims growing from the destruction of a gun factory in the draft riots, had made illicit profits in war contracts, and had despoiled Frémont of much of his California property.[1]

---

[1] This trial is fully treated, with verbatim testimony, in a pamphlet published by the American News Company: "New York Supreme Court: The Great Libel Case of George Opdyke *vs.* Thurlow Weed, 1865."

From the intricate testimony which occupied the next fort-night, it is possible to piece together a story which would have made a fitting theme for one of Balzac's novels of business life. Evarts struck the dominant note of the tale when he said, in summing up: "The one phrase on everybody's lips is 'poor Frémont!'" It is a story of the Mariposa estate, 44,386 acres, from which many millions had been taken in placer gold and 3 million dollars in quartz gold, and which was valued on a production basis at 10 million dollars; of Frémont as the owner of this estate, unworldly, a rash enthusiast, quite uninformed upon the sharp practices of a shady era of business; of his trust in Opdyke, a slippery speculator long known as hungry for money and political preferment; of his confidence in David Dudley Field, an astute lawyer later identified with some of the most outrageous operations of Jim Fisk and Jay Gould, and the counsel of Tweed; of his faith in a financier well named Ketchum—Morris Ketchum—and others of similar stripe. He was among friends, said Evarts sarcastically; "and he may thank God that he did not fall among thieves"—at which the courtroom laughed. It is a story of the Mariposa estate involved, while Frémont was commanding in Missouri and West Virginia, in heavy debts for litigation and the expense of development—debts that bore 2 or even 2½ per cent interest a month, in some instances compounding; of the manipulation of the estate by Opdyke, Ketchum, Hoey, and others, always to their own benefit; of a fee of $200,000 charged by Field; and of attempts, legal but barefaced, to deprive the owner of his just rights and revenues.

Frémont himself took the stand, his hair grizzled, his face, according to the reporters, showing a touch of genius and poetry, his eyes still lit by a deep smouldering blaze.[2] He had a natural reluctance to accuse old associates and expose himself as a victimized man. When, on cross-examination, he was asked whether a harsh advantage had been taken of him by his "friends," he stammered slowly: "I—I—I think not." When

[2] New York *Herald; World; Tribune;* December 14 and later issues, 1864.

Field himself asked if the gentlemen named did not fairly and honorably execute their agreement, the General answered: "You will remember, Mr. Field, there were controversies which were adjusted that grew out of our different interpretations of the agreements." The indignation of the spectators was especially aroused by the testimony regarding one transaction. It was shown that Frémont had been induced to transfer $2,500,000 of his stock in the Mariposa estate to Ketchum by proxies so that Ketchum, acting as his deputy, could control it. But when Frémont wished to recover some of his proxies, he was told that he had signed a document which amounted to a deed of trust, and he had to commence a suit to get his shares back. On the settlement of the suit, his opponents offered to give him 2 million dollars of the stock if he would sell them the remaining $500,000 at 25 cents on the dollar, though it was then rated at 50 cents on the market. "His hand was in the lion's mouth," as Edwards Pierrepont put it, "and he got out the best he could. He made this sacrifice of $125,000."

Family papers show that Frémont had gone to Europe in 1861, with his lawyer, Frederick Billings, in the hope of selling an interest in the estate, or at least procuring a favorable loan to pay its debts; and that he had talked with the Rothschilds and the Paris bankers without avail. They show that the debts at the beginning of 1862 or thereabouts were estimated at a total of $1,250,000, but actually came very close to $2,250,000, and that interest charges were about $13,000 monthly. Tormented by anxiety, the General was eager to shift the growing burden from his shoulders. At this time he held a five-eighths interest in the estate, Billings one-eighth, A. A. Selover of California one-eighth, and Trenor W. Park, who had advanced a large sum against the debts, the remaining eighth. It became imperative to raise money and stop the drain of interest-payments. Frémont was finally forced into a very bad bargain. As a result of complicated negotiations in New York, in June, 1863, a company was formed with 100,000 shares of stock, of $100 par value each. Of these 12,500 each went to Billings, Selover, and a creditor named Parker; while 25,000 were turned over to three men who engaged to pay off the debts, Ketchum, Hoey, and Opdyke. This nominally left 37,500 shares to Frémont. But he paid 2,000 (of par value $200,000!) to Field for legal services; and he placed 25,000 in the hands of Ketchum, who represented that he needed power to vote them to insure control for the New York group. They were to be held in trust until the bonds for clearing off the debts were repaid, and then returned to Frémont. Meanwhile, the explorer kept only 8,500 shares in his own hands. As we have seen, the task of getting Ketchum, Hoey, and Opdyke to disgorge the other 25,000 proved anything but easy.

Writing long after the event,[3] Mrs. Frémont asserted that if her husband had not carried through this desperate and costly transaction when he did, "those interested in accumulating the indebtedness on the property, and so depriving him of the estate, would have succeeded." As it was, she added, in every way feasible by litigation they tried to hamper the actions of the company and, if possible, obtain control of parts of its property. She and her husband believed that the sweeping away of the costly dam which he had built across the Merced River was attributable to the treachery of an agent who deliberately neglected to open the sluice-gates in flood time. Legal expenses ran up to a total of $600,000! There is no doubt that he did well to get out of the mess when he could, and with what money he could. He had not the cold, calculating business sagacity which was needed to rescue Mariposa from the ravenous sharks circling about it. Judge Pierrepont told the jury (which incidentally refused to convict Thurlow Weed of libeling Opdyke) that "this genius of a man once worth $10,000,000 and more" would testify that it had almost all "been stripped away from him, and he has but little left."

[3] MS. *Memoirs*, Bancroft Library. Trenor W. Park, who played the part of a rapacious creditor in the affair, was later the principal promoter of the Emma Mine, and induced General Schenck to discredit himself by lending his name to the mine promotion while Minister to England.

This was not quite true. When he sold his shares, he was still a rich man. But he had only a fragment of his once-great fortune.

It would have been well if, recognizing that the ruthless hurly-burly of business in the seventies was no place for him, Frémont had invested his money in safe securities and devoted himself to some professional pursuit. But such a course was alien to his temperament. He was too active, ardent, and imaginative. Always some great object, wealth or fame or power, floated just before his outstretched hands. The great spaces of the West still called to him for conquest. His dream of leadership in opening the gates upon their vast resources still burned in his brain, and it led him into an inevitable field. As the war closed, construction gangs began racing westward across the plains and eastwards across the Sierras to join the two sections of the first transcontinental railroad, the Central Pacific-Union Pacific. Plans were already on foot for the Northern Pacific, which soon enlisted Jay Cooke. Frémont had devoted two expeditions to exploring for a south-central or southwestern route, and it was natural for him to turn eagerly to various projects for railroads in that quarter.

With characteristic impetuosity, he hastened to throw not a quarter, not a half, but all his money into these enterprises. His first step was to purchase the franchise and property of the infant Kansas Pacific and begin its construction; then he bought the Missouri Pacific, and induced Congress to rename it the Atlantic & Pacific, extend its line, and give it a large land-grant. But his interest in these lines soon became subordinate to another undertaking, and he surrendered his holdings in both of them. This other undertaking was built about the Memphis & El Paso, of which he bought control, shortly becoming president. He writes in his manuscript *Memoirs:*

The Memphis & El Paso had a large segregated grant of lands from Texas, in no wise connected with the [Federal] Government. I procured from the Texas Legislature a large grant of lands, which was all in the interest of the Memphis & El Paso, which was planned to run from the harbor of Norfolk to San Diego and San Francisco, and its extended name was the Transcontinental, and I had acquired for it franchises in South California, Arizona, and Arkansas. An interest had been bought by me in the Memphis & Little Rock Railroad, and arrangements were being made with the intervening lines.

This is correct. The unbuilt Memphis & El Paso, chartered in 1856 by Texas, had received from the State promises of about 18,200,000 acres in all, a small principality. Frémont believed that with this line as a beginning he could bring into existence a mighty system from Memphis through to San Diego. Before him floated the vision of finally extending his southern transcontinental to the Atlantic at Norfolk—that vision which Collis T. Huntington ultimately realized.[4]

With this object in view, Frémont and other heads of the Memphis & El Paso in 1867-68 offered two bond issues totaling 10 million dollars. He acquired franchises in several States and Territories, bought lands for terminals at San Diego, and made tentative arrangements with a projected western line called the San Diego & Fort Yuma Railroad. While it built east from San Diego to the Gila, the Memphis & El Paso would build southwest through Arkansas, Texas, and the Territories to a junction at Yuma. What could be simpler? General Rosecrans and Sedgwick inaugurated work on the San Diego & Fort Yuma in September, 1869, when it was announced that sufficient funds were in hand to build to the Gila.[5] Frémont expected his bond issues to carry his own line forward rapidly, and while fifty miles of Texas track were being graded and the first locomotives ordered, he placed surveyors at work in the mountain passes of New Mexico.

In planning this southern transcontinental, he asked for no Federal land-grant; he believed that the Texas grant was sufficient. He did go to Congress for a right of way through the

[4] Frémont's railroad ventures are somewhat fully and very harshly analyzed in Cardinal Goodwin, *John Charles Frémont*, Ch. 13. The transcontinental venture, which had a separate existence from the Memphis & El Paso, was called the Memphis, El Paso, & Pacific Railroad.

[5] New York *Herald*, September 16, 1869.

Territories, and the House passed the necessary measure in February, 1869, by a vote of 121 to 41. The bill then went to the Senate, where Oliver P. Morton and Roscoe Conkling pressed it earnestly, but Howard of Michigan was instrumental in strangling it. This misfortune precipitated a wordy battle between Greeley's New York *Tribune,* which had been praising Frémont's enterprise in the highest terms, and Senator Howard. The *Tribune* not only declared Howard's motives selfish, but hinted that they might be corrupt. He was chairman of the committee on the Pacific Railroad. One transcontinental had been built with a large Federal subsidy; at least two more must be added, with various branches: "There are always crowds in the lobby of either House raving for more subsidies." Indeed, said the *Tribune,* only President Grant's intervention had prevented a steal at the previous session. Now came Frémont offering to build a transcontinental line without costing the nation a cent—threatening to spoil the subsidy business; and Howard, holding a position "in which a corrupt man may make a great deal of money," hampered his undertaking by quibbles and sharp manœuvers. When Howard explained that he had threatened a filibuster against the bill because he questioned the continued validity of the Texas land grant, the *Tribune* pooh-poohed his excuse, remarking that if any such doubts existed they were for the financiers of the road, not for Congress, to consider.[6]

That summer of 1869 witnessed efforts, much more strenuous than discreet, to float the bonds of the Memphis & El Paso in France. They were fairly successful; a total of $5,343,000 worth of securities was sold in Europe, almost wholly to French investors. But of this the French agents of the road, after the custom of the time, paid only three-fifths into the company treasury, taking two-fifths for their trouble. The money came in slowly and irregularly, much of it being used in France to buy rolling-stock and rails; obligations at

[6] For the controversy between the *Tribune* and Howard, see its issues for August 5, 11, and 17, 1869.

home meanwhile rose steadily. Moreover, unexpected physical obstacles were met; a freshet blocked the channels of the Red River and steamboats could not come within fifty miles of the point where construction had begun. The cost of grading the first seventy miles far exceeded the early estimates. Nevertheless, Frémont's faith in his road remained undiminished. So did that of the *Tribune*. Senator Howard's Pacific Railroad Committee early in 1870 showed fresh hostility, for on April 22nd a subcommittee reported that it believed the road had forfeited its land-grant by tardiness in construction. The *Tribune* scolded this report vigorously while praising Frémont's undertaking anew. Greeley was always a staunch friend: [7]

The proposition of a railroad on the 32d parallel of latitude has been before the public in various shapes for twenty years, and yet the enterprise is still struggling desperately for existence. Then Texas was the only State of the Gulf region, to whose prosperity the completion of the road is of almost vital importance, which gave it the least encouragement. Louisiana was cold because New Orleans was passed by, and Arkansas offended because Memphis was aimed at. But so earnest was Texas in its desire to see the road built that its several legislatures under rebel and loyal rule affirmed and reaffirmed the grant of lands made to the road in 1856. California on the Pacific Coast was desirous of making the port of San Diego the western terminus of the line, chartered and aided the partial construction of another line. The Texas route is the Memphis & El Paso line; the California route is usually called the San Diego & Fort Yuma Railroad. Of the former more than fifty miles are graded, and twenty-three miles laid with rails. Of the latter we know only that work is in progress. Without doubt the two lines have more of finished work, larger land grants, and better prospects of being eventually completed than any other Southern Pacific Rrd. These two roads are under the control of Gen. John C. Frémont; and he has asked Congress to consolidate, charter, and aid them under the title of the "Southern Transcontinental Railway.

[7] New York *Tribune*, May 25, 1870.

The Senate Committee on the Pacific Railroad has not only reported adversely to this consolidation, but has proposed to authorize an entirely new line, to be called the Texas Pacific Railroad, with branches and connections; and the bill makes large land grants....

Frémont's enterprise, while ambitious, was not more grandiose than many others in the Gilded Age, and the methods by which he tried to finance his scheme were merely typical of these flush and optimistic years. In view of the apparent security which 18,200,000 acres (10,240 for each mile built) offered, they were not reckless.[8] Compared with Jay Cooke's methods of booming the Northern Pacific or "banana belt" route they were conservative; compared with the operations of the Credit Mobilier in building the Union Pacific, they were decidedly decent. They differed little from the financial arrangements made for dozens of other lines which went bankrupt in or before 1873. To be sure, the Memphis & El Paso actually laid down only short stretches of track, and only three locomotives were placed on them, but the land grants were, as the press agents wrote, "an empire in themselves." However, high construction costs, the ebbing flow of French money, Senator Howard's doubts as to the land-grant, and other factors all sapped the credit of the company. In midsummer of 1870 the blow fell. The road failed to meet payments, mortgage-holders applied for a receivership, and the Federal courts appointed John A. C. Gray to take possession of the property.

To Frémont this meant ruin—ruin utter and irretrievable. His Kansas Pacific enterprise had already shaken his position, for after paying $200,000 for this road and investing large sums in construction, he had lost it all. Now his remaining money was gone. Family tradition describes the blow as paralyzing in its completeness.

Throughout these years of railroad-planning, the General's household had lived on a lavish though hardly ostentatious scale; he was a millionaire, and he had dwelt like one. During

[8] *Commercial and Financial Chronicle,* August 9, 1873.

the war he had bought a commodious brownstone mansion at what is now 21 West 19th Street, between Fifth and Sixth Avenues. This was a fashionable part of town, and his neighbors included Theodore Roosevelt, Sr., and (for a time) Senator John Sherman. Early in the sixties he had also bought a comfortable summer home on the Hudson, "the old Webb place," some two miles north of Tarrytown—later a part of John D. Rockefeller's estate. Here, amid more than a hundred acres of lawn and woodland, he had a fine house of rough gray stone, commanding a view of the broad Tappan Zee. Both houses afforded every comfort—a good cuisine, presided over by a French chef, well-drilled servants, flowers, music, and handsome furniture. Frémont, keeping a spirited horse, rode much in Central Park with Colonel Zagonyi and others, while his daughter Lilly drove a pair of Kentucky thoroughbreds. The children had tutors, and Lilly in especial became an excellent linguist. Mrs. Frémont, interested in many charities, gave to them with a generous hand.

At all times Frémont's personal tastes were simple, and in some ways he maintained a Spartan existence even when his wealth seemed greatest. He ate astonishingly little, never touched spirits, and drank wine—a glass of claret or Matrai —only when he was tired. He did not smoke, saying that he had taken warning from his men on his expeditions, who seemed to suffer as much from the deprivation of tobacco as of food. He dressed plainly. He used to say that he preferred "old garments, old books, old friends." His library was large, filling from floor to ceiling, in these years, all sides of a room twenty by thirty feet; indeed, after Humboldt's death in 1859 he had purchased the books of the great geographer. Here were also other volumes in beautiful bindings, including a set of the Audubon which had so fascinated Jessie as a child in the Congressional Library. His own room held a special set of cases covering the art of war from the earliest time to his own day. But books and horses were his chief indulgences. He belonged to no clubs, costly or otherwise; he cared little for the theater and nothing for elaborate social entertainments; and he liked to go to bed by ten or earlier, rising at the glimmer of dawn. The household was hospitable, for nothing pleased Frémont more than having friends about him. At the estate on the Hudson—which Mrs. Frémont christened by the local Indian name Pocaho—guests were usually present, and in town an extra plate was always laid at dinner for the chance comer. But balls, receptions, and large dinner-parties were avoided. The general liked better a good fencing-match, a long country walk, or a quiet chat with some congenial friend like N. P. Banks, Thurlow Weed, or John Sherman. A young woman, Nellie Haskell, who lived with them for a time at Pocaho has described his routine:

The general was often away in the West on his railroad business, but when home he usually read quietly or took evening walks with Mrs. Frémont or long rides through the woods and along the post-roads with the boys, Lil, and myself. He loved to listen to what he called home-made music. He went occasionally to the theatre when Mrs. Frémont asked him, which was seldom, because she knew he preferred to play chess or chat with the neighbors, the Phelpses, Schuylers, Aspinwalls, or Beechers, who dropped in often. As to formal dinners, he attended them only when Mrs. Frémont said: "You really must go this time." She attended many such functions when he was West on business, going to Washington for dinners and musicales. She was present at Mrs. Grant's first White House reception.... But when Mr. Frémont was at home, she tried to have only the sort of guests in the house agreeable to him.

In these years he and Mrs. Frémont spent much time and money in travel. In 1869 they visited France, Germany, Austria, and Scandinavia, the General combining pleasure with a certain amount of business; and they left two of the children in Dresden for schooling. As a railway president, he was in Washington, Texas, or California—everywhere that affairs called him. Both he and Jessie were personages, and they moved with dignity. The summer of 1868 they visited St. Louis to witness the unveiling of a statue of Thomas Hart Benton. In Mrs. Frémont the event awakened the deepest emotion. A holiday crowd of 40,000 filled the park, and thousands of school-children carrying roses were massed about the pedestal. A band played in the hot afternoon sun. As Jessie pulled the cord and the white drapery fell away the children threw their flowers at the base of the statue; an outgoing train to San Francisco halted and saluted with whistle and waving flags; and she gazed through a mist of tears at the bronze image of her father, facing westward, with the words carved below: "There Is The East. There Lies the Road to India." To both Frémont and Jessie, movement, action, and the sense of important pursuits were the breath of life; and Jessie in especial delighted to live with a certain largeness and splendor.

Now the spacious, luxurious days were suddenly gone forever. There was no money for travel, for tutors, or for servants. The Nineteenth Street home and the much dearer Pocaho on the Hudson were both swept away. Even prized personal belongings had to be sold. Bierstadt's painting of the Golden Gate with the sun setting behind it was bought by a friend for $4,000, just what Frémont had paid for it. The library, portraits, and mementoes of California, Washington, and Paris in large part disappeared. Land which had been held in California in the name of Mrs. Frémont and the children was sold with the rest. For a brief period the two could not even live together, Mrs. Frémont going into the country to take refuge in one friendly household, and Frémont staying at another in the city. It was a chilling plunge from wealth to penury.

It could not be said that Frémont had fared better than other investors in the Memphis & El Paso, for he was the last man in the world to use his inside knowledge to escape scot-free from the crash which ruined others. Yet about his name there instantly collected the atmosphere of a scandal. The reason for this lay in the means used to sell the Memphis & El Paso bonds in France. Frémont, with his usual poor judgment of men, had been unfortunate in his agent. The French consul-general in New York, Frémont's brother-in-law Gauldrée Boileau, had introduced to him a M. Henri Probst, whom he endorsed as a well-known businessman in Paris. Probst had in fact been connected with the French Government in supplying the troops engaged in the Mexican occupation; Frémont liked the man, and at his instance the executive board appointed him agent in France. It was agreed that for the first series of bonds issued 60 per cent of the face value was to be paid to the Company, 34 per cent was to be given to the banking house selling the bonds, and 6 per cent was to go to the agent.[9] Probst, after associating with himself a prominent French railway engineer, Antoine Lissignol, to lend an appearance of technical strength to the enterprise, arranged with the great brokerage house of Paradis et Cie. to float the bonds. This house made harsh stipulations, requiring that all possible materials be purchased in France or Belgium; and one reason why the road shortly failed was that contracts for 100 engines and 45,000 tons of rails, costing 14,000,000 francs, were let in France.

Going from New York to Paris late in 1867, Probst had concluded this arrangement with Paradis et Cie. during the latter part of 1868; and either Probst or Paradis et Cie. then indulged in a series of remarkable misrepresentations. A full-page advertisement in *La Liberté* of May 15, 1869, is typical of the extravagant claims made for the enterprise. This described the company as the "Transcontinental Memphis Pacific," and pictured its line as running from Baltimore, Norfolk, and Charleston, the three Eastern termini, westward through Chattanooga, Memphis, Arkansas, Texas, and the Territories to San Diego. The roads from the Eastern seaports to Memphis were spoken of as "that part of the transcontinental railroad which is finished and in operation," while it was stated that the section from Memphis to Little Rock was in working order and the line from Little Rock to the Red River was being

[9] *Commercial and Financial Chronicle*, September 4, 1875; Frémont, MS *Memoirs*.

"pressed forward actively." Part of the advertisement reads like some dream of Tartarin of Tarascon. "Entering the territory of New Mexico," it declared, "the Transcontiental meets the great commercial route from Guaymas and the interior of Mexico at Santa Fé. It will, for the future, suppress the dangerous marches of caravans from Santa Fé to San Francisco, New Orleans, and St. Louis. It then reaches California, after receiving at Arizona City the traffic of the great River Colorado." [10]

This was bad enough; but there were still worse misrepresentations. In *La Liberté* and other newspapers the brokers stated that "the company with the approbation of Congress has fused itself with the lines constructed and at present working from Memphis to Chattanooga, Chattanooga to Washington and Baltimore, Chattanooga to Norfolk, and Washington to Norfolk through Richmond." They also declared that the Federal Government had subsidized the Memphis & El Paso as it had the Union Pacific. "Besides the grants of land," ran the advertisements, though there were no congressional grants, "the Federal Government has voted a guarante of interest of six per cent in favor of the ordinary construction bonds." Of course this was preposterous. The American minister, Elihu Washburne, promptly sent copies of the advertisements and the placards which were stuck up over Paris to the secretary of state, suggesting that he investigate and take remedial action. He was the more ready to act because ever since his visit to St. Louis in 1861, and his formulation then of charges which the Committee on the Conduct of the War declared unfounded, he had keenly disliked Frémont. By this time, fifteen million francs' worth of the bonds had been sold.

Of these falsehoods circulated in Paris, Frémont knew nothing till later. "At the time the misstatement was made," he writes, "I was in Washington asking Congress for the right of

----

[10] A full history of the Memphis, El Paso & Pacific, and of the methods used to sell the bonds in France, is given in *Senate Misc. Doc.* 121, 41st Cong., 2d Sess.; this contains more than a hundred pages of data and testimony.

way for this road through the Territories to the Pacific. This
fact was widely known—spoken of in the newspapers in editorials and otherwise; and a telegram from Paradis et Cie.
to any banker in New York would have corrected an error
which the face of the bonds should have suggested." The bonds
declared explicitly that they were based upon lands granted
by the State of Texas, and in no way indicated any connection
with the Federal Government. No doubt some of the material
for the glowing account of the "Transcontinental" as a system
running from Norfolk to California was drawn from the hopes
and imaginings of Frémont and his associates, who believed in
the line. But even the mildest representations of the French
agents were made without his authority or knowledge, on their
own responsibility.[11]

Reaching Paris in the summer of 1869, Frémont published a
letter in an influential French journal in which he tried to set
the public right on the main facts as to the bonds. "It is completely false," he wrote, "that we have ever declared that our
mortgage bonds enjoy a Federal guarantee of six per cent
interest." On the contrary, he declared, the security for the
bonds was the mortgage placed upon the state land-grant.[12] In
a supplementary statement published on September 27th he
added that the company was pressing Congress for a Federal
charter, the result of which would be a new land subsidy from
the states which had not disposed of their public domain, and
the recognition of the line as a postal and military railroad. His
optimism unquestionably operated, like Jay Cooke's optimism
about the Northern Pacific just before its collapse, like the
optimism of many an enterpreneur, to lead investors into a
highly speculative enterprise. He should have been more indignant, explicit, and thorough in contradicting the lies cir-

---

[11] Fremont's full statement in self-defense on the sale of the bonds, in the
form of a letter to Senator Howard, is published *Senate Misc. Doc.* 96, 41st
Cong., 2d. Sess. It is complete and explicit, filling nine pages. It contains no
date, but was apparently written about March 25, 1870. One feature is Frémont's sharp attack on Washburne.

[12] *La Phare de la Loire,* September 18, 1869.

culated by Probst. He should also have included a warning
that some question had recently arisen as to the continued
validity of the Texan land-grant. But his sanguine temperament conspired with his desire not to injure the bonds un-
necessarily.

The bankruptcy of the Memphis & El Paso caused an indignant outcry in France and a feeling of dismay among right-
thinking Americans. For some time the press devoted much
space to the affair. Three years later such failures were to become commonplace. But the post-war boom still endured, and
many Americans were anxious to determine who was blameworthy for these losses. They agreed with Senator Howard's
emphatic statement that "a more stupendous fraud never was
committed or attempted upon a friendly people," and that
"it is one which, if the work of Americans, should make every
American blush." They turned back to the published report
of April 22nd upon the railroad, with its mass of testimony by
Frémont, Corwine, and others upon the operations of the company.

Senator Howard, who compiled this report and who had
shown a hostile attitude to Frémont from the beginning, now
told the Senate that while he could not hold him "personally
responsible" for the misrepresentations, he did not "think Gen.
Frémont's skirts are clear in reference to these transactions."
Many Representatives and not a few Senators were ready to
defend Frémont. In debate half a dozen champions challenged
Howard's statement with asperity.[13] Sumner declared that it
was highly unjust, for there was no evidence of privity on the
part of the explorer. Lyman Trumbull of Illinois, James Nye
of Nevada, and Simon Cameron of Pennsylvania all took the
same side. Trumbull demonstrated that Howard's statement
represented only his individual judgment, that it was based
chiefly on one-sided French and American newspaper reports,
and that a majority of the subcommittee had dissented from it.
He also made the valid point that the French themselves were

---

[13] For this debate see *Congressional Globe,* June 20-23, 1870.

largely blameworthy for their losses—that they had no excuse for not learning the truth:

> Sir, he [Howard] brings no fact against Frémont that I have heard. He brings charges against the Memphis & El Paso Railroad; he complains that its bonds were puffed up. I understand that a single party in France was the purchaser of those bonds, and afterwards put them upon the market in Paris, and he had various publications inserted in the papers in order to sell them for as much as he could get. Is General Frémont responsible for that? ... The bond itself shows what its security is; and the Senator will hardly make the Senate or the country believe that capitalists do not look to see what security the bond is issued on. Capitalists understood this thing quite as well as the Senator from Michigan did. They knew what they were buying.

Nevertheless, the episode left an unhappy blemish upon Frémont's reputation. It is evident that he had acted with entire honesty in the matter, but it is also certain that he had shown a lamentable lack of discretion and care. It was his business, in the conscientious discharge of his duties, to scrutinize the advertisements of his company's bonds in all markets, to insist upon fair statements, and to caution his agents against exaggeration. His fault was of omission, not commission, but it was nevertheless real. When he learned of the false statements he should have been more emphatic in denying them. We cannot believe that a man of his sense of honor consented to an improper act, but he did not sufficiently guard against such acts by others. Once more his precipitancy and lack of circumspection betrayed him.

Irate Frenchmen came to America and filed affidavits demanding his arrest; French bondholders commenced suits in New York against him and his associates. The Paris office of the Memphis & El Paso was closed by the authorities, and all books and papers were seized. Criminal proceedings were begun against the men supposed to be responsible for selling bonds under false pretenses, including Frémont. After a thorough official examination, lasting more than two years, his name was removed from the list of those accused; but just before the trial commenced it was suddenly restored. Later he was told that this was at the instance of our minister, Elihu Washburne, whom he had attacked in his published defense. He was given inadequate time to appear before the *juge d'instruction*—only ten days after the summons was served in New York; he had scanty funds for travel or for hiring counsel, and in his absence was condemned for failing to reply. Though his French counsel, M. Allou, was in the courtroom, in accordance with French law the judge refused to hear him. The publicity given to this condemnation left a totally unjust impression.

Some years later, in closing his work as Federal receiver for the Memphis & El Paso, John A. C. Gray wrote the General on the subject. "I deem it fair to say," he stated, "that throughout the long and careful scrutiny which I have made into the affairs of the company, I have found no proof that would sustain the charges brought against you regarding the fraudulent sale of the company's bonds in France." Gray's testimony is the more important in that he was an attorney of marked distinction. The Marquis de Chambrun, who represented the French bondholders in America, gave the same testimony. He also wrote for Frémont a letter explaining the condemnation in Paris. "The judgment pronounced against you," he said, "was nothing more than a judgment by default resting upon the *prima facie* case submitted to the tribunal of *police correctionale* by the judicial officer or officers who had directed the preliminary investigation. Under this state of affairs no defense could be offered in your behalf." He added that these ex parte proceedings were an absolute nullity in the eyes of American law, were in direct conflict with the safeguards of personal liberty in the American constitution, and "are now void in France." [14]

[14] The letters of Gray and Chambrun are in the Frémont MSS. Gray went on to say: "The misrepresentations under which the bonds were sold to the

As the wreck of the Memphis & El Paso was cleared up, and the Texas Pacific Railroad took over its debts and assets, Frémont beyond doubt felt that his honor remained unblemished; that his motives and aims had always been of the highest character. Jessie shared this conviction. "It is an inextricable mass," she told a friend, "out of which I can glean only an impression of millions of dollars of railroad bonds floated abroad which brought profit only to the agent, advertisements published abroad that misrepresented the whole railroad picture, of which Mr. Frémont knew nothing.... He has had no part in any dishonest transaction. Certain of that, I am strong for whatever is to come." But he had little left but his self-respect. His career as a financier was as decisively ended as his career as an explorer. The demonstration that he was unfitted for business affairs was so complete that no acceptable employment was open to him. He was past sixty; he had three dependent children; he was almost penniless. All the courage that he had shown in facing the snow-choked Sierras and the storm of wartime obloquy in St. Louis was needed again; all of it and more.

public, were made by parties in Paris to whom the entire issue of bonds had been sold by the Company, and my examinations fail to show any proof that these misrepresentations were made with your authority."

XXXV

Poverty and Labor

IN this family crisis, it was Mrs. Frémont who, with characteristic vigor, came to the rescue. "I am like a deeply built ship," she used to say; "I drive best under a stormy wind." She had already discovered that she could earn money with her pen. During the Civil War she had set herself, with a frenzy of energy, to write the history of Zagonyi's brave troopers who made the charge at Springfield; and within ten days, according to family tradition, had produced the spirited little book called *The Story of the Guard,* the profits of which she devoted to the Sanitary Commission. Now, while the family went to live first on Madison Avenue, far uptown at Seventy-second Street, and then scraped together its resources to rent a cottage on what was called "the Esplanade" on the waterfront of Staten Island, she became a breadwinner.

Spurred on by the illness of her younger son, who was threatened with tuberculosis, and who must—the physician said—be sent to a dry high climate, she approached Robert Bonner of the New York *Ledger.* He offered her $100 each for a series of articles. Doubtless he thought it would be months before they were all completed, but she went home, sat down at her desk, and for days labored almost incessantly, hardly pausing for food or rest. When they were all done, she took them to the Ledger office and demanded payment in a lump sum to meet her son's needs. At once she began contributing to other magazines. In the fifteen years between 1875 and 1890, she produced article after article, story after story. She contributed tales for children to the *Wide Awake,* popular essays to the *Ledger,* historical sketches to *Harper's* and the *Century.* Some of this magazine work was made over into books: *A Year of American Travel,* dealing with California and Panama in the gold-rush days; *Far West Sketches,* concerned chiefly with Mariposa life; *The Will and the Way Stories* for juveniles; and most important of all, in 1887, the *Souvenirs of My Time,* an episodic review, brightly written, of her eventful life from the Bodisco wedding to the last tour of Europe.

Frémont was one of the incorporators of the Texas Pacific, which took over the wreck of the Memphis & El Paso, and till March, 1878, when the receivership was terminated, he was largely occupied in helping adjust the affairs of his dead railroad enterprise. For his labors, he received only a slender compensation. He hence had reason to be glad when, in 1878, upon the intercession of Zachariah Chandler and other old friends, he received from President Hayes the appointment as territorial governor of Arizona. The salary was but $2,000 a year, yet that sum meant much to the General. So, too, did the opportunity to revisit the wild West, and to see his surviving friends, including Alexis Godey, who traveled with him from San Francisco to Los Angeles.[1] There was still a halo of legend about Frémont's head, and his journey along the transcontinental line was a modest ovation. In Chicago and Omaha, he was offered banquets; in San Francisco the Pioneer Association of California gave him a reception; in many smaller towns, the stations were crowded with people eager to see him once more; and the friendly demonstrations continued through lower California to the end of the railroad at Yuma. Thence he had a "camping-out journey," as Mrs. Frémont called it, to Prescott, the territorial capital.

Frémont enjoyed such administrative opportunities as the post offered, and busied himself with recommendations regarding mining development, railway building, and irrigation by storage reservoirs. With his characteristic liking for large projects, he raised also the question of using the Colorado River to flood the depressed region above the head of the Gulf of

[1] I. T. Martin, *Recollections of Elizabeth Benton Frémont,* p. 136.

California known later as the Salton Sink, where a great inland sea could easily be recreated. The climate and vegetation of Arizona, he believed, might be essentially affected for the better. There was a congenial if narrow social life at Prescott, where a number of army officers were stationed. He delighted in the return to an outdoor life, and was capable of being in the saddle for twelve hours at a stretch. He thought nothing of riding eighty miles in two days. But poverty remained a sore burden even in the distant Southwest, where house rent was ninety dollars a month and provisions were atrociously high. It is an eloquent fact that although Mrs. Frémont and her daughter knew that the wonders of the Grand Canyon were at hand, it was a financial impossibility to visit them. After a time the high altitude of Prescott told so heavily on Jessie's health that she returned to a small house on Staten Island, and there continued writing stories and essays.

In 1883, hopeful of reëstablishing himself in the business life of New York, Frémont resigned and joined Jessie on Staten Island. On the day of his arrival Mrs. Frémont wrote a friend: "There is only one piece of news in the world to-day, the General is here. He tells me I am beautiful, but I tell him the truth. He looks young, rested, and as handsome as that day in '41 when I saw him swinging down the avenue in his new uniform." [2] One undertaking which floated elusively before him was a plan for enlisting the Barings and other English capitalists in the development by irrigation of the rich Imperial Valley in California. While in Arizona he had become interested, in association with Judge Edward Silent, in various mining enterprises, notably in the rich copper area now known as the Verde—enterprises which ultimately made Judge Silent rich. He was as eager and hopeful as ever. He believed that fortune always lay just ahead. But of actual monetary returns, there was pitifully little.

These trying years brought into relief some of the best qualities of Frémont and his wife. They did not conceal their strait-

[2] Catherine Coffin Phillips, *Jessie Benton Frémont*, p. 305.

ened lot. Newspaper reporters who visited their cottage for a "story" exclaimed over their evident poverty.[3] Yet they made the most of their few paintings, their bric-a-brac, their books, and the many trophies of Frémont's work as an explorer and soldier—the presentation swords he had received from the people at Charleston, the Germans of St. Louis, and Captain Cathcart; his foreign medals; the flag he had unfurled from the Wind River Peak, and the campaign banners of '56. Their pride permitted not the slightest recognition, by word or gesture, that they had fallen in fortune, or the slightest intimation of regret. In dignity of bearing, Mrs. Frémont was as much the *grande dame* as ever; her husband was the same grave, reserved, courteous gentleman, a little quieter as the years passed, but with the same piercing eye. Their devotion was, as always, beautiful to see. Observers who were much with them have said that they seemed never to need to discuss a question to reach the same conclusion; they intuitively knew each other's wishes and mental processes. They appeared to have some strange spiritual bond, such as that which Mrs. Frémont suggested when she described for the Psychical Research Society the telepathic message which she believed she had received, after long days of emotional prostration, of Frémont's safety at Parowan in 1854.[4]

Both of them struggled valiantly to make the best of their position. The two sons were educated at the Naval Academy and the Military Academy. Constant but unavailing efforts were made to obtain from the Government some compensation for the house and land seized at Black Point, near San Francisco, in 1863, for the erection of a fort; compensation which should have been made without hesitation, and which would have rescued them from all their difficulties. Mrs. Frémont wrote with unresting pen. In 1886, her husband also turned to literary labors. The *Personal Memoirs* of General Grant were then being read with intense interest, and the explorer was

[3] Compare Leander Richardson in Boston *Herald*, August 14, 1884.
[4] Described also in *Far Wes' Sketches*, pp. 29-41.

seized by the idea that his own reminiscences would be of considerable value. Going to Washington, the Frémonts took a house for a year so that he could have access to official papers and reports, and set to work. A newspaper writer has given us a picture of them at their labors:[5]

The Frémonts live in a commodious house that overlooks the wooded grounds of the British Legation, the trees of Nineteenth Street, and the shrubbery of Dupont Circle. The family at present here consists of the General and Mrs. Frémont and their daughter. The two sons are married. One is in the navy, the other lives in Montana. The workroom is on the second floor of the house.... There is a bay window in the east end of the room, on the right of which is placed the General's table, surmounted by a tall set of pigeonholes, where letters, notes, and papers are kept. On the other side of the window is placed Mrs. Frémont's table, a large plain affair, covered with green leather. The General dictates and Mrs. Frémont writes down each word of the story as it falls from his lips. The family group is, however, not yet complete. In the alcove is placed a typewriter, and with it Miss Frémont transforms her mother's manuscript into neat, legible print. Here they all work together...all day long. The rule of the house is to rise at seven, take a cup of tea and a roll, and begin at eight, and continue until twelve, when breakfast is taken. At one o'clock they resume work and forge ahead until six, when the stop for the day and for dinner is made. In the evening the copy is sent out, and in the morning the proof-sheets are received from the printer. Gen. Frémont is now seventy-four years old, but looks scarce sixty. His hair, short beard, and moustache are white, but his brown eyes are clear and bright as stars, and his complexion has the ruddy, healthy glow of childhood.

To find a publisher was not easy, but at last Belford, Clarke & Co. of Chicago and New York entered into a contract. The first of the two volumes, a ponderous 650-page work, appeared in 1887 under the title of *Memoirs of My Life: A Retrospect of Fifty Years,* with a sketch of the life of Benton written by

[5] New York *Evening Post*, September 7, 1886, quoting the Washington *Star*.

Jessie. Based largely upon the reports of the exploring expeditions, much of which was reprinted almost verbatim, the first volume came down only to the capitulation of Couenga in 1847. Its full detail proved wearisome to general readers. Some of the numerous plates, from paintings and drawings based upon the daguerreotypes made by Carvalho in the fourth expedition, were admirable, but others were weak. The price of the book, ranging from $5.75 to $12.50 according to binding, was too high for ordinary purchasers. As a result it was a commercial failure, and the second volume was never published. For all his labors on the *Memoirs* Frémont received almost nothing. He spoke occasionally in public, as when in 1884 he campaigned in Michigan for Blaine, but he never lectured for pay. There were still times when the wolf howled very near the door.

At last a sudden crisis arose, Frémont's health seemed to break under the strain of writing, and late in 1887 he was seized with so severe an attack of bronchitis that his physician declared he must be taken at once to a warmer climate.[6] There was no money. In desperation—doubtless also in humiliation— Mrs. Frémont went to her old friend, the eminent railway builder Collis P. Huntington, who was all concern. "It must be California," he said; "you should have my private car, but it is already lent." That night he came in person to bring tickets, letters to officials of different railways, and a generous sum for expenses. Frémont was reluctant and almost angry, but Mrs. Frémont insisted. So did Huntington, who tactfully remarked: "You forget our road goes over your buried campfires and climbs many a grade you jogged over on a mule; I think we rather owe you this." A day later they were in a Pullman, running out of the stormy December weather into the bright sunshine of Kentucky:

It had been a trial to see the General's sad, unsmiling face [wrote Mrs. Frémont afterward], but toward evening he beckoned me across to his section, and holding my hand said, "You were right to come.

[6] I have received much material on this period of family life from the late Major Frank P. Frémont.

I feel better already." Whereupon I cried heartily. Instantly a young conductor was beside me with words of genuine compassion. "O, it is not that," I said, "I am so happy, the General says he feels better." "We all know who you are," the tender-hearted man said, "but we respected General Frémont's wish for silence."

This was the beginning of the end, though Frémont's long rest in California—they settled in a cottage on Oak Street in Los Angeles—seemed to restore his health. He returned to New York in 1889 to look after what he still proudly called his business affairs, leaving Mrs. Frémont on the Pacific Coast and writing to her daily. He had high hopes that he would yet induce Congress to make a proper payment for the Black Point property. Moreover, he had been deeply touched and gratified when his friends (prompted, it must be confessed, by Jessie) set on foot a movement to have him restored to the Army as a major-general, and placed on the retired list with pay, and he now gave them every assistance that was proper. He had outlived most of his enemies—the Blairs, Elihu Washburne, and others—and all the ill feeling of the past. Public sentiment supported the measure, and in April, 1890, Congress, "in view of the services to his country rendered by John C. Frémont, now of New York, as explorer, administrator, and soldier," duly made the appointment. It secured to him, for the first time in more than fifteen years, an adequate income, $6,000 annually, and enabled him to look forward to his last days in peace.[7]

His relief and pleasure, his friends in New York have said, were childlike. He proposed to go back as quickly as possible to Los Angeles, and there make his permanent home. Early in July, 1890, he wrote Mrs. Frémont that he would set off the following week and spoke of "living out our years together in a content most absolute." He had become involved with Josiah Royce in a controversy over his rôle in the conquest of Cali-

[7] Jessie, who believed the government owed them more than $40,000 for the Black Point property, declared with her usual spirit that this allowance was "small payment on account," and "sadly delayed" at that.

fornia, and wished to complete an article for the *Century Maga-zine*. But he had less strength than he or his sons, with whom he had spent much time in Washington, supposed.

The end came as a direct result of a kindly act. On a hot July Sunday, he made a pilgrimage to the grave of a little boy friend in Brooklyn. The English mother had obtained from him a promise that he would lay flowers there in memory of the child's birthday, and he kept the promise. That night occurred a sudden fall in temperature, and his boarding-house bed had insufficient coverings. Frémont had been overheated and fatigued, and was seized with a violent chill. His physician and close friend, Dr. William J. Morton, was called, and immediately upon arriving telegraphed up the Hudson to Ossining for the only son in reach, John C. Frémont, Jr. When the latter arrived, it was evident that peritonitis had set in, and that in a man seventy-seven years old it could only terminate fatally. Within a few hours it was all over. There was little time to warn Jessie. A telegram had gone to her from Charley: "Father is ill." Three hours later came another: "Father is dead." But the suddenness was perhaps best. "The end came painlessly," wrote the son to his sister Elizabeth, in words which recall Kent's exclamation over the dead Lear, "and without knowl-edge to him. It was blessedly quick and easy, and as I looked at him lying there so still and peaceful I questioned whether I was not heartless, for I could find no sorrow or pity for him at all, but a feeling of relief that his life was over. And how thank-ful I am that the last few months were made more peaceful and happier for him." The date was July 13th. He added: "Of what the effect is going to be on mother, I don't dare think. And when I do think, I doubt whether the cruelest result would not be the kindest. They lived in each other so that I don't think there is any life for the one left."

It was a characteristic end for a life full of misfortune—almost alone in a cheerless Manhattan boarding-house, with no friends near, and with Jessie three thousand miles away; his hope of their comfortable days together, all financial anxiety at last removed, never to be realized. Doubtless he knew, as his life ebbed away, that his wife would be plunged back again into utter poverty. When he was placed in his coffin—he had instructed that it be a plain pine box, and that he be buried in an ordinary black suit, not his uniform—his son took a miniature of Jessie as she had been in the days of her youth, and the telegram that was her last message to him, and folded them in one of his crossed hands. It was the end of the romance that had begun in Washington in the bright autumn days of 1840.

* * *

Mrs. Frémont was destined to outlive her husband by a dozen years, residing constantly with her daughter in Los Angeles. The death of the General, who had received only two months' pay since his restoration to the army lists, left her in sorely straitened circumstances; but her friends and admirers came at once to her aid. Within a few months, in the latter part of 1890, she was presented with a handsome cottage in the newer part of Los Angeles. At the same time, Congress, spurred on by exaggerated press stories that she was in actual destitution, passed a bill giving her the ordinary pension of $2,000 allowed to widows of major-generals. Her future was thus secure. For many years, she was one of the prominent figures of Los Angeles, deferred to on all public occasions. When President McKinley and John Hay visited the city in 1901, one of their first acts was to drive to Mrs. Frémont's home to pay her their respects. "My goodness, John," Mrs. Frémont said with a twinkle to the portly Secretary of State, whom she recalled as a slender stripling in the White House in Lincoln's time, "how you have grown!" She was then confined to her chair, and on December 27, 1902, she died.

They are buried together at Piermont on the Hudson, near the brink of a bluff looking out over the broad Tappan Zee to the old home, Pocaho, where they spent some of their happiest years together. Over their grave, the state of New York in 1906 erected a dignified monument, with bronze flag, sword, and a medallion head of the explorer against a granite stone, and on it are recorded his many achievements and titles. He would have chosen for himself a shorter, simpler inscription—perhaps the sentence in which Buchanan declared that to him more than any other belonged the credit for the conquest of California. Some of his friends would have chosen the line of Whittier—"Frémont, who struck the first brave blow for liberty." But the most fitting epitaph, recalling his happiest achievements, and his most remarkable services to the nation, is furnished by the words of Jessie Benton Frémont—"from the ashes of his campfires have sprung cities."

XXXVI

Character and Fame

IN this varied and energetic career, so full both of achievement and frustration, there is much which appears psy-
chologically puzzling. The fact that to many of Frémont's
contemporaries his personality seemed alien and impenetrable
helps to explain why his aims and motives were frequently mis-
judged, and his acts aroused such violent antagonism. He made
ardent friends who loved him (some of them) just this side of
idolatry; he made enemies who found no condemnation too
harsh. Many who attempted to measure him in a detached way
formed, after long study, an impression that he was a genius
manqué, a distinguished and valuable man who just fell short
of being effectively great. Josiah Royce, not the friendliest of
observers, wrote that the most transient personal intercourse
with this romantic and fascinating figure left a sense of a peculiarly hidden and baffling character. "The charming and courtly
manner, the deep and thoughtful eyes, the gracious and self-
possessed bearing, as of a consciously great man at rest, awaiting his chance to announce his deep purpose and to do his decisive deed—all these things perplexed one who had any occasion
to observe, as some did, that the deep purpose seemed always
to have remained in reserve, and that there had been some
reason in his life why the decisive deed had never been done."
Other men, like Schurz, felt strongly attracted to him at first
sight, and yet retained, in a sense of some subtle deficiency combined with great capacities, an unwillingness to give him their
complete confidence.

Yet Frémont's character and mind are essentially simple and
clear, and both his talents and limitations are susceptible of as

close analysis as those of most men of reserved temperament. He has sometimes been described as a showy and pretentious personality. Nothing could be further from the truth. All his closest associates testify that the outstanding qualities of his character were sincerity and simplicity. For ostentation—despite certain appearances to the contrary when in 1861 he tried to impress his strength upon hostile St. Louisans—he not only had no taste, but a decided distaste. He dressed with the utmost plainness. He avoided public appearances, and would go far to avoid a reception or civic dinner. He disliked public speaking, and it required a strong attachment to a man or cause to induce him, as in his brief tour for Blaine, to appear before an audience. He was simple in all his private habits: he liked plain food, gave a plain hospitality, and found his chief amusements in horseback riding and walking. In Mrs. Frémont's tastes there was always a strong element of liking for the dramatic, but of this Frémont himself showed not a trace.

Frémont's habits and impulses were essentially restless and kinetic. His friends noted that, beneath his quietness and dignity, he was always active, always moving, always concerned with action rather than thought. In his leisure at Pocaho he was incessantly busy outdoors. Though he had a large library, especially strong in military works and exploration, he was seldom observed sitting with a book in his hand. His friends remember him eagerly mastering one of the high-wheeled bicycles just coming into vogue, going on long botanical excursions, and overseeing the gardens and stables. He was extremely fond of dogs and horses. The years in which he furiously organized the mining activities at Mariposa, building flumes, stamp-mills, and roads, were as congenial to him as the years of outdoor exploration. Rather strangely, he had little aptitude for mechanical contrivance; as one of his family expressed it, he was "not a putterer." But he loved activities in the open and had little taste for study; in his later years, when master of his time, he retired early that he might be outdoors with the dawn. Yet there was no nervousness in this; when he was induced to take his seat in the circle indoors, his restlessness abruptly left him, and his dignified immobility, his perfect quiescence, with never an unnecessary gesture or motion, impressed all who saw him.

His social needs were fully met by a family life which was singularly attractive in its warmth and devotion, and in which he displayed the knightliest side of his character. It is significant that he not merely refrained from joining any clubs, but that he took no part in the activities of such bodies as the Grand Army of the Republic, in which he might have been a prominent figure; he was honored by the Royal Geographical Society, but joined no American scientific body. His circle of friends was limited, for his love of home life and his native reserve kept him from making new acquaintances readily. Yet with the men and women whom he knew best his reserve gave way to animation and even fun. His son writes that there was—

A sharp division between the two sides of his character; the questing side, which was expressed in his explorations, and the human side, which was companionable, cheerful, and with a tendency to gaiety accounted for by his French forbears. He heartily enjoyed a joke or a bright story, so long as it was keen and clean. Though in no sense pharisaical, he instinctively avoided the unclean, both physical and moral; and with all this, he was intensely human and understanding. One trait, or it might be said fault, was an indifference to what the general public might think, so long as he was sure that his action was right. Appearances are sometimes more important than facts, and I am sure that it was this indifference which has left him to a certain extent a misunderstood figure. Perhaps a sentence I remember may explain what I mean more clearly. One day when I was commenting upon the injustice of the government toward him in a certain case, he checked me by saying: "No! The United States and its government are all right. The fault lies in the fact that the conscience of the people is delegated to the members of Congress, and a delegated conscience never functions."

Frémont's primary talent was as an explorer; and just as he was rarely fortunate in the circumstances which threw him as a youth so quickly and effectively into the field of exploration, so he was unfortunate that later circumstances cut him off from all achievement therein. He was only rarely a "Pathfinder"; for the most part he was a Pathmarker. At times, particularly in his explorations of the Great Basin, he really made a new area known to the world. But in general he traveled over trails which had been found before by trappers, hunters, and traders, and through regions that were at least partially known to frontiersmen. His distinction lay in the scientific equipment he brought to the task of surveying, observing, and describing these trails and regions. For his period he was an excellent topographer, surveyor, and mathematician, and a good amateur geologist and botanist. For zoölogy, which was less important, he showed slighter aptitude. It would be hard to overemphasize the zeal and conscientiousness which he gave to the work of mapping his routes, collecting specimens, noting geographical and topographical facts, and at night taking his observations of the stars. He had a true scientist's reverence for his calling. Few distinctions pleased him so much as his medal from the Royal Geographical Society, and he spoke warmly of that body as his "alma mater"; while he took pride in naming one of his rivers after Alexander von Humboldt. "I am given by myself," he wrote, "the honor of being the first to place his great name on the map of this continent."

As an explorer he showed qualities of precision, industry, and resourcefulness that are quite incompatible with the conception of a flashy, unstable nature, a man of meretricious parts. His expeditions had no picnic aspect. For every member they were full of toil, hardship, hunger, fatigue, and peril; for Frémont they were full of constant and heavy responsibility. The romance of the western explorer's life, like that of most adventurous callings, largely vanishes on close examination; as the British soldier said of trench service, it was damned dirty, damned uncomfortable, and damned dangerous. To rise in the chill gray dawn; to tramp all day, twenty-five or thirty miles, over rough country; to eat half-raw, inadequate food and drink dirty water; to enforce discipline at every step; to be responsible for every animal, every piece of equipment, every life; to remain awake even to midnight in the harshest weather, after benumbing toil, in order to take astronomical observations; to sit up later still with cramped fingers noting the day's results; to rouse himself to see that watches were duly kept—such was Frémont's lot. It was his lot to frighten cowards out of his expedition before it got into the wilderness; to rise to sudden emergencies—now to replace the broken glass of the barometer without any glass, now to cross a rushing torrent without boats or material to make them; to hearten his men in undertakings that made even Indians quail, as in the winter passage of the Sierras; to be first on his feet in a surprise attack, as when the Klamath Indians struck. No poseur could have lasted ten days on these expeditions. The explorer deserved Kit Carson's heartfelt tribute of 1856:

I was with Frémont from 1842 to 1847. The hardships through which we passed, I find it impossible to describe, and the credit which he deserves I am incapable to do him justice in writing.... I have heard that he is enormously rich. I wish to God that he may be worth ten times as much more. All that he has or may ever receive, he deserves. I can never forget his treatment of me while in his employ and how cheerfully he suffered with his men when undergoing the severest of hardships.

Two contrasting traits are evident in Frémont the wanderer and explorer. He brought to his labors an enthusiasm which had in it more than a touch of poetry. The grandeur of the West became a passion with him. When he speaks of valley flowers "in brilliant bloom," of some lake "set like a gem in the mountains," of a camp where "the rocks lit up with the glow of our fires made a night-picture of very wild beauty," of Mount Hood rising "like a rose-colored mass of snow," he is recording an emotion that touched his innermost being. After the hardest day's march, he could write of some strange landscape that "the interest of the scene soon dissipated fatigue."

To many this poetic enthusiasm over the fresh beauties of the West will seem the most attractive element in Frémont's character. The other trait is represented by his skill as an organizer, his iron discipline, and his fierce contempt for cowardice or shirking. The poet gave way to the martinet when it came to mounting guard against Indians, protecting camp equipment, barring liquor, or demanding the intensest exertions in Nevada deserts or Sierra snows. Himself uncomplaining and indomitable, he could not forgive the quitter. There is an undertone of scathing contempt, in his letter to Mrs. Frémont after the calamitous expedition of 1848-49, describing how one man gave up. "Proue laid down in the trail and froze to death. In a sunshiny day, and having with him means to make a fire, he threw his blankets down in the trail and laid there till he froze to death."

To the end of his life Frémont retained his ardent enthusiasm for wild nature in all its aspects. He read nothing with so much interest as accounts of travel in uncharted lands, from the penetration of tropical Africa to polar expeditions. He never hunted or fished, and taught his children not to take animal life except under necessity.

Out-of-doors was life to him [writes his son], indoors, a place sheltered from the elements. Stormy weather appealed to him as well as fair. Trees were to him sacred, and he would not let them be cut down on our property, unless dead or dying; then he would do the cutting himself. Flowers especially appealed to him; being a botanist, he took a double interest in them. Travelling with him through the mountains of Arizona on horseback, when he was governor, I have noticed he would guide his horse so as to avoid crushing a flower or ant-hill; all life had a significance for him. Once we were climbing in the mountains near Innsbruck, and I came across a snake. Boylike, I started to kill it, but he would not permit it. "No, let it go! It has not harmed you and probably enjoys life," he said, adding: "Besides, any Indian knows that to kill a snake causelessly will bring rain and a wet camp."

The two salient faults in Frémont's composition, as the fore-going chapters amply illustrate, were his impulsiveness or rash-ness, and his weak judgment of men and of critical situations. The two faults were closely allied. A greater endowment of caution or practical sagacity would have saved him from expulsion at college; it would have withheld him from descending the dangerous Platte cañon with his instruments and records in a frail boat; it would have prevented the unnecessary clash with Castro on his first entrance into California. His midwinter crossing of the Sierras was an act of reckless impetuosity, in which he brilliantly succeeded because of favorable weather and the aid of two of the best frontiersmen of the time, Carson and Fitzpatrick. His attempted midwinter crossing of the San Juan and other mountains in 1848-49 was another impetuous act, which this time ended in irretrievable disaster. If Carson had been with him here when the storms smote him with irre-sistible force, he would have urged Frémont to make camp, gather wood, put up shelters for the men and animals, weather the storm, and at its termination go back instead of forward. A different decision on Frémont's part would have saved hu-man lives. But his most unfortunate display of imperfect judg-ment was in St. Louis in 1861. He surrounded himself with poorly selected men; he treated tactlessly men and forces re-quiring careful conciliation; he disregarded the wise and kindly efforts of Lincoln to counsel him. It is but a partial excuse to say that his judgment, with all its defects, was in many respects better than the judgment shown by Cameron, the Blairs, and others in Washington.

Our statement as to his deficiencies requires a certain elab-oration. Lack of judgment frequently means lack of general ability; but not so with Frémont, who had extreme quickness of mind and some very brilliant abilities. It sometimes means lack of foresight, a tendency to live too narrowly in the pres-ent; but Frémont if anything lived too much in the future. With him it meant a disproportion between his ardent imagina-tion, and his mediocre grasp of practical means to achieve the

goal he so vividly saw—to measure the hard, practical, intermediary steps separating him from it. He was a man who
dreamed dreams and saw visions. They fired his heart and
carried him, always intense and dynamic, into well-intentioned
action. They were such dreams as others might have brought to
practical fruition. His dream, when commander of the Department of the West in Missouri in 1861, of marching through
Arkansas to Memphis, living on the country as he went—it was
such a dream as Sherman realized in his march to the sea. His
dream of throwing a railroad from Little Rock or New Orleans
to the Pacific—it was the dream that the builders of the Santa
Fé and Southern Pacific made reality. But once transported
outside his true scientific vocation into the hard world of clashing human interests, he lacked the shrewdness, the grasp of
human nature, the insight into ways and means, to give his
grandiose plans effect. Without the imagination, he would have
been a more useful though a far less striking man. If fate had
gifted him with strong practical grasp as well as soaring imagination, he might have been one of the dominant figures of his
time. He was not a rudderless ship, but a ship whose swelling
sails made its rudder seem feeble.

The result was a career that was never quite tragic, never
quite victorious, but often midway between the two as he played
out an elaborate drama of frustration. Again and again he
was placed in situations where he seemed on the eve of some
great triumph, his wife watching with elation by his side. Again
and again the promised triumph turned into sorry futility, and
the indomitable Jessie steeled herself once more to meet disaster with queenly dignity. He might have scored a resounding
success in 1853 in finding a practicable winter route for a railway through the Sangre de Cristo range—but he lost his men
and some starved to death. He might have carried Pennsylvania
and the Presidency in 1856—but the election left him no happier a figure than many another defeated candidate. He might
by rapid marches and masterly maneuvering have swept Mis-

souri and Arkansas free of Confederates; but a subordinate
was thrown back at Wilson's Creek, and a rash defiance of
Lincoln's wishes brought about his removal. He might have
made a fortune from the Mariposa grant—but financial harpies
snatched it from his hands. He seemed about to become a commanding figure in the railroad world; but the result of all his
effort was heavy financial loss and the discredit of a French
indictment. "It was as if a character of pure poetry," writes
Royce, "some Jaques or some lesser Round Table Knight, had
escaped from romanceland and were wandering about amongst
live men on the Earth. Always his promises and gifts would
vanish, as by the stroke of an enchanter's wand, when men
stooped to pick them." His career remained thus frustrated to
the end—to the time when the leader who had come so close to
the Presidency was glad to accept a territorial governorship,
and when he gained his long-sought retirement pay in the Army
only to die before he could collect it.

In studying this strange career we can readily understand
why it excited the harsh censure of many observers. Frémont
seemed after 1850 to seek easy success in a world where true
success almost always comes hard. His great achievement for
the American nation, his geographical work, followed upon ten
years of severe practical training under the ablest masters; it
was well earned by that and additional years of peril and effort
in the field. The Frémont of the first three expeditions every
one must admire. But by 1850 the tide of events had moved
so rapidly that his geographical vocation was gone; and like
Othello, he knew not where to turn. He sought the laurels of
the Presidency without the stern practical preparation which
men like Lincoln gave themselves during half a lifetime of
political labor. He sought the glory of a Civil War general,
never having commanded five hundred men, without that protracted and often bitter training which men like Grant and Lee
had received in military academy, camp, and field. He sought
the rewards of a railroad-builder without passing through that
grim business tuition which Cornelius Vanderbilt and Collis P.

Huntington had gained long before they constructed their first short railroad line. Frémont tried too often to reap where other men had sown, and it was not surprising that he met with scathing condemnation from critical onlookers.

Yet the fault was not all his own. His associates, and the American people as a whole, bear no little responsibility for his failures. The people after 1847 created a legend, and this legendary Frémont bore as remote a relation to the real man as the legendary Grant in 1870 bore to the real President. Nor can we altogether regret the many vicissitudes of this half-frustrated, half-successful career. Although the legend has been dissipated, Frémont, himself a man of imagination, must appeal poignantly to the imagination of successive generations. If he was not always heroic in defeat, he was unfailingly picturesque; and because picturesqueness has an ineffaceable charm, we cannot but deal leniently with the figure who offers it.

His greatest definite contribution to American life was his geographical work—his careful mapping of old paths, his discovery of some new ones, his revelation of the true character of what he was first to call the Great Basin, his share in dispelling the myth of a wide desert in the Platte country, and his encouragement to well-planned emigration. The maps on which he and Preuss collaborated and the reports which he wrote with Jessie's assistance were models of their kind. But we must not think of Frémont's services in purely definite and practical terms. His life is memorable partly because it so strikingly illustrates the possibilities of adventurous action in the wide American scene. Where is a career with more of contrast, of vicissitude, of wide-ranging effort, of varied participation in national life? His name evokes a series of scenes which appeal irresistibly to the imagination: the great untamed West in the era of the buffalo herds and roving Indian, of Kit Carson and Johann Sutter; the clash of Mexicans and Americans over the imperial domain stretching from the Rio Grande to Shasta; the excited rush of Forty-Niners to the gold fields; the idealistic crusade for freedom which gave birth to the Republican

Party; the anguished years of civil conflict, with armies grappling in Missouri and the Shenandoah Valley; the desperate political intrigues of 1864, and the railway building and financial speculation of the Gilded Era. His name evokes, too, the fragrance of one of the truest love stories in American history. To have lived so daringly and completely, to have written so many pages fascinating in their dash and color, to have touched so many important events, makes him a contributor not only to the history but to the romance of America.

XXXVII

Some New Light on Frémont

Ancestry and Birth

Two bits of evidence indicate that Charles Frémon was an excellent French teacher. Samuel Mordecai, in "Richmond in Bygone Days: Being Reminiscences of an Oldtime Citizen" (1856), states that early in the century a large brick building on Carey Street was occupied by Haller's Academy, a private school. Haller was a Swiss or German of a little learning and a good deal of address and pretension. But "he also had judgment enough to enable him to select good teachers. Among these was Mons. Frémont, the father of Col. Frémont, of Pacific and warlike celebrity." The civil engineer R. B. Osborne, in his life of Moncure Robinson, privately printed in 1889 and later republished in the *William and Mary College Quarterly* for 1921, writes that Robinson, by studying under Frémon at William and Mary, gained a "remarkably perfect" knowledge of French.

Frémont's birthplace in Savannah is preserved and still shown to visitors. It is a two-story and basement house, rectangular, of solid brick construction, with a door and a full-length French window on the first floor, two windows on the second.

The Third Expedition and the Bear Flag War

The New York *Herald* gave a good deal of attention to the start of Frémont's Third Expedition. It carried a front-page article and map on October 19, 1845, followed by articles on October 26 and November 2 of that year. While these contain no new information, they indicate that Frémont already had a certain renown. Another article on November 11, 1846, dealt with the explorer's travels in Upper California.

The question of the exact tenor of Archibald Gillespie's message to Frémont remains unresolved. We might assume that it contained nothing that was not in the instructions which Gillespie carried to Sloat and Larkin, bidding them pursue a policy conciliatory to the Californians, but for one fact: Why, if that were true, should Gillespie push on posthaste hundreds of miles to the north, through dangerous Indian country, to overtake Frémont homeward bound to the Atlantic Coast? Actually, the instructions sent Commodore Sloat were two-headed. One part required him to treat the native Californians with great friendliness. The other part ran: "If you ascertain with certainty that Mexico has declared war against the United States, you will at once possess yourself of the port of Saint [sic] Francisco, and block and occupy such other ports as your force may permit." Sloat had five warships. The text of the letter to Larkin is known only from a copy sent by ship around Cape Horn; Gillespie, before landing in Mexico, committed it to memory and destroyed it. Of Frémont, Gillespie later testified that he had been instructed by Secretary of State Buchanan to "confer" with him, and "make known my instructions." These again were two-headed. One part told Frémont "it was the wish of the Government to conciliate the feelings of the people of California, and encourage a friendship towards the United States." The other part, said Gillespie, called upon him "to watch over the interests of the United States, and counteract the influence of any foreign agents who might be in the country with objects prejudicial to the United States."

Obviously, when Gillespie began to "confer" with Frémont, he might emphasize the conciliatory side of the instructions—a side not pertinent if Frémont continued to travel east. Or he might emphasize the Government's desire that Frémont watch over American interests and counteract foreign machinations— a side very pertinent if Frémont turned back. And then there were oral messages from Benton and others.

A dim ray of light is thrown on the subject by a letter of Benton's in the Buchanan Papers in the Pennsylvania Historical Society. Senator Lewis Cass on February 17, 1848, wrote Buchanan that the Senate Military Committee were investigating the origins of the military operations in California against the Mexican authorities before the news of war; that they had examined Gillespie; and that if no state reason existed to the contrary, they would like to see a copy of the instructions. Buchanan evidently consulted Benton. The Missouri Senator wrote back February 18, 1848:

I do not think it necessary, nor desirable, to publish the instructions, nor in fact, any part of them. The depositions of Frémont and Gillespie are brief and general, and only go to the general point of observing and counteracting foreign designs in California and conciliating the people towards ourselves. No authority for hostilities is claimed under them; and as they stand, they only showed the natural and proper desire of the government to frustrate the prejudicial designs of foreigners in Cal.—which designs were found to be far more dangerous than known of here and requiring a remedy of a much stronger kind than the govt. contemplated; and fortunately, we have the full proof now here to show the danger of the designs which were then on foot, and the necessity for the strong remedy which was applied.

For the downright Benton, this has an evasive ring. We now know that the British had no "designs" on California. Yet the matter cannot be dismissed with that statement.

When Secretary Buchanan wrote his message of October 17, 1845, to Consul Larkin, and when Gillespie left Washington the next month, relations between Britain and America were gravely strained by the Oregon issue. Polk had declared in his inaugural message that the United States had good title to all Oregon. Withdrawing previous offers of compromise, in December, 1845, he called for ending the joint occupation. When the following April he gave notice of this termination, the two powers were at an impasse. War between them was possible, and to many seemed probable. One reason why the Mexicans attacked Taylor's troops was that they expected Anglo-American hostilities. Earlier, in 1844, an influential body of native Californians had asked Alexander Forbes, the British agent in the province, whether they could obtain a British protectorate. The British Foreign Office wrote Forbes (December 31, 1844) that Britain would not assent to this, for it would be a breach of faith. But it added: "Great Britain would view with much dissatisfaction the establishment of a protectual power over California by any other foreign state." Sir George Seymour, who commanded the British warships on the Pacific coast, asked the Admiralty in March, 1846, for an increased force.

Thus Gillespie might well have got the impression in Washington, in Mexico, and in Monterey that a British threat was real and powerful. Not until June 15, 1846, was the memorable treaty settling the Oregon question signed in Washington— some five weeks after Frémont turned back from Klamath Lake. In 1848, when Benton wrote Buchanan, the impression of a British threat still lingered in many quarters. Indeed, Buchanan in a letter to T. Miller as late as January 15, 1866, speaks of the acquisition of California to keep it from Great Britain (Buchanan Papers, Pennsylvania Historical Society). It is certain that the State Department late in 1845 and early in 1846 feared action by the British as soon as they heard (1) that California had declared its independence of Mexico, or (2) that war between the United States and Mexico had begun; such action being perhaps a mere recognition of California's independence, in line with the Foreign Office's letter to Forbes. Had Gillespie emphasized the importance of Frémont's being on the scene "to watch over the interests of the United States, and counteract the influence of any foreign agents," this might account for the explorer's turning back. Pressure from American settlers would account for his ensuing activities.

The Court Martial

That the events leading up to Frémont's court martial contained much that was discreditable alike to Frémont, Kearny, and the Administration (whose orders led to a conflict of authority), is plain. But Benton, Jessie, and Frémont never wavered in their conviction that the verdict was a gross injustice to the explorer. After it was rendered Secretary Buchanan urged the young officer to resume his command. On March 7, 1848, Frémont replied from the Benton residence (Buchanan Papers, Pennsylvania Historical Society):

I have to make you many thanks for the kind interest which you have manifested in my behalf, and would take great pleasure in conforming my conduct to your opinion, if it were possible. But it is not possible. I *feel* the sentence of the court martial against me to be unjust; and while that feeling remains I can never, by any act or word whatever, even by the remotest implication, admit, or seem to admit, its justice.

One of the main results of the court martial was to confirm the hostility of West Point graduates to Frémont. They resented his rapid rise to fame, his strong political support first from Poinsett and later from Benton, and his position as a brilliant amateur in military affairs. This hostility had been patent in California before and after his arrest by Kearny; it was plainly manifested, according to the press, by officers at his trial. It would cost Frémont dear in the Civil War. Other Civil War generals, like Jacob D. Cox and John A. McClernand, complained bitterly of the jealousy, arrogance, and clannishness of West Pointers in dealing with high volunteer officers. From John Pope and others Frémont was destined to suffer much.

Frémont later (September 4, 1856) wrote T. S. King, editor of the San Francisco *Bulletin*: "From the day when my connection with the army was dissolved, I have considered my life consecrated to the construction of this Pacific [rail] road."

The Fourth Exploring Expedition, 1848–49

That devoted member of the expedition, Micajah McGehee
—according to Stark Young's article, "Cousin Micajah," in
the *Saturday Evening Post,* April 13, 1935—was "shy and silent,
taller than medium, with fine hair of a golden brown, and a fine
white skin." When graduated from the University of Virginia
he did not go home, for he was in love with the girl his brother
courted, and did not wish to complicate affairs. So he joined
Frémont to see the West. His father owned the Bowling Green
plantations in Mississippi.

McGehee wrote in his MS Journal that the object of Frémont's expedition "was to finish his exploration of California
and the Rocky Mountains, particularly of the Great Interior
Basin, of which so little had hitherto been known. It was considered a vast, barren desert, inhabited by savage tribes, and
rarely entered by trappers. He wished also to discover a direct
practicable traveling route, and, if possible, railway route, from
the Mississippi Valley to the Pacific on the 38th degree of latitude." St. Louis lies between the 38th and 39th degrees. It is
evident from various sources that Frémont confided a good deal
in McGehee.

On this disastrous fourth expedition, Benton wrote in the
National Intelligencer of November 8, 1853, Frémont was
turned out of his right path by his guide. Some of the reasons
for believing that Old Bill Williams misled the party are stated
in the text. Additional evidence to that effect is furnished by the
letter of one of the most intelligent members of the party,
Edward M. Kern, dated Taos, New Mexico, February 11, 1849,
to A. Robidoux, published in the St. Joseph *Gazette* and reprinted in the *Missouri Statesman* of April 27, 1849. It
ran:

My dear Robidoux:
    I arrived at this place last evening from Rio Colorado, from about
as hard a trip and as total destruction of an expedition as possible.

As rumors will reach you I thought it would be as well to give you some little correct information on the subject, though my time will scarcely allow of anything like detail.

As far as Bent's we met with no obstacle or loss and everything bade fair to give us a tolerable pleasant trip, considering the season. Our animals were in good condition; and procuring corn at Hard Scrabble for the worst part of the road, we calculated passing the mountains with success. Old Bill was with us as a guide, and that of course gave confidence, supposing none so capable as he to carry us through. Leaving Hard Scrabble, we continued up its creek into the mountains. As we advanced the snow increased. Crossing the first range we fell upon the waters of the Wappanah [Huerfano], passing through the mountains to the Del Norte by your old wagon road— the snow still increasing.

We continued a couple of days on the Del Norte, and then turned up what Williams called your pass on to the Compadne [Uncompahgre?]. In this he was evidently mistaken, for a worse road I never saw. If you ever got over it with wagons, I should like to have seen the operation. We went on up the canon, our animals failing and the snow deepening every step we took, bidding fair, as it subsequently turned out, to defeat our crossing. On the 15th of December we attempted to cross what we supposed to be the dividing ridge between the St. Johns [San Juan] and the waters of the Del Norte, but were driven back by the storm. The next day we returned to it again, and were successful enough to get on the other side to a small clump of pines. We unpacked our animals on a bare point and drove them to the hill top in hopes of their finding sufficiency of food for a day, as the snow had drifted from it in places. From this hill they never came again; the storm continuing, and having no shelter, they perished.

Camp then commenced making portages, in hopes of reaching the river. This you may suppose was a severe undertaking in the cold, and no positive hopes ahead of reaching any place, even should we have been able to get out our effects. By hard labor we worked our way gradually down. On the 26th, King was sent ahead with Old Bill to Abaque to bring us relief, while we were to continue down. On the 11th of January, he not arriving, the Colonel became anxious and started with his mess and Godey in hopes of meeting the relief party. Our provisions had given out, and we were living on parfleshes and tug ropes. Already Proulx had perished from hunger and exposure.

On the 16th, all having reached the river, we made our little packs of bedding and with our rifles started for—God only knows where. Here commenced our greatest suffering. The company had for its head Vincut Hatter [Vincent Haler], about as contemptible and cowardly a fellow as ever walked: his own lack of courage quickly diffused itself among the men—so you may suppose how things went on. Probably up to the 27th we had lost nine men. Our mess and another had made our final camp. A dead wolf was all we had to sustain life among nine men. I had closed all my affairs and felt that a day or two more would end my troubles, when, about noon on the 28th, we heard a shout, and Godey entered camp. Here ended our troubles. From him we learned the fate of King's party who had been found by him on the way down on the 16th. Poor King had died from exhaustion somewhere on the 9th; and the rest were in a miserable condition—frozen and partly crazed. They had given up all hopes of returning to us with relief.

Thus has ended the expedition—commenced, so far as outfit was concerned, under as flattering prospects as ever one started. The loss in dollars has mounted to over 10,000—in life 10.—My brothers and myself will winter somewhere in this vicinity, and return home early in the spring, when I shall pay you a visit at your pleasant town of San Jose.

Adios,

NED KERN

This letter apparently convicts Old Bill Williams of completely mistaking the pass up which he turned the expedition.

The Fifth Exploring Expedition, 1853–54

Intended to support the demand of St. Louis interests for full consideration of a Pacific railway route lying somewhere near the 38th or 39th parallel, this expedition deliberately tried a winter journey. Frémont had told Benton after returning from California in 1850 as Senator that only two sections of this Central Route remained to be explored. One extended from the head of the Rio Grande across the valley of the Upper

Colorado; the other from Las Vegas de Santa Clara west to the Sierra passes. He felt confident that a good roadway and good land for settlement existed in both areas.

Benton in a letter published by the *National Intelligencer,* October 13, 1853, declared that the recent journey of Harris Heap and Major Edward F. Beale had proved Frémont correct with respect to the first section. As for the second section, Benton believed that a still more recent crossing by an emigrant party which included the Rev. J. W. Brier had again proved Frémont right. Brier's party, after leaving Salt Lake, made use of a Mormon "way bill of a new and better route to California." This led from a point on the Old Spanish Trail about seventy-five miles southwest of Little Salt Lake, called "The Divide," to Owen's Lake, Walker's Pass through the Sierra, and Tulare Valley. Brier estimated the entire distance from "The Divide" to Walker's Pass as about three hundred and fifty miles, and found the pass itself easy, with no snow in January.

Benton, continuing to beat the St. Louis drum for the Central Route, sent a new letter to the *National Intelligencer* of November 8, 1853. A Virginia emigrant had just written him from Fort Massachusetts (a small post established the previous year in the San Luis Valley, at the foot of Blanca Peak, to protect settlers on the upper Rio Grande from the Ute Indians), praising the Beale-Heap route. This emigrant had found the country for seven hundred miles from the Missouri frontier largely rich and beautiful, and the San Luis Valley—which lies in present-day southern Colorado—very attractive. "In short," wrote Benton, "I now feel emboldened to repeat what Frémont has often told me, that in the central part of the Rocky Mountains covering the Three Parks, the headwaters of the South Platte, the Arkansas, and the Del Norte, and the headwaters of the East Fork of the Great Colorado of the West, and about halfway between them, there is good country enough to make a mountain State double the size of all the Swiss cantons put together, and presenting everything grand and beautiful to be found in Switzerland, without the drawbacks of glaciers and avalanches, and consequently without its cold." Benton is writing of what is now south central Colorado, the area roughly bounded by Aspen, Leadville, Colorado Springs, Pueblo, and Telluride, with Frémont County at its heart.

Frémont meanwhile was toiling westward. He wrote Benton, November 25, 1853, from "Big Timber" on the upper Arkansas, about the site of present-day La Junta, Colorado, that the expedition had made successful progress and had found large beds of coal:

I am determined to carry the enterprise through to the end, contending with the winter and every obstacle, prudently and cautiously, but never giving way. I have presents to conciliate the Indians, and our vigilance will prevent attacks. Our movement now will be a struggle with the winter. We have December and January, the mountains and the strength of the winter before us, and shall move slowly, but do good work. The astronomical, barometrical, and topographical work all go on well. After surmounting some difficulties with our *daguerre* (which it required skill to do), it has been eminently successful, and we are producing a line of pictures of exquisite beauty which will admirably illustrate the country. We hope to get through in two months, and to make a complete winter exploration of the route.

The news of Frémont's emergence at Parowan, completely across the Colorado and Utah mountains and near the Nevada boundary, and of his subsequent arrival in San Francisco, reached the East by way of the Isthmus and New Orleans. It included the absurd statement that Frémont, on reaching San Francisco, had been accompanied "with only twenty men, the greater part of them having deserted after leaving the Colorado." This elicited from Benton an irate letter to the *National Intelligencer*, with some sharp animadversions on West Point hostility to the explorer, and on the frequency of desertion in the regular army. He scored the "Telegraphic" or telegram which brought this San Francisco news from New Orleans:

I have to remark upon this Telegraphic that, like all the first reports given out about Col. Frémont, it is disparaging to him; and,
like all such disparaging accounts is false to the extent of the dis-
paragement. This is so upon its face. It says he arrived in California
with *"only"* twenty men. Very well: that much is true. He set out
with only twenty from Paroan; and, as he went through a wilderness, he had no chance to get more. He set out from the United
States last fall with "only" twenty-one men, and one of them died
after he reached the valley of the Paroan, which leaves "only"
twenty.

Now for the *deserters.* The Telegraphic says *"the greater part of
his men deserted after crossing the Colorado."* This is false. Frémont
was not educated at West Point, and his men—whether Americans,
Germans, Irish, French, Indian, mulatto, or black—do not desert
him. They die by him, but never *"desert."* As for this particular story
of "desertion," it is as ignorant as false. Frémont and his twenty men
were seen by Babbitt after they had crossed the Upper Colorado at
Paroan, nearly two hundred miles west of the Colorado; and Frémont
wrote letters home (which were published) showing that his entire
company (21) had all arrived there—one to fall dead from his
saddle.

The Telegraphic is probably true in this, that Col. Frémont had
arrived in California the 16th of April. He left the Mormon settlements of the Little Salt Lake and the Santa Clara meadows [Parowan
is near Little Salt Lake] about the 20th of February to explore a
new route (in that part of its course) for the CENTRAL ROAD,
and would be occupied some two months in this new exploration. It
is probable, therefore, that he had got through by the 16th of April.
We rely upon that much of the Telegraphic to be true; but repulse
the *"desertion"* part of the story as false, and as an aspersion upon
Frémont from which the conduct of his men in all time past should
exempt him. No man ever deserted from him. His men die with him,
as for him; but never desert. He was not educated at West Point.
And if any person wishes to know why the United States army has
been in a state (nearly) of dissolution for some years past they have
only to read a brief letter from Mr. Mason to me, printed in the
Thirty Years' View, at page 182, at the beginning of the chapter
headed "MILITARY ACADEMY."

Frémont sat down in Parowan on February 9, 1854, to write Jessie and Benton. He reported that the winter had been exceedingly severe; in that valley the severest since it was settled. But when he found only four inches of snow on the Cochetopa Pass in Colorado, even among the pines and in the shade of rock walls, he decided that the expedition had successfully proved its point. "I congratulate you on this verification of your judgment, and the good prospect it holds out of final success in carrying this road by the central line." He spoke of the large supplies of coal, iron, and timber near at hand in present-day Colorado. "In making my expedition to this point I save nearly a parallel of latitude, shortening the usual distance from Green River to this point by over a hundred miles." He expected to blaze a new line from Parowan to the Tejon Passes in the Sierra, and into the head of the Joaquin Valley; passes "through which in 1850 I drove from two to three thousand head of cattle that I delivered to the Indian Commissioners. I shall make what speed I can, going light, and abandoning the more elaborate survey of my previous time. . . ."

A good deal of publicity attended Frémont's emergence from this winter journey. C. L. Smith of Parowan wrote the *Deseret News* of Salt Lake City an account of the arrival. Frémont, he added, "was sanguine in his opinion that he had found the best route for the great national railway." On the explorer's arrival in San Francisco the *Alta California* carried a long news story, reprinted in the *National Intelligencer* of May 26, 1854. Other newspaper accounts could easily be found.

Frémont himself published in the *National Intelligencer* of June 15, 1854, a full statement, of perhaps 3,000 words, on his journey (see also the New York *Herald* of the same date). He was sure that his explorations contradicted the Southern leaders who insisted that winter snow and storms made a central railroad impracticable. He wrote of the central chain of the Rockies in what is now southern Colorado, just beyond San Luis Valley:

Across these wooded heights—wooded and grass-covered up to and over their rounded summits—to the Coo-che-to-pe pass, the line followed an open easy wagon way, such as is usual to a rolling country. On the high summit lands were forests of coniferous trees, and the snow in the pass was four inches deep. This was on the 14th of December. A day earlier our horses' feet would not have touched snow in the crossing. Up to this point we had enjoyed clear and dry pleasant weather. Our journey had been all along on dry ground; and travelling slowly along waiting for the winter there had been abundant leisure for becoming acquainted with the country. The open character of the country, joined to good information, indicated the existence of other passes about the head of the Sah-watch. This it was desirable to verify, and especially to examine a neighboring and lower pass connecting more directly with the Arkansas valley, known as the Poow-che.

But the winter had now set in over all the mountain regions. . . . We were moving in fogs and clouds, through a region wholly unknown to us, and without guides; and were therefore obliged to content ourselves with the examination of a single line, and the ascertainment of the winter condition of the country over which it passed; which was in fact the main object of our expedition.

Our progress in this mountainous region was necessarily slow, and during ten days which it occupied us to pass through about one hundred miles of the mountainous country bordering on the eastern side of the Upper Colorado valley the greatest depth of the snow was, among the pines and aspens on the ridges, about two and a half feet, and in the valleys about six inches. The atmosphere is too cold and dry for much snow, and the valleys, protected by mountains, are comparatively free from it, and warm. We here found villages of Utah Indians in their wintering ground, in little valleys along the foot of the higher mountains, and bordering the more open country of the Colorado valley. Snow was here (December 25) only a few inches deep—the grass generally appearing above it, and there being none under trees and on southern hillsides.

The horses of the *Utahs* were living on the range, and, notwithstanding that they were used in hunting, were in excellent condition. One which we had occasion to kill for food had on it about two inches of fat, being in as good order as any buffalo we had killed in

November on the eastern plains. Over this valley country—about one hundred and fifty miles across—the Indians informed us that snow falls only a few inches in depth; such as we saw it at the time.

In present-day Utah the Frémont river, with the town of Frémont on its headwaters, empties into the Colorado. Frémont described the southerly reaches of the Wasatch and connecting ranges, which again he thought no impediment to easy railroad operation:

They lie between the Colorado valley and the Great Basin, and at their western base are established the Mormon settlements of Parowan and Cedar City. They are what are called fertile mountains, abundant in water, wood, and grass, and fertile valleys, offering inducements to settlement and facilities for making a road. These mountains are a great storehouse of materials—timber, iron, coal—which would be of indispensable use in the construction and maintenance of the road, and are solid foundations to build up the future prosperity of the rapidly increasing Utah State.

Salt is abundant on the eastern border mountains, as the Sierra de Sal, being named from it. In the ranges lying behind the Mormon settlements, among the mountains through which the line passes, are accumulated a great wealth of iron and coal and extensive forests of heavy timber. These forests are the largest I am acquainted with in the Rocky Mountains, being, in some places, twenty miles in depth of continuous forest; the general growth lofty and large, frequently over three feet in diameter, and sometimes reaching five feet, the red spruce and yellow pine predominating. At the actual southern extremity of the Mormon settlements, consisting of the two enclosed towns of Parowan and Cedar City near to which our line passed, a coal mine has been opened for about eighty yards, and iron works already established. Iron here accumulates in extraordinary masses, in some parts accumulated into mountains, which comb out in crests of solid iron thirty feet thick and a hundred yards long.

In the interest of St. Louis and its central route, Frémont was exaggerating the resources a bit. He closed by praising the advantages of Walker's two passes and the Tejon Pass in the southern Sierra over those farther north. "The low dry country and the long slope, in contradistinction to the high country and short sudden descent and heavy snows of the passes behind the bay of San Francisco, are among the considerations which suggest themselves in favor of the route by the head of the San Joaquin."

Railroads from the east today ascend the Arkansas River on Frémont's route past Pueblo and Canon City, one line crossing the Rockies just above the Sangre de Cristo Range near Salida, and thence running down the Gunnison River (mainly between the 38th and 39th parallels) to the Colorado River and the Utah boundary, whence it pushes on west and northwest to Provo and Salt Lake City. No railway crosses southern Utah to any point near Parowan; but a line does run down from Provo and Nephi a little west of Parowan, and on into Nevada. Had it not been for the Civil War, Frémont's route might have received more consideration for a central railroad. The Union Pacific-Central Pacific line built with government aid was not preferable from an engineering standpoint; the main reason for its selection was that it better suited Chicago and the Northwest.

The Mariposa Estate

Some additional details on Frémont's close escape from losing this estate in 1851–52 are supplied by a letter which Edwin A. Post, a New York attorney, sent the New York *Courier and Enquirer* early in 1852 (reprinted in *National Intelligencer*, February 21, 1852). This shows that in July, 1851, Frémont's agent, Eugene Flandin, made a sale of the Mariposa estate to T. Denny Sargent of Washington, subject to Frémont's ratification. In October, Frémont sent Benton a power of attorney to give this ratification; and on January 31, 1852, Benton completed the sale. G. Harris Heap then sailed from New York in the *Empire City* in February to take possession of the estate for Sargent, while Sargent left the same month for London to obtain funds to finance the development of the mines. In cancelling this sale Frémont was no doubt aided by the Federal suit against his title.

When early in 1852 one Dr. John B. Trask of California attacked Frémont on the ground that he had allowed exaggerated representations of the value of the gold veins on his estate, the explorer wrote the assayer, John L. Moffat, a German geologist, S. C. Wass, and a mining expert, Frederick Goodell, all of San Francisco, for written opinions. The answers were highly favorable. "I have twice visited the Mariposa vein," stated Moffat on January 15, 1852, "in March and July last. In both instances, I judge from what I saw and what I learned, that it was producing then, and had averaged for several months, forty dollars per ton, worked with close mortars and shaking tables. With better amalgamators, I am of opinion twice that amount could have been saved from the same ore." Goodell wrote on the same date: "The veins upon your property in the Mariposa and Agua Frio districts are numerous, and rich in gold; and I am confident that large results can be realized by a judicious outlay of capital and the use of heavy and well-constructed machinery." This correspondence, and an editorial in the *Alta California* defending Frémont, are published in the *National Intelligencer* of February 24, 1852.

The great extent and irregular bootlike shape of Frémont's estate, covering some of the richest mineral lands in Mariposa County, resulted in inconvenience to many settlers, some of whom alleged real grievances. Details of the way in which the owner, supported by Governor J. B. Weller, maintained his Mariposa rights against the Merced Mining Company, may be found in the interesting two-column narrative of Bear Valley troubles in the New York *Weekly Tribune* of August 14, 1858, and in a shorter article in the *National Intelligencer* of August 21, 1858, taken from the Boston *Transcript*. Someone interested in the reputation of California for law and order sent the *Intelligencer* of November 3, 1857, a paper on Frémont's return to his estate. After remarking that vigilante troubles had given the State a bad name, the anonymous writer continued:

All have heard of the numerous settlers on the Frémont estate (the Mariposas), and of the violent language and conduct of some of the intruders, so conducting themselves as to pass for all—holding public meetings, adopting resolutions, charging the Supreme Court with bribery when they heard that it had confirmed Frémont's grant, burning Chief Justice Taney in effigy, binding themselves to stand together to resist the decision, and menacing Frémont himself if he came upon the place. Well, after three years' absence he returns to California, lands at San Francisco, and without accompaniment of force proceeds directly to the Mariposas, to the heart of the estate, and arrives at the town of Mariposas, 3,000 souls, and which is the seat of justice for the county. There are 16,000 settlers on the estate, and not one molested him! On the contrary, all received him kindly, and with the deference due to a proprietor; many asking for leases, or purchase of parts; and all wishing him to take charge of the property, and make it more productive by conducting streams of water through it.

Frémont made his return to Mariposa more welcome by bringing some capital and the promise of much more. During his European sojourn and the campaign of 1856 Bear Valley operations had become confused and inefficient. He paid judgments against his property reaching nearly $18,000, hired men, imported machinery, and planned the construction of two canals, the Merced and the Frémont.

The Mariposa difficulties had the effect of stirring up in California much ill-founded criticism and belittlement of the explorer. The Mariposa *Gazette* of December 3, 1858, in an editorial copied by the Sacramento *Union* of December 7, declared that "he is and has been the subject of more bitter personal enmity and abuse than any man we ever heard of. So far as we know, there is no reason for it, and for the benefit of all concerned, it should stop until it fully appears that he *is* the autocratical swindler, scoundrel, and rascal that it seems the heart's desire of some men to make out." Feeling over the Mariposa boundaries perhaps helps to explain a letter which Henry A. Wise, naval officer and author of *Los Gringos,* wrote his father-in-law, Edward Everett, from Washington, February 1, 1851. Describing a Congressional debate on a California land title bill in which Benton had pertinaciously defended the claims of Frémont, he added: "We who knew the latter gentleman on the field of his California exploits, regarded him as a very unscrupulous character. I would at the same time, however, award him the real merit he has hardly won in his scientific explorations, and admiration for the indomitable energy, perseverance, and skill with which he accomplished them." (Everett Papers, Massachusetts Historical Society.)

The Blairs and the Frémonts

After Thomas Hart Benton's death on April 10, 1858, Francis P. Blair, Sr., sent Jessie at Mariposa a paternal letter of affection and sympathy. She replied in May, thanking him and his daughter Elizabeth for their kind messages. She had known her father was dying when she left the East, but he had forbidden her to stay. She was thankful that his period of extreme suffering had been short and that no cloud had dimmed his great mind:

I had a letter from Father the day I left New York. In it he tells me I ought to go—that it is not right for a family to be divided. It was a hard choice—one that left lasting regret for whichever was set aside but it is done and I am more than justified in being here when I see how much I do to keep Mr. Frémont where his interests require—the children too are so strong and well here and so entirely free from any influence but our own. . . .

Mr. Frémont has a great deal to do—for the present lawsuits carry him occasionally to San Francisco, but a few weeks more will give order and then he enters regularly on his writing—it is quite impossible until he is through these interruptions. With all he finds more time to take care of me than ever in all the time we have been together, and when I remember that my father's last days were untroubled about me and my children because he could rely on Mr. Frémont's care for us, it gives a new value to my home here and a new reason for making it every way pleasant to Mr. Frémont.

She described the scenery near their house, and a mountain excursion on which Frémont had hurried them away from a bear they heard growling in the brush. They had killed rattlesnakes near their door:

But snakes and sounds of grizzly bears do not follow us indoors where everything looks as secure and peaceful as at Silver Spring. When the cool evenings come now we shall sit around a fire of oak and pine. . . . This range back of us and nearest the Sierra was named years ago for Father and the tallest peak is Mt. Bullion. On its summit a bonfire had been prepared by Mr. Frémont's friends (there are more friendly than unfriendly here) and it was lit the evening of our arrival. It was Friday the 16 April. At the same time he was laid in the ground at St. Louis his mountain was a blazing beacon of welcome to us. You know how fond Father was of the classics and classical comparisons. It seems to me he would have liked to hear me—his favorite scholar—tell him what thought links itself with that day—how as the old Greeks sculptured a jet of flame on the tomb to typify the soul purified and ascending so that great flame rising from the mountain of gold rock is to me an image of his great heart and mind freed from the clay and rising to the great Master. . . .

We had a last talk together the Sunday of his birthday. When he saw my heart too full he changed the topic for he evidently dreaded excitement or emotion. But he knew he would not see me again and I did not know the end was so soon, but I saw his changed face and evident pain and his voice was like a death knell while he was telling me of his will and his motives in making it. Mr. Frémont will be steady and faithful to his trust as Trustee and so must Montgomery and Mr. Lee. . . .

This letter in the Blair-Lee Papers at Princeton University is accompanied by a note from Montgomery Blair, August 8, 1858, to his sister Elizabeth Blair Lee:

The old gentleman asked me to take the enclosed letter out of his desk this morning and send it to you and tell you he would write you soon. By the by he seems a good deal out with Jessie. She has not written to him for a long time and now that she does write there is merely a tedious description of her camp—no reference to his heart out pouring, wishing her to make his home her home, consider him her father etc. etc. He does not say much about it but I think he is hurt by her proceedings and rather inclined not to give himself so much concern about her in future. But I have no doubt she will come to presently and greet him affectionately and then his big heart will forget all this.

Later, Montgomery Blair, as one executor of the Benton estate, received a complaining letter from Baron Gauldrée Boileau, one of Benton's sons-in-law; and he concluded that Jessie Frémont, who had expressed keen disappointment over the condition of the estate, was equally discontented. "I do not know how such expectations were created," he wrote his sister Elizabeth of the hopes of the Benton children for a larger inheritance (July 22, 1859; Blair-Lee Papers). Relations between the Blairs and Frémonts were thus under a certain strain even before 1861.

Frémont's Operations in Missouri, 1861

To a remarkable extent the accounts of Frémont's Missouri command have followed the narrative of Nicolay and Hay, subsequent authors failing to give the subject fresh research. This has resulted in an endless repetition of certain misinterpretations and misstatements. The older history by the Comte de Paris is fairer, more accurate, and more penetrating than that of Lincoln's biographers. Frémont's worst errors were political: his proclamation freeing the slaves of Missourians who aided the enemy, and his final agreement with the Confederate leader Price for a joint prohibition of the formation of partisan bands. These political blunders and his quarrel with Frank P. Blair, Jr., fully justified Lincoln in removing him. His military career, however, offers a more complicated, difficult, and creditable story than most writers have supposed. A careful book devoted to all its ramifications is much needed.

It seems anomalous that the Confederates in Missouri were

able to concentrate their forces more efficiently than the Unionists, and to strike two heavy blows, the defeat of Lyon at Springfield and the capture of Mulligan's little force at Lexington, before Frémont could prepare a counterstroke. The explanation lies partly in the fact that Missouri was an exposed salient of the North, partly in the superior strength of secessionist sympathizers outside St. Louis, and partly in the length of the Northern lines in that region. From southern Kansas, Arkansas, Tennessee, and Kentucky, all contiguous, the Confederates could pour forces into Missouri. The Missouri River tier of counties across the State was heavily slaveholding and secessionist in sentiment. Frémont had to hold the Missouri River from Kansas City to its mouth, the capital at Jefferson City, the railhead at Rolla, and the Mississippi as far as Cairo. He was essentially on the defensive; the Confederates could mass against any point, while he had to maintain his grip everywhere. His most vital positions were Cairo, Jefferson City, and St. Louis; to lose any one of them would be a disaster indeed. All were held.

Among secondary reasons for the Federal reverses in Missouri were shortage of weapons; the persistent preoccupation of Washington with the Virginia theater, and its readiness to deprive the West of troops to strengthen McClellan—who made no use of them in 1861; the inexperience of Frémont and other commanders in handling large bodies of men; the rashness of Lyon; the violent quarrel between Frank P. Blair, Jr., and Frémont; and the practical insubordination of General John Pope and General Samuel D. Sturgis.

The want of arms was lamentable. Before leaving Washington, Frémont had received an order for 7,000 stand, but it was at once countermanded; he then got a new order for 5,000 to be delivered from the St. Louis arsenal, but on reaching the West discovered it no longer afforded more than 1,300 arms. His total force when he arrived in St. Louis on July 25 was nominally 25,000, but was actually only about 15,000 when the departing three months' men were deducted. Of these about 7,000 had no weapons at all; indeed, Governor Richard Yates of Illinois had told Frémont in Washington that Illinois troops were largely defenseless (Committee on the Conduct of the War, III, 44, 45). "We must have arms—any arms, no matter what," Frémont telegraphed Major P. V. Hagner, in charge of War Department purchasing, on July 29. No response came. To meet the deficiency and arm incoming volunteers he made emergency purchases, including 25,000 Austrian muskets for the quality of which his Hungarian chief of staff, A. S. Asboth, vouched. Nevertheless, the shortage continued all summer and fall, his troops using "all kinds of arms" when they had any. Three officers who examined the weapons of John A. McClernand's regiments at Cairo shortly reported that his queer mélange included Prussian muskets, English Tower muskets, French minie rifles, three patterns of American muskets, and English contract muskets made by Lacy & Co. Only a trifle over half his force was armed at all, reported McClernand on September 30, "and they with dangerous and insufficient weapons, and without a supply of available ammunition." (McClernand Papers, Illinois State Historical Library.)

Lyon's rash precipitancy was the cause of his own defeat. Southwestern Missouri being largely Unionist in sentiment, he had pushed down to Springfield, in the Ozark country, to sustain the loyal inhabitants. But this was too far. His movement entailed a dangerous stretching of Union lines, a wide scattering of Federal units in his rear, and a risk of being overwhelmed by superior forces. On July 27, Lyon asked Frémont for reinforcements—"a few regiments." (Committee on the Conduct of the War, III, 96.) That same day (when Frémont had been in St. Louis only forty-eight hours) 10,000 Confederates were concentrating at Warsaw just to the southwest, and he needed an additional regiment. On the 28th, General B. M. Prentiss telegraphed that more than 12,000 organized Confederates were within fifty miles of Cairo, while he had but 6,350 men at Cairo and Bird's Point to meet them. On August 1, a telegram from Colonel C. C. Marsh in southeastern Missouri announced that G. J. Pillow had been at New Madrid the previous day with 11,000 well-armed Confederates, including cavalry and artillery, while 9,000 more troops were coming up to assist him. In these circumstances sound strategy required a retreat by Lyon, and the reinforcement of Cairo, capture of which would have imperilled a wide area in Kentucky, Missouri, and southern Illinois (Committee on the Conduct of the War, III, 96–99).

Frémont hastily reinforced both Cairo and Cape Girardeau. Meanwhile, ordering various units to Lyon's aid, he instructed that general, if not strong enough to hold his position, to fall back toward the railhead at Rolla until met by these detachments. On August 9, Lyon wrote from Springfield that he was "at present unable to determine whether I shall be able to maintain my ground or be forced to retire." Retreat, though difficult, would have been feasible, and his shrewd adjutant-general John M. Schofield urged it. But stung by being superseded in the chief command, Lyon probably thought that retirement would discredit him (a West Pointer) and strengthen Frémont; he attacked with disastrous results. Colonel John M. Palmer of Illinois, stationed at Rolla, wrote his wife on August 15 that the Union forces were winning until "Gen. Lyon made the terrible mistake of ordering Col. Totten's artillery to open on Sigel's command who had changed positions without his knowledge. They fired upon Sigel and killed many of his men and scattered his prisoners." Like Schofield, Palmer thought Lyon's attack a deplorable blunder in the first place. "The truth is that the battle of Wilson's Creek was a folly which the gallant death of Gen. Lyon does not atone for." (Schofield, *Forty-six Years in the Army;* Frémont, MS Memoirs; Palmer Papers, Illinois State Historical Library.)

Early August found a majority of the ninety-day troops first called out by Lincoln, and especially the foreign-born elements, leaving the service. "The new levies," Frémont wrote Montgomery Blair, "are literally the rawest ever got together." (August 9, 1861; Committee on the Conduct of the War, III,

119.) Nearly all the recruits sent to St. Louis from various parts of the Northwest were unarmed, and all lacked transport. One regiment after another lay for days in the city without weapons, ammunition, accoutrements, or wagons. As in Washington, soldiers patronized the grog shops heavily and disgusted residents by their rowdy behavior. "It is a rehearsal of the state of affairs in Washington before the fight at Manassas," exclaimed Frank Blair (Frank to Montgomery Blair, St. Louis, September 1, 1861; Blair-Lee Papers). Some officers were outrageously unfit. More than half the six Illinois regiments at Cairo, Gustave Koerner reported to Lyman Trumbull, would ultimately re-enlist, but never under their former colonels. Governor Yates's thirteen new regiments, he predicted, "will be officered in the usual way by incompetent men." (July 29, 1861, to Lyman Trumbull; Trumbull Papers, Library of Congress.) One Illinois brigadier-general whom Frémont had to use in northern Missouri, Stephen A. Hurlbut, was grossly intemperate; before joining his command, testified the editor, Joseph Medill, he was drunk every day in Chicago (Medill, July 13, 1861, to Trumbull; Trumbull Papers).

To help drill what he called his "unmanageable mob" of raw recruits, Frémont asked Washington to authorize him to collect veteran soldiers throughout the Northwest, and use them as a framework to form an army. Receiving permission, he brought to the field a considerable number of such drillmasters. He also created a special infantry unit, the Benton Cadets, which he expected to make a school for infantry officers; and he intended to make his so-called Frémont Bodyguard (an unfortunate name for what was a very efficient cavalry unit) a school for cavalry officers. He came nearer the idea of officers' training camps than anyone else in this early period of the war.

His energy also did much to give the troops a partial supply of arms. The statement of Frank P. Blair that it was impossible to get the Administration to give any attention to Western needs (Frank, as head of the House Military Committee, knew the facts) was for a time literally true. Frémont's contracts later came under fire. But it appears that the Austrian arms which he bought were quite serviceable, became excellent when rifled, and cost but $11.50 each when finally ready. His purchase of 5,000 breech-loading Hall carbines at $22.50 each, an emergency order which at a later period was given much publicity because J. P. Morgan was involved in it, was also defensible, the government's own commissioners pronouncing the price entirely fair. Some field artillery was supplied by a Cincinnati firm at the same price for which it had made guns for the State of Indiana. The Frémont Hussars, under Major George E. Waring, bought some 500 horses under special contract, while nearly 6,000 more were purchased in the open market. Both East and West, in 1861, intolerable confusion and waste, and much corruption, accompanied the purchase of arms, munitions, and stores; but the waste was chiefly attributable to frenzied haste and War Department inefficiency, while corruption never touched Frémont's skirts (37th Cong., 2d Sess, House Exec. Doc. No. 94, and House Report No. 2; Gordon Wasson, *The Hall Carbine Affair*; Committee on the Conduct of the War, III; Anon., *Vindication of Quartermaster General McKinstry*).

In the opinion of shrewd observers, one main cause of confusion, shortages, and excessive costs in the Western Department lay in the failure of the national government to provide adequate funds. When the time of the three months' men expired, Frémont kept many of them only by a personal guarantee of their fourth month's pay. He had to buy large quantities of material on credit. Colonel I. C. Woods told the Committee on the Conduct of the War that for every dollar of unnecessary cost arising from collusion among contractors or suppliers, ten dollars were lost for want of ready money. As soon as the Western Department had to use credit, control over prices passed into the hands of banks, brokers, speculators, and moneyed merchants, the intermediary links between the army and its sources. In buying mules, the government lost heavily because it did not furnish money for proper corrals, feed, shoeing, and attendance in St. Louis; in buying wagons, because it supplied no money for repairs. Treasury policy was responsible. "Chase," Montgomery Blair explained to Frémont on August 24, "has more horror of seeing Treasury notes below par than of seeing soldiers killed, and, therefore, has held back too soon. . . . It is better to get ready to beat the enemy by selling stocks at fifty per cent discount than wait to negotiate [stocks] and lose a battle." (Committee on the Conduct of the War, III, 115 ff., 222 ff.; Frémont Papers.)

John Pope, one of the West Pointers who gave Frémont the most trouble, burst out August 22, 1861, in a letter to V. B. Horton, in the following violent denunciation of the Lincoln Administration (Civil War MSS, New-York Historical Society):

They [the Illinois troops] find themselves neglected, abandoned and humiliated by the President they have themselves put into the White House, and they have resolved to endure it no longer. A deputation reached Washington yesterday representing the State authorities and the military which will force upon Mr. Lincoln either an open rupture or a redress of their wrongs. They warned him that neither Banks nor Hunter will be suffered to take command of Illinois troops and that if it is attempted the whole of the Illinois forces will march back into the State and have no more to do with the war.

We are certainly cursed with rulers in this country and especially at such a time. This Administration will do in a different manner what Jeff Davis is doing directly. I mean that by neglect, corruption and outrage, the States of the West will be driven to group together and act without reference to the authority of the General Government. You would be surprised to find how prevalent this idea is today and unless some change is made in Washington I fear we shall see before long Illinois, Iowa, and perhaps Indiana carrying on this war in defiance of any authority or control from Washington.

Frémont's staff came under much captious criticism. Actually it was an able staff. When first appointed he was allowed only three officers, but the Act of August 5, 1861, permitted major-generals to nominate for presidential appointment as many aides as they needed. General Orders No. 15, dated headquarters St. Louis, September 20, 1861, announced a sensible list. Chief of staff was Brigadier-General A. Asboth. General John A. Dix wrote the elder Blair on September 23 that he voted with Jessie on the question of Asboth. "I think him a very able man as an engineer and he is certainly very intelligent on general subjects." (Blair-Lee Papers.) Frémont's military secretary was Colonel John H. Eaton, later noted for his work with the freedmen. Among the others were Brigadier-General Justus McKinstry as assistant quartermaster-general, and Colonel John T. Fiala as chief topographical engineer. George E. Waring thought highly of the staff. "Frémont," he wrote Frederick Law Olmsted on October 31, 1861, "is hampered in every way, but he has good heart of it, and does more than could be expected under the circumstances. Asboth is a good engineer and plans well. Fortunately General Albert, his confidential adviser, is a man of excellent executive ability, and our Division is consequently in excellent condition for a fight." (Olmsted Papers, Library of Congress.) The most dubious element in the staff were several politicians, notably Representative Owen Lovejoy, who were probably forced on Frémont.

The origins of the quarrel between Frémont and Frank P. Blair, Jr., were complex. Frémont, General Justus McKinstry, Colonel I. C. Woods, and others declared that it began when McKinstry refused to make a $750,000 contract with two of Blair's friends, one Gurney of Chicago and ex-Mayor How of St. Louis, after Blair had strongly pressed the matter (Committee on the Conduct of the War, III, 202). Frémont also emphasized the elder Blair's arrogant demand that Frank be given an appointment which was outside Frémont's power—"I shall expect you to exert your utmost influence to carry my points, and now, to begin, I want to have Frank made a militia major-general for the State of Missouri." (This Blair letter is in the Frémont Papers at the University of California.) Frank, for his part, declared that he became convinced of Frémont's incompetence (as Schofield and John H. Eaton also declared). On both sides this oversimplifies the dispute. The two men were temperamentally incompatible. Frank was shrewd, direct, practical, aggressive, and imperious; Frémont was erratic, impetuous, and imaginative. Both were proud and hot-tempered. Frank, now recognized nationally as the principal savior of the Union cause in the State, expected to continue to dominate Missouri; Frémont had no intention of letting his own authority be weakened. In dealing with the lukewarm General Harney, Frank had shown how quickly, using his father and brother in Washington, he could break an opponent. Returning to Missouri in August from Congress, he expected to have his wishes treated as commands, and was irritated by the independent course of Frémont and Jessie. Motives on both sides were mixed. But essentially both men were ambitious for power and prestige; each became jealously suspicious of the other; and in the confused Missouri situation, with radical and conservative parties already forming, "charcoals" and "claybanks," it was easy for each to misconstrue the other's actions.

Frémont's proclamation announcing that the property of Missourians actively aiding the Confederacy would be confiscated, and their slaves, if any, freed, was in part a military measure designed to help stamp out the horrible guerrilla warfare then raging; in part a declaration that he stood with the radicals or "charcoals." To what extent it was encouraged by Lovejoy, who on July 8 had offered in Congress a resolution forbidding Union soldiers to halt or return fugitive slaves, we do not know. To what extent it was the product of sheer impetuosity—the impetuosity of a harried, overworked general who sat up all night worrying over guerrilla outrages, worrying over demands for troops, arms, and wagons when he had none to give, worrying over the clamor of soldiers for pay when money was lacking, worrying over the problem of keeping rebellious counties in check once he concentrated his army to march against Price—we can only guess. It was a cardinal blunder. Confiscation was a subject for Congress, and emancipation Lin-

coln rightly regarded as a question for himself. Perhaps Frémont did not realize how his action would reverberate through
the country.

That proclamation at once made a new enemy for Frémont
in the Administration. Attorney-General Bates, who hated all
the Blairs as a set of "tricky politicians" (*Diary*, 291), but
who stood with the conservatives in Missouri, now turned violently against the general. "I have demanded the recall of
General Frémont—possibly with too much emphasis, and too
often repeated," he wrote J. O. Brodhead of Missouri on September 28 (Brodhead Papers, Missouri Historical Society).
Of course the radicals in Washington vigorously defended the
proclamation. William Pitt Fessenden of Maine wrote that it
had electrified the country as a statesmanlike stroke. Ben
Wade, when Lincoln overruled it, burst out angrily to Zack
Chandler that the President was universally condemned and
execrated in the North. "I have no doubt that he has done more
injury to the cause of the Union, receding from the stand taken
by Frémont, than McDowell did by retreating from Bull Run."
Lincoln's sagacious friend, Orville H. Browning, himself far
from a radical, and later in Andrew Johnson's Cabinet, sent
the President on September 30, 1861, a letter warmly defending
the general. He wrote (Browning Papers, Illinois State Historical Library) from his home in Quincy, Illinois:

My acquaintance with him has been very limited, and I have had
no personal feeling in the matter. If he was honestly and faithfully
doing his duty, justice to him and regard for the country alike required that he should be sustained.

There was much complaint and clamor against him, and as I am
not quick to take up evil report I went twice to St. Louis to see and
learn for myself all that I could. It is very probable he has made
some mistakes, but in the main he seemed to be taking his measures
wisely and well. Many of the charges against him appeared to me
frivolous, and I do not know of anyone who could take his position
and do better amid the surrounding difficulties, and was confident
his removal at the time and under the circumstances would be dam-

aging both to the administration and the cause. Hence I wrote you, as I thought it my duty to do, certainly not intending any impertinent interference with executive duties, or expecting what I said to have any greater scope than friendly suggestion.

His proclamation in my opinion embodies a true and important principle which the government cannot afford to abandon, and with your permission, and with all deference to your opinions so clearly stated, I will venture a few suggestions in regard to it.

It is very important that the law which governs the case should be certainly and clearly understood, but either you have greatly misunderstood it, or I have. According to my understanding of it, it does not deal with the relations between the government and its citizens at all. It does not deal with citizens, but public enemies. It does not touch a legislative function, but only declares a pre-existing law, and denounces consequences which that law has already attached to given acts, and which would follow as well without the proclamation as with it. It was neither based on the act of Congress of August 6th nor in collision with it, but had reference to a totally different class of cases, provided for long ago by the political law of nations. . . .

It . . . rests upon the well ascertained and universally acknowledged principles of international law as its foundation.

But the power of the Blairs and of Bates, with their free access to Lincoln, far outweighed that of Browning, Wade, and Chandler. When Frank's formal charges against Frémont came, Montgomery Blair took them to the White House and read them to the President. Frémont's family later believed that the three Blairs, plotting the general's fall, enlisted General David Hunter and Adjutant-General Lorenzo Thomas for the purpose. Frémont had seven large boxes, full of wartime letters and documents, which were destroyed in a fire in the Morrell Warehouse in New York in 1877. "If you could have seen the statements of prominent men of that era, their conversations with Lincoln and others high in authority," Major Frank Frémont wrote the author in 1927, "you would know that the above combination was not to examine, but to determine on the best way to get rid of Frémont without implicating Lincoln." Much more credible is the statement of George E. Waring, writing from Missouri to Frederick Law Olmsted, October 31, 1861, that several regular army officers, notably John Pope and David Hunter, deliberately acted against Frémont through jealousy.

Frémont always believed that Brigadier-General John Pope, given orders a week before the fall of Lexington to march to its relief, could have done so but for his desire to injure his commander. Pope's capacity for negligence later proved extraordinary. When in 1862 he was removed from command of the Army of the Potomac, McClellan hailed this as "retributive justice." (W. S. Myers, *McClellan*, 351.) This boastful officer held peculiar political ideas, believing that Illinois should maintain a State army, and use it to gain a dominant position in the nation. He had written Senator Lyman Trumbull, July 6, 1861 (Trumbull Papers):

Illinois, if properly cared for, occupies today a most peculiar and commanding position in this country. On the one side Missouri has as much as she can do to take care of herself, while Iowa, Minnesota, and Wisconsin have had their troops drawn off for service eastward. On the other hand, Ohio and Indiana have been depleted of their volunteers for service in Western Virginia. Illinois so far stands nearly intact with a powerful force of nearly 20,000 men in the field.

If this force can be kept together and properly officered and commanded, upon Illinois will devolve largely the reconquest of the Valley of the Mississippi. Where she moves, with such a force, she will of necessity stand first—and hers will be the voice which controls the warlike operations in this valley.

If we can be kept together we shall constitute two-thirds of any army sent south from this region and our position and influence will dominate in any settlement of affairs west of the Alleghenys. To secure this vital object to our State I have been working from the beginning for some *head* to our troops, even if it be a wooden one— some commander who shall be a citizen and native of this State, and who shall move to the execution of any great military operation with the concentrated forces of Illinois.

For this reason also I have objected whenever I could exercise any influence to the separation of any isolated regiments from our

troops. I deem this object vital to our military reputation and efficiency, and I appeal to you to interfere against the system which is
now demoralizing us—frittering away our strength—subjecting our
volunteers to the most obscure and odious service—and absolutely
destroying the identity of the State. We want a military commander
of our own troops, who shall have full authority in this State.

Although we have force enough on foot for two Major Generals
and at least four Brigadiers, only two Brigadiers have been appointed
and neither of them has been assigned to duty. Give us a Major
General and one of our own people, to whom the welfare and reputation of our State are dear, and who can enable us to move with the
whole military force of Illinois.

I feel deeply on the subject. . . .

Pope believed that *he* should be the major-general of the
dominating Illinois army. He was perhaps just as lukewarm in
Frémont's service as Fitz-John Porter later proved to be in
John Pope's. He at any rate escaped the court-martial that
befell Porter; but Frémont felt so strongly that he declined to
serve under Pope in the Virginia theater.

Samuel D. Sturgis was also accused by Frémont of insubordination. Ordered to march from Mexico, Mo., to the relief
of Lexington, he approached the town, heard rumors of Price's
superior force, and hastily retired. Grave as the charge is, we
have reason for crediting it. Sturgis, though a Northerner by
birth, had strong social sympathy for Southerners. "He has
been accustomed, we are assured," said the New York *Tribune*
editorially on June 30, 1862, "to protest that the only gentlemen in the country are those of the South, and that when he
died he intended to have his body carried to the South and
buried there." When Senator Zack Chandler of Michigan criticized McClellan, Sturgis got considerable publicity by calling
the radical leader "a liar, scoundrel, and coward." As a West
Pointer and a strong Democrat, Sturgis had reasons for wishing to see Frémont fail.

At Second Manassas, Sturgis distinguished himself by a display of malevolence toward his commander, John Pope, whom

he hated as McClellan's successor. As that terrible battle closed, Pope and his defeated troops found themselves on Sunday, August 31, moving under a drizzling rain back into the entrenchments built at Centreville the year before by the Confederates after Bull Run. The terrible toils and sufferings of the campaign had ended in futility; the death and maiming of hosts of northern soldiers had all been in vain. As darkness fell, Sturgis, with his reserve division, reported to Pope's headquarters. According to Franz Sigel, the commanding general called out to him in the despairing voice of a man for whom the game is lost: "Too late, Sammy, too late!" And Sturgis harshly replied: "Damn it, didn't I tell you that all that was necessary for you to hang yourself was to give you plenty of rope?" (Jacob Picard, MS Life of Franz Sigel.)

Sturgis was one of the men with whose conduct at the battle of Fredericksburg General Ambrose E. Burnside was dissatisfied; and on January 23, 1863, in General Order No. 8, which Lincoln did not approve and which therefore remained ineffective, Burnside included Sturgis among a group of officers relieved from duty because they "can be of no further service to this army." (*Battles and Leaders*, III, 216.) The evidence shows that when Sturgis served a commander he liked, such as McClellan at Antietam, he fought well; but under a commander he disliked, he fought badly or not at all.

The condition of the Union forces in Missouri by October was one of real and rising efficiency. Frémont concentrated a large command at Jefferson City, which he and his staff reached September 27. Though a thousand rotten wagons sent him from the East broke down, by October 7 all his troops were on the march to Tipton. Supply depots were established at Jefferson City (two million rations) and Tipton (one million), but the general expected to subsist largely on the country, paying loyal citizens and confiscating from the disloyal. He intended to move with great rapidity to the Arkansas line.

Sterling Price, with booty and prisoners, had quickly retreated from Lexington to join Ben McCulloch's forces in southwestern Missouri. Taken together, they would have but about 17,000 men, and Frémont believed that by bringing them to battle in that area he could crush them. He had written Winfield Scott just after Lexington that he hoped to crush Price either before or after his junction with McCulloch. His five divisions under Pope, Sigel, McKinstry, Hunter, and Asboth were directed to concentrate at Springfield, and all but one of the five commanders gave energetic cooperation. The exception was Pope, whose letters show a spirit approaching insubordination. Even after the main force reached Springfield in southwestern Missouri, the lagging Pope was convinced that the march was preposterous. "The prospect before us is appalling, and we seem to be led by madmen," he wrote Hunter on October 26, 1861. The fact was, however, that Frémont's troops were in high spirits, enthusiastically loyal to their general, eager for battle, and expectant of victory. Many in St. Louis held the same faith. The journalist, John F. Hume, in his reminiscences (*The Abolitionist*, 1905), declares that if Frémont had been permitted to hold his Western command a little longer, he would have scored a brilliant military success.

That was also strongly the opinion of the St. Louis educator William T. Harris, who defended Frémont's military record at every point. (Kurt F. Leidecker, *Yankee Teacher: The Life of William Torrey Harris*, 201–204.)

It is a fact, though one denied or ignored in most histories, that the Confederate forces were ready to give battle. Price wrote Albert Sidney Johnston on November 7 that although Frémont's estimated force of 35,000 to 40,000 men, with 100 guns, far outnumbered his army, he and McCulloch had agreed to make a stand at Pineville, trusting to the rugged country to compensate for their inadequate numbers. Price actually could not retreat farther than the Arkansas line, because his troops would not fight outside Missouri. The two generals, McCulloch states in his report on the campaign, dated December 22, 1861, met midway between their forces; "where it was agreed upon by all the Mo. Genls that we should await an attack from the enemy, the ground to be selected by Genl Price and myself." (Price in *Official Records*, I, III, 732; McCulloch's report in *Missouri Historical Review*, 1932, p. 354 ff.)

Both Confederate leaders were disheartened by the bad state of their commands. "Our combined forces cannot cope with them (the Federals) in numbers," declared Price to the governor of Arkansas. "Men, men are now what we want. . . ." His Missourians, he informed Jefferson Davis, were half-fed, half-clothed, half-armed. McCulloch, speaking contemptuously of the Missouri militia as undisciplined, officered largely by politicians, and ill-equipped, states that the Arkansas men got on badly with them—"but little cordiality of feeling between the two armies." (*Official Records*, I, III, 731–734.) Nearly 5,000 Missourians, their time up, were ready to disband. It is evident that Frémont risked far less than Washington supposed by his advance toward Arkansas. He might have cleared all Missouri of the enemy, and by a battle at Pineville have won the victory that early the next year was won at Pea Ridge near by. But on November 2, Frémont, to the wrath of his troops, was relieved.

President Lincoln, in his assignment of the command to Hunter, had left future operations to the judgment of that commander, but had stated his opinion that the best plan would be to give up the pursuit, divide the main army into two corps, post one at Sedalia and the other at Rolla, and drill and equip the men. Hunter consulted his subordinates. McKinstry, Asboth, and Sigel were for advancing; Pope was noncommittal (Committee on the Conduct of the War, III, 240). Hunter turned back. Sigel later called this decision "an outrage without parallel in history." As soon as the retreat of Hunter and Pope became known, he wrote, the Union people of southwestern Missouri were struck with terror and despair. Within a radius of more than fifty miles, abandoning all nonportable property, they flocked into the Union lines at Springfield. Then, as the Federal forces retreated from Springfield, the woebegone, impoverished mass of fugitives, including nearly every family in the city who had sympathized with the national cause, took to the roads with the troops—refugees and beggars, without shelter, clothing, or adequate food.

A friend of Sam Ward's, writing from St. Louis, November 25, similarly declared that Hunter's retreat had plunged Missouri into a sorry mess. Price and McCulloch were rapidly reoccupying the country they had evacuated; they could threaten Rolla, Jefferson City, and Leavenworth as they had done after Wilson's Creek; they could lay waste the country up to the Union encampments (S. L. M. Barlow Papers, Columbia University). Sigel believed that if the Union army which Hunter took from Frémont had thrust hard at the enemy at Cassville and Pineville, it might have won a great victory and completely liberated the State. As it was, the Confederates had their will of southwestern Missouri for months.

Thus the Missouri chapter of the war in 1861 remained a dreary series of blunders to the end. For the miscalculations, errors, and failures blame has to be widely distributed. The War Department was blameworthy for failing to supply arms, and the Treasury, money, to the West. McClellan was blameworthy for detaching an important part of Frémont's force, at a critical moment, to meet an entirely imaginary threat in Virginia. Frémont and Frank Blair were censurable for quarreling so violently and for thinking almost as much of their private feud as of defeating the enemy. Francis P. Blair, Sr., and Montgomery Blair were at fault for throwing themselves so headlong into Frank's duel. John Pope was to blame for a disaffected spirit which approached insubordination. Hunter could be criticized for his eagerness to replace Frémont, and his hurried reversal of Frémont's orders—he knowing well that a victory with Frémont's army would have gone far toward showing that the replacement was a mistake. The patient, generous Lincoln appears better than anyone else in this unhappy scene. He did his best to inform himself upon the tangled situation in that distant area, and acted with sagacity upon the facts as he saw them.

Senator Ben Wade of Ohio went too far when he told Charles A. Dana, February 3, 1862: "No public man, since Admiral Byng was sacrificed by a weak and wicked administration to appease the wrath of an indignant people, has suffered so unjustly as General Frémont. His persecution will prove the darkest page in our history." (Dana Papers, Library of Congress.) But Greeley had some warrant for writing his wife, October 27, 1861, that Frémont had accomplished *something* with eight or ten million dollars, whereas McClellan had done nothing with ten times the sum. And Senator James W. Grimes of Iowa, who had not wanted to see Frémont appointed, decided, after a minute scrutiny of his record in Missouri, that he was guiltless of the main allegations against him, and the victim of "a regular conspiracy to destroy his influence in the country and with the army." (William Salter, *Life of Grimes*, 152–156.)

Frémont's Withdrawal from the Presidential Campaign, 1864

For the history given in Chapter XXXIII, two corroborative pieces of evidence have been unearthed. One is a long-forgotten letter by David H. Jerome, a close associate of Senator Zachariah Chandler, in the New York *Nation*, September 26, 1889; the other a manuscript letter of Montgomery Blair's to John A. C. Gray of New York, December 12, 1864, of which the late Henry G. Gray sent the author a copy.

Jerome's explicit statement supports the account in this book at every point. It asserts that Ben Wade, when approached by Zach Chandler early in September, 1864, agreed to desist from his opposition to Lincoln and support the President, if only his colleague in assailing Lincoln's Reconstruction plans, Henry Winter Davis of Maryland, should be satisfied. Chandler then approached Congressman Davis, who agreed to rally to the Republican standard on one condition—that his personal enemy and political antagonist, Montgomery Blair, should be dismissed from the Cabinet. Chandler went to Lincoln. He assented. Thereupon Chandler journeyed to New York, accompanied by Jerome, to open negotiations with Frémont and his associates. The two made their headquarters at the Astor House; they were efficiently aided by George Wilkes, editor of *The Spirit of the Times*; and they prevailed upon the Frémont group to agree to the general's withdrawal, without condition or reward.

"At one time during the negotiations," writes Jerome, "Mr. Bryant of the *Evening Post,* feeling the necessity of harmony, and fearing that the opposition to Mr. Lincoln in certain quarters might prove disastrous to his reelection, had in type an editorial for his paper advising Mr. Lincoln's withdrawal, and a united Republican support of Gen. Frémont or some other available candidate; but, by the vigorous assurances of Senator Chandler that harmony could better be reached in the support of Mr. Lincoln, the editorial was withheld from publication."

The night after they had made the arrangement with Frémont's friends, Senator Chandler and David H. Jerome went to Washington, arriving in the morning. They at once called at the White House, where they were "anxiously and eagerly received by the President." When Chandler had announced the result of his negotiations, "Mr. Lincoln at once fulfilled his part by addressing a note to Mr. Blair asking his resignation (which was promptly tendered), thereby closing the dangerous breach, and making certain his reelection."

It is clear from this explicit letter, which Jerome writes is based on both his personal recollection and the authority of Senator Chandler, that Frémont made no bargain and asked no price. It was Henry Winter Davis, reinforced by Ben Wade, who demanded Montgomery Blair's head.

This conclusion is reinforced by Montgomery Blair's remarkable letter of 1864 to his friend Gray. Blair, licking his wounds and nursing his wrath, was eager for a bit of revenge upon Secretary Stanton. He wrote:

Mr. Sumner told me on Friday last that Senator Chandler had told him that I had been removed in consequence of his reporting to

Lincoln a conversation between himself and Gen'l Frémont, the purport of which was that Frémont agreed to withdraw in the event of my removal.

I have two reasons for discrediting this so far as it relates to Frémont. The first is your statement to me. Second, W. O. Bartlett, who has always had a kindness to Frémont, met me and told me that Frémont denied having made any such proposition directly or indirectly. My impression is that it was a suggestion of Stanton acted on by Chandler who has been very intimate with Stanton for some time. I wish you could see Frémont and report the matter to him and see what he says about it. If it is false, I would like you to get him to write you a letter denying it as broadly as the facts will admit of his doing. Frémont owes nothing to Stanton and he is aware of that I presume and would not be unwilling to see him bite the dust. Having got his revenge on me through Stanton he may now be willing to have Stanton come to grief also.

I don't know that I can fix the lie on Stanton, but I shall bring it pretty near when I get it fixed on Chandler. I want you to show Frémont's letter to Old Abe when you come on and tell him the whole story.

To this discreditable epistle Montgomery Blair appended the form of the letter which he wished Frémont to sign! Of course he was mistaken in thinking Stanton the prime mover; mistaken also in thinking that Chandler was not concerned. But his letter brings in two witnesses, John A. C. Gray and W. O. Bartlett, to add their testimony that Frémont never stooped to bargain with Lincoln in this matter.

Frémont and His Retired Pay

Our last glimpse of Frémont, in a letter to John A. C. Gray, February 27, 1889, is as a petitioner in Washington for his pay as a retired major-general of the army. "I find good will here," he wrote, "and plenty of it, but I am afraid that we are too near the end of the session. I could not get away from New York until yesterday afternoon. Senator Palmer's carriage met me at the station here and I am staying with them. I went with him to the Capitol this morning and we saw some members of the Committee on Rules. All are friendly except Reed of Maine, who says he will interpose no obstruction. But the difficulty is in the mass of business which interferes to prevent the Rules Committee from discriminating in favor of any particular bill. I think I shall know positively tomorrow." The morrow brought postponement. It was not for more than a year, within a few months of his death, that he was placed on the retired list with pay.

APPENDIX I

Frémont's Children

JESSIE BENTON FRÉMONT'S Bible lists the births and deaths of her children. The roster is as follows: Elizabeth Benton Frémont, born Washington, November 13, 1842; Benton Frémont, born Washington, July 24, 1848; John Charles Frémont, born in California, April 19, 1851; Anne Beverley Frémont, born Paris, February 1, 1853; Frank Preston Frémont, born Washington, May 17, 1854. Benton Frémont died on the Missouri River, October 6, 1848—his being the grave that lay between Jessie and General Kearny; Anne Beverley Frémont died at Silver Spring, Maryland, July 12, 1853. Below the list Jessie wrote: "Care and sorrow and childbirth pain."

APPENDIX II

Corruption in St. Louis, 1861

AT THE OUTBREAK of the Civil War few men foresaw the wide scope or prolonged duration of the conflict. Lincoln appointed to the Secretaryship of War a politician, Simon Cameron, who was quite incompetent for the proper discharge of his duties. The result was that, amid general confusion, months passed before the government in Washington appreciated the necessity for setting up a central purchasing agency for ordnance stores, and months more elapsed before order began to appear in government buying. Immediately after the firing on Fort Sumter volunteer military units sprang up all over the North under state and city auspices. Union Defense Committees sprang up alongside them. The state and local governments and these Defense Committees began frantically buying arms, clothing, and other equipment. In an ill-stocked market, they drove prices sky-high.

Not until July was far advanced did the highly competent Chief of Ordnance, James W. Ripley, delegate Major P. V. Hagner to take charge of War Department purchases from private contractors in New York. Hagner was a blunt, sharp-spoken, conscientious military man, impatient with the inefficiency and chicanery about him, and so stubborn in his business dealings that, as he himself later testified, other buyers often took arms away from him by topping his price. When he reached New York on July 13, 1861, he found a scene of wild confusion. States, cities, Defense Committees, generals, colonels, and speculators were bidding frantically against each other and the Federal Government. The market was plagued with middlemen and profiteers. Men who had no arms were struggling to land government contracts at high figures, hoping afterwards to make a profitable arrangement with some manufacturer. The confusion spread to Europe; it was said that five northern agents took the same boat to England and were soon bidding against each other there! The same confusion spread to St. Louis.

In St. Louis the principal purchaser was Justus McKinstry. He had been assigned to that city as quartermaster by Secretary of War Floyd; removed by Secretary Holt; and replaced by Secretary Cameron long before Frémont arrived. Frank and Montgomery Blair were responsible for his reappointment, the latter going personally to Cameron to obtain it.[1] Before Frémont reached St. Louis, McKinstry had practically been given *carte blanche* in purchases by the authorities in Washington. E. S. Sibley, Acting Quartermaster-General, wrote him early in June: "You are authorized without reference to this office, under his direction [the commanding general's] to procure such means of transportation as he may deem neces-

[1] House Exec. Doc. No. 94, 37th Cong., 2d Sess., p. 15.

sary, practising a sound economy in making your purchases, and if the exigency is not immediate or pressing, conforming to the law or regulations in relation to the manner of making purchases or contracts for supplies."

On June 25th the newly appointed Quartermaster-General Meigs wrote again: "The department approves your course, ...but desires that while economy is right, there be no room left for charging the failure of any military movement upon a want of promptness and efficiency in the quartermaster's department." [2] McKinstry was shortly brought under great pressure by Frank P. Blair to award contracts and make purchases from a long list of Blair's friends and political supporters.[3] Meanwhile Frémont himself, earnestly trying to find supplies for ill-clothed, ill-mounted, and totally unarmed troops, made purchases on his own responsibility with greater regard to speed than economy. Some were very indiscreet; none was dishonest.

The most famous was the Hall carbine purchase, given much publicity because it involved J. P. Morgan, Sr. Frémont knew when he returned home to America of the appalling shortage of arms. He spent much of early July in New York trying to obtain guns, and did order 23,000 stand which were never delivered to him.[4] When he reached St. Louis he found his recruits defenseless. On July 29th he telegraphed Hagner: "We must have arms—any arms, no matter what." But Hagner replied that after Bull Run the government had ordered all arms diverted to the Potomac! The 23,000 stand Frémont had bought went there. From that moment Frémont in desperation bought arms wherever he could find them. On August 5th an eastern arms dealer named Simon Stevens telegraphed Frémont that he had "five thousand Hall's rifles, cast-steel carbines, breech-loading, new, at $22, government standard, fifty-eight," and invited an order.[5] Frémont had used Hall's carbine on

[2] See pamphlet, *Vindication of Quartermaster-General McKinstry*, p. 12.
[3] See appendix to the *Vindication*.
[4] *Battles and Leaders*, I, p. 278, 279.
[5] War Department records.

one of his western expeditions and liked it. Stevens's telegram seemed manna from heaven. On August 6th he telegraphed that he would take the 5,000 pieces, and wanted them by express, not by freight. For them he promised to pay the $22 demanded. Before the end of August, 2,500 of the carbines had been shipped to Frémont, and the second 2,500 were all in St. Louis by Sunday, September 15th. When Frémont bought them he did not know that they had recently been sold by the incompetent and confused War Department itself to a man named Eastman, who had in turn let Stevens (financed in part by J. P. Morgan, Sr., have them. How could Frémont know it? The government's sale of these pieces, thoroughly good though slightly outmoded, was a piece of the grossest idiocy.

This transaction was subsequently inquired into by a number of government bodies. A select committee of Congress reported on the subject December 17, 1861.[6] It cleared Frémont, saying that he had acted unwisely but probably "under some misapprehension as to the nature of the purchase of the arms." It estimated that the pieces were really worth $12.50 each. Early in 1862 Stanton created a special Commission on Ordnance Claims and Contracts. In June, 1862, this body held that $65,228 was a fair price for the carbines and should be paid. Later still, in the Court of Claims, it was decided that Frémont had acted with full legal right and no impropriety in buying the arms.[7] Those who declared he had acted illegally were thus confuted.

Whether he paid too much for the carbines is a matter on which judgments might well differ. Government records showed that while he was paying $22 for newly rifled carbines (pieces that had cost the government $17.50 when new and been rifled subsequently), the Ordnance Bureau in Washington was paying $35 for Sharp's carbines, $32.50 for Smith's, and $35

---

[6] House Report No. 2, 37th Cong., 2d Sess.

[7] Stevens vs. U.S., Cases Decided in the Court of Claims, December term, 1866, Vol. 2, pp. 95-103.

for Burnside's.[8] The Bureau bought 10,000 of Smith's pieces at $32.50 on August 27, 1861, and 7,500 of Burnside's at $35 the same day. Yet it did not need arms so badly, and did not have to have them in such a hurry, as Frémont.

Beyond doubt there was great waste and some corruption in St. Louis, as in Washington and New York, in connection with arms purchases; but none of the corruption was Frémont's, and the waste was largely attributable to the War Department's own inefficiency.

APPENDIX III

The Writings of John Charles Frémont, with Related Material

A REPORT on the Exploration of the Country Lying between the Missouri River and the Rocky Mountains on the Line of the Kansas and Great Platte Rivers, by J. C. Frémont, of the Corps of Topographical Engineers. 27th Congress, Third Session, Senate Document 243. Washington, 1843. Pp. 207.

Report of the Exploring Expedition to the Rocky Mountains in the Year 1842, and to Oregon and North California in the Years 1843–44, by Brevet Captain J. C. Frémont. . . .. under the Orders of Colonel J. J. Abert, Chief of the Topographical Bureau. 28th Congress, Second Session, House Executive Document 166. Washington: Blair & Rives, Printers, 1845. Pp. 583, maps.

The Same. 28th Congress, Second Session, Senate Executive Document 174. Washington: Gales & Seaton, Printers, 1845.

(Both editions of the Report contain scientific materials by John Torrey on botany, and James Hall on geology and organic remains. The Senate edition only contains the astronomical and meteorological observations. Other editions of the Report are those of H. Polkinhorn, Washington, 1845; D. Appleton, New York, 1845; G. S. Appleton, Philadelphia, 1846; and Hurst & Company, New York, 1885.)

Charges and Specifications and Findings and Sentence of a General Court Martial in the Case of Lieutenant Colonel John C. Frémont. U.S. War Department General Orders No. 7, February 17, 1848. Washington, 1848. Pp. 28.

Defence of Lieutenant Colonel J. C. Frémont, Before the Military Court Martial, Washington, January, 1848. Washington (?), 1848. Pp. 78.

Message of the President of the United States Communicating the Proceedings of the Court Martial in the Trial of Lieutenant Colonel Frémont. 30th Congress, First Session, Senate Executive Document 33. Washington (?), 1848. Pp. 447.

Geographical Memoir upon Upper California, in Illustration of his Map of Oregon and California: Addressed to the Senate of the United States, by John C. Frémont. Washington: Wendell & Van Benthuysen, Printers, 1848. Pp. 67, with folding map.

Oregon and California. The Exploring Expedition to the Rocky Mountains, Oregon, and California, by Brevet Colonel J. C. Frémont, to which is added a Description of the Physical Geography of California, with Recent Notices of the Gold Region from the Latest and Most Authentic Sources. Buffalo: G. H. Derby & Company, 1849, 1851. Pp. 456.

Central Railroad Route to the Pacific. Letter of J. C. Frémont to the Editors of the *National Intelligencer*, Communicating Some General Results of a Recent Winter Expedition Across the Rocky Mountains, for a Survey of a Route to the Pacific. 33rd Congress, Second Session, House Misc. Doc. 8. 33rd Congress, First Session, Senate Misc. Doc. 67. Washington, 1854. Pp. 7.

The Mariposas Estate. Papers by J. D. Whitney, J. Adelberg, Frederic Claudet, and T. W. Park, Showing the Condition and Resources of the Estate. Preface by J. C. Frémont,
Frederick Billings. London: Whittingham & Wilkins, 1861.
Pp. 63, with folding map.

Memoirs of My Life, by John Charles Frémont. Including
in the Narrative Five Journeys of Western Exploration during
the Years 1842, 1843–44, 1845–46–47, 1848–49, 1853–54. Together with a sketch of the life of Senator Benton in connection
with western expansion, by Jessie Benton Frémont. A retrospect of fifty years covering the most eventful periods of mod-
ern American history. With maps and colored plates. Volume I.
Chicago and New York: Belford, Clarke & Company, 1887.
Pp. 655 + xix, with maps, in part folding.

BIBLIOGRAPHICAL NOTE

The first three books written upon Frémont were campaign biographies. John Bigelow's *Life of John Charles Frémont* (1856) is a hasty compilation of about five hundred rather dull pages, eulogistic throughout. It, however, contains some documents of permanent value, including Commodore Stockton's report on his Pacific Coast operations, Frémont's defense before his court-martial, his letter from Taos in January, 1849, the Frémont-Wilkes correspondence, and his letter to the *National Intelligencer* on his expedition of 1854. S. M. Smucker issued *The Life of Colonel J. C. Frémont* in 1856. Charles Wentworth Upham's *Life, Explorations, and Public Services of John Charles Frémont* (1856), is a brief, clear, undistinguished compilation, also eulogistic. Two later volumes have been published. As a scientific and critical account of Frémont's explorations, Frederick S. Dellenbaugh's *Frémont and '49* (1914) is invaluable. The author is well acquainted with most of the country traversed. He identifies localities, furnishes information on topography, climate, and Indians, corrects many of Frémont's minor observations, explains others and presents a wealth of maps and pictures. The book, which virtually closes with 1850, is sympathetic. It contains a valuable bibliography. Cardinal L. Goodwin's *John Charles Frémont, An Explanation of his Career* (1930) is a brief and studiously hostile estimate.

Frémont's own *Memoirs of My Life* (1886) is based directly upon his reports, and chapters four to eleven inclusive add little to them. The first three chapters contain a rapid account of his education, early adventures, and work with Nicollet. The last four chapters deal, often sketchily yet with evident sincerity, with the events of 1845-46 in California up to the Capitulation of Couenga. The government published for Frémont in 1845 his *Report of the Exploring Expedition to the Rocky Mountains in the year 1842, and to Oregon and North California in the years 1843-44* (Senate Doc. 174, 28th Congress, 2d Session). It also published in 1848 his *Geographical Memoir upon Upper California, in Illustration of his Map of Oregon*

671

and California (Senate Doc. 148, 30th Congress, 1st Session). Numerous commercial editions of Frémont's reports for 1842-45 were issued by publishers in the United States, England, Ireland, and Germany. References in the text are to the edition of George H. Derby & Company, *The Exploring Expedition to the Rocky Mountains, Oregon, and California* (1849), used because a copy furnished by the Frémont family contained certain corrections in Frémont's hand. This contains also the official report of Colonel Richard B. Mason on the gold regions.

Catherine Coffin Phillips has written an excellent biography of *Jessie Benton Frémont, A Woman Who Made History* (1935). All Jessie's own books, while highly readable, must be used with care, for she wrote rapidly and with an eye to dramatic effect. The most valuable are *The Story of the Guard* (1863), *A Year of American Travel* (1877), *Souvenirs of My Time* (1887), and *Far West Sketches* (1890). *The Recollections of Elizabeth Benton Frémont* (1912) compiled by E. T. Martin, have material of interest upon the years at Mariposa and at Prescott. A fairly full list of magazine publications by Jessie Benton Frémont is given in Mrs. Phillips's biography, pp. 350-352.

The Frémont manuscripts used by the author in preparing this volume were supplied him by Major Frank P. Frémont and other heirs, and were later sent by the author (with collateral material) to the Bancroft Library at the University of California. They fall into four groups: (1) a few letters of Thomas Hart Benton to his daughters; (2) a body of letters and autobiographical writings by Jessie Frémont; (3) a number of letters and memoranda by Frémont himself; and (4) the manuscript of perhaps 100,000 words to which I have referred as MS *Memoirs*. This was written chiefly by Mrs. Frémont, with some assistance from Major Frank P. Frémont upon the military chapters. In part, these memoirs were composed with General Frémont's direct assistance and supervision, and among his papers are a number of loose sheets dealing with moot points in his career. It is greatly to be regretted that these *MS Memoirs* are not more complete, and that the first volume of the published *Memoirs* did not meet with a sufficient sale to justify the issuance of the second.

The author has also made extensive use of manuscript material from other sources. The courtesy of Professors Herbert I. Priestley and Herbert E. Bolton enabled him to obtain much that was valuable from the Bancroft Library. The more important narratives by American settlers and others thus used are the *Narrative of John C. Frémont's Expedition in California in 1845-46, and Subsequent Events in California Down to 1853,* by Thomas S. Martin, one of Frémont's men (Cal. MSS. D. 122); the *Statement of William F. Swasey* (Cal. MSS. D. 200); the recollections of John Fowler of Napa County upon *The Bear Flag Revolt in California, 1846* (Cal. MSS. D. 83); and *California in 1846,* as related by William Hargrave, of Napa. The letters and reports of Thomas O. Larkin in the State Department in Washington were used, and Mr. R. L. Underhill of Berkeley kindly allowed the author to see his excellent manuscript life of Larkin. The author also saw the Larkin Papers in the Bancroft Library and obtained some copies. The long-lost papers of Edward Kern, recovered and now kept in the Huntington Library in San Marino, California, have been reprinted as the *Fort Sutter Papers* in a small edition edited by Seymour Dunbar; I have consulted the originals at the Huntington Library. In New York I have used the John Bigelow papers and Bigelow's unpublished diary. In the Library of Congress I have used the Welles MSS, the John Sherman MSS, the Washburne MSS, the Chase MSS, and other papers. The Gamble Papers in the Missouri Historical Society have kindly been searched for me by Miss Marguerite Potter.

Lists of printed books upon Frémont and the many events he touched are easily available. In my original two volumes on Frémont I included an eight-page bibliography. Good bibliographies may also be found in Mrs. Phillips's *Jessie Benton Frémont* and in Cardinal L. Goodwin's *Frémont;* while there is an excellent list of titles on the trans-Mississippi in E. W. Gilbert's *The Exploration of Western America, 1800-1850* (1933). H. R. Wagner's *The Plains and the Rockies: A Bibliography of Original Narratives of Travel and Adventure, 1800-1865* (1921), is, of course, invaluable.

INDEX

Abert, J. J., as head of Topographical Corps, 49, 88; orders Frémont to return, 131; and Mrs. Frémont, 131-133.

Abert, Lieutenant James William, and third expedition, 207, 208, 212n.

Abolitionists attack Frémont in 1856, 450.

Adams, C. F., and arms purchases, 475.

Adams Express Company, 490.

Adams, J. Q., death of, 341.

Adams, Reverend Jasper, 12, 16.

Adelberg, Dr. Festus, 461.

Albuquerque, Frémont at, 369.

Alcatraz, Frémont purchases, 314.

Almonte, J. N., as Mexican minister, 189, 200.

Alvarado, Gov. Juan, and Sutter, 162ff.; rule of, 151, 170ff.; and California sectionalism, 218; Frémont visits, 224; Frémont buys Mariposa from, 371.

American Fur Company, traders' work, 123; assistance to the Nicollet expedition, 37.

American River, Frémont reaches, 159; Sutter's ranch on, 163, 164, 215.

Ames, George Walcott, articles by, 222.

Ames, Oakes, supports Frémont, 569.

Andrews, Israel D., 427.

Andrew, John A., 573.

Arago, Frémont meets, 457.

Aram, Captain, on Frémont, 416.

Arcé, Lieutenant, under Castro, 266, 267.

Arcé, Mme., entertains Jessie, 375; nurses the Frémonts, 390.

Archilette camp-ground, 178.

Arizona, Frémont governor of, 603, 604.

Arms, Frémont's purchase of, in Civil War, 474-476, 490ff.; see Appendix II.

Asboth, Alexander, as Frémont's chief of staff, 476, 477; and river gunboats, 492; as division commander, 530.

Ashley, W. H., as explorer, 75ff.; use of cannon, 130.

Astor, John Jacob, and western explorations, 76.

Atlantic & Pacific Railroad, 587ff.

Baker, Senator E. D., meets Frémont, 468, 470, 471.

Bancroft, George, and western expansion, 202; and third expedition, 203, 204; instructions to Frémont, 202, 203; to Sloat, 240; letter to Frémont, 245, 246; memorandum, 246, 247.

Bancroft, H. H., as critic of Frémont, 281.

Banks, N. P., and Frémont's nomination, 425ff.; and Native Americans, 431, 432; campaigns for Frémont, 441; commands in Shenandoah, 555ff.; defeated, 556; as Frémont's companion, 593.

Bartleson-Bidwell party of pioneers, 217.

Bates, Edward, attitude toward Frémont, 470, 530, 539; hostility to Blairs, 567.

Beale, Mayor Edward F., befriends Frémont, 368, 369; visits him, 389; and Pacific Railroad, 409.

Bear Flag, raising of, 271.

Bear Flag War, history of, 254-286.

Bear River, Frémont follows, 139.

Bear Valley, Frémont's home at, 383.

Beckwith, E. J., his survey, 406.

Beecher, H. W., in 1856, 452; supports Frémont, 547; opposes Lincoln, 568.

Belford, Clarke & Co., 606.

Belmont, August. 453.

Bennett, J. G., on Washington dullness, 333; and Frémont courtmartial, 336; supports Frémont, 340, 341, 443, 445; endorses proclamation, 504; attacks Lincoln, 568; Blair pleads with, 577.

Bent's Fort, and second expedition, 137; return to, 184; third expedition, 207, 208; visit to in 1848, 350, 351.

Benton, Randolph, with Frémont, 90; death, 405.

Benton, Thomas Hart, duel with Jackson, 9, 10; Washington position and character, 51-55; friendship with Frémont, 52, 55; opposes him, 57, 58, 68; relations with Jessie, 63; consents to marriage, 59; belief in western development, 83, 125; plans second expedition, 127; visits St. Louis, 128, 185; concern over Jessie, 185, 186; takes in Frémont, 190ff.; and the third expedition, 201ff.; anger against Kearny, 329ff.; relations with Polk, 328ff.; and the court-martial, 327-342; Mount Bullion named for, 383; and Pacific railroad, 406, 408ff.; loses Senate seat, 422; opposes Frémont for President, 448, 455, 456; death, 459, 460; statue to, 594.

Bidwell, John, as Sutter's aide, 217.

Bierstadt, A. H., Frémont own painting by, 594.

Bigelow, John, on Frémont in 1856, 426ff.; writes campaign life, 443; campaign manager, 450; distrusts Frémont, 472.

Bigler, John, as governor, 397.

Billings, Frederick, as Frémont's lawyer, 471; in Civil War, 491; and loss of Mariposa, 583-586.

Bissonette, Joseph, interpreter for Frémont, 112.

Black, Jeremiah, Frémont confers with, 458.

Black Hills (Laramie Mountains), Frémont describes, 122.

Black Point, purchase, 467; life at, 468ff.

Blair, Francis P., Sr., friendship with Benton's, 186; Mrs. Frémont at his estate, 407; and Frémont in 1856, 427ff.; takes defeat hard, 456; dislike of Frémont, 470; family pride, 507, 508, demands on Frémont, 509, 510; sees Mrs. Frémont, 519.

Blair, Frank, in St. Louis, 186; and campaign of 1856, 427ff.; organizes forces in Missouri, 479, 480; family pride in, 507-510; at Frémont's headquarters, 509, 510; demands on Frémont, 510-512; doubts Frémont's capacity, 512; quarrel with Frémont, 513ff.; arrest and release, 520, 526; files charges against Frémont, 526, 527; assails Lincoln's Cabinet, 529; attacks Frémont in Congress, 554; attacks Chase, 571, 572; military command, 572; Congress rebukes, 575; Republican convention hostile to, 576.

Blair, Montgomery, in St. Louis, 186; as Frémont's counsel, 396, 462; Frémont appeals to, 485; on Frémont's delays, 481; family feeling, 507, 508; criticizes Chase, 509; visits St. Louis, 513, 514; and Mrs. Frémont, 515-519; and Cabinet antagonisms, 566, 567; enmity of Chase to, 572; Republican convention attacks, 575, 576; resignation, 581, 582.

Blenker, General, reinforces Frémont, 560.

Boileau, Baron Gauldree, marries Susan Benton, 459; as business intermediator, 593.

Boisé, Fort, Frémont visits, 144.

Boonville, battle of, 480.

Botts, John Minor, on disunion, 448.

Boutwell, George S., attacks Montgomery Blair, 581.

Brackenridge, Thomas E., with fourth expedition, 349ff., 357.

Brady, his photographic studio, 420.

Brant, Henry, on Frémont's first expedition, 93.

Brant, Mrs. Sarah Benton, entertains Frémont, 92; Jessie with, 551.

Brant Mansion, as Frémont's headquarters, 493, 494.

Frémont—(Continued)
writes memoirs, 605, 606; last days
and death, 607ff.; character, 612ff.
Frémont, Elizabeth Benton (Lilly),
mentioned, 343; and Frémont's defeat for presidency, 456; life after
the war, 606; and Frémont's death,
609.
Frémont, Frank P., birth, 423; education, 605.
Frémont, Jessie Benton, Frémont
meets, 56; character, 63; their attachment, 58; training and abilities, 63-67; marriage, 69; reconcilia-
tion with father, 70, 71; first child
born, 116; assists with report, 117-
119; and second expedition, 131ff.;
disobeys Col. Abert, 131-134ff.; life
in St. Louis, 185, 186; Frémont's
return, 187ff.; assists with second
report, 190ff.; reunion with Frémont
in 1847, 326; and Polk, 327ff.; her
anxiety, 330; goes West, 343; crosses
Panama, 374, 375; reaches California, 376; life in California, 377ff.;
slavery issue in California, 387; in
Europe, 401ff.; and Democratic offer to Frémont, 425; in campaign of
1856, 442; and Frémont's defeat,
456; in Paris again, 459; in California, 460ff.; and death of father,
460, 461; and the Mariposa War,
463-466; and Black Point home,
467, 468; carriage accident, 471; letter by, 472; with Frémont in St.
Louis, 481ff.; and emancipation
proclamation, 503ff.; travels east,
515; interview with Lincoln, 516-
518; in St. Louis, 520ff.; her bitterness, 551; and White House reception, 552, 553; and West Virginia,
554; relieved by Frémont's 1864
withdrawal, 582; in California, 608,
609; last days and death, 610, 611.
Frémont, John C., Jr., education of,
605; and Frémont's death, 609.
Frémont, Nina, her education, 444; at
Mariposa, 461.
Frémont's Peak, ascent of, 105, 124.
Frenière, Louison, as scout, 39, 40.
Fuller, Oliver, with Frémont, 418.

Gabilan Mountains, Frémont in, 228.
Gabriel, Benton's servant, 187, 188.
Gamble, Governor Hamilton R., hostility to Frémont, 499, 510, 515; re-
fuses Frémont's request, 510; criti-
cizes Frémont, 514, 515.
Garde, Comte de la, Jessie's friendship
with, 402ff.
Garfield, James A., opposes Lincoln,
565.
Garrison, W. L., derides Republican
party, 450; in 1864 attacks Fré-
mont's candidacy, 573, 574.
German-Americans support Frémont,
443; applaud his proclamation, 504;
support him in St. Louis, 542; for
presidency, 570-577.
Gerolt, Baron, 200.
Ghent, W. J., quoted, 212.
Geyer, Charles, as botanist, 32, 34, 38.
Gila River, Frémont on, 369, 373.
Gillespie, A. H., as despatch-bearer,
222, 229, 233, 237, 238ff.; letters
to Navy Department, 258; with
California troops, 293.
Gilpin, William, on second expedition,
129, 196.
Girardin, Louis, his school, 5, 6.
Godey, Alexis, on second expedition,
138; punishes Indians, 177ff.; on
third expedition, 207, 208, 276, 284;
at court-martial, 333; and fourth
expedition, 349; on Williams's responsibility, 357-359; bravery of,
363; brings relief, 366; defends Frémont, 369; goes to California, 369,
370; at Mariposa, 394; on Frémont
as leader, 416, 417; Frémont meets
in West, 603.
Gody, F. W., letter to Frémont, 69.
Golden Gate, named by Frémont, 278.
Graham, Isaac, arrest of, 170.
Grand River, 412, 413.
Grant, U. S., in St. Louis, 186; and
Mexican War, 289; takes field command, 521; on the Chickahominy,
575; in fighting of 1864, 576; nomination proposed, 578.
Gray, John A. C., receiver of Texas
& Pacific, 591; exonerates Frémont,
600.

Whittier, J. G., supports Frémont, 443; poem praising Frémont, 546; begs him in 1864 to withdraw, 579; Jessie's letter to, 582.

Wilkes, Charles, Pacific explorations of, 127; Frémont's controversy with, 348.

Wilkes, George, assists Zach Chandler, 579.

Williams, Old Bill, with fourth expedition, 351; described, 352, 353; responsibility for disaster, 357ff.; goes for aid, 363; fails, 364; adventures of, 365ff.; errors of, 367, 368; death, 369.

Williams, Captain W. S., Frémont serves under, 25.

Wilmot, David, and Republican Convention, 433, 434; campaigns for Frémont, 453.

Wilson, Henry, supports Frémont, 426, 427; calls on Lincoln, 569; offers Frémont a bargain, 580.

Wilson's Creek, battle of, 487-489.

Wind River Mountains, Frémont explores, 105; beauty of, 106.

Winthrop, Robert C., opposes Frémont, 450.

Wise, Henry A., campaign attacks on Frémont, 451.

Wood, William, quoted, 549.

Wootton, Richard, 359.

Wyeth, Nathaniel J., his western expedition, 196.

Yates, Richard, on defenseless West, 476, 495.

Yerba Buena (see also San Francisco), 222.

Young Brigham, and Frémont's report, 142.

Zagonyi, Charles, and his battalion, 494; charge at Springfield, 536.

Zagonyi Guard, mustered out without pay, 550.

Zindel, Louis, and the Nicollet expedition, 37, 39; and Frémont's second expedition, 129, 138.

Zollinger, James Peter, cited, 162.

(1)

From *Frémont and '49*, by F. S. Dellenbaugh; reprinted by courtesy of Harper & Bros.